11-5-73

Politics in War

Lam Son Square, Saigon

Photo: M. Lyall Breckon

Politics in War

The Bases of Political Community in South Vietnam

Allan E. Goodman

Harvard University Press   Cambridge, Massachusetts   1973

In memory of John Christopher Wood

1776745

Preface

This book provides an alternative to views of Vietnamese politics that stress its fragmentation as an immutable barrier to the emergence of effective political organizations. To ignore the role of politics in war has meant that military victory rather than political mobilization was sought as the primary means to end the present conflict. The cost of this blunder has been immense. Particularly characteristic of the outlook of American officials in Vietnam, this view obscured the fundamental importance of involving the population in an organized way in the processes of social and economic change. American Agency for International Development officials, for example, might regard the decentralization of power in the Government of Vietnam to the local level as essential to improving its performance, but, considering themselves administrative technicians, they made a practice of steering clear of politics.

The irony of this approach was that American assistance to the Government of Vietnam, rather than facilitating the involvement of the population in government programs, too often tended to make it unnecessary. Failure to comprehend what decentralization and a host of other suggested reforms meant to Vietnamese politics obscured the fact that before power could be decentralized it had to be created; this required the political mobilization of the population. Such mobilization is a function of politics not warfare, and, thus, the importance of politics cannot be ignored even during war. My aim has been to write a book that advances understanding of Vietnamese politics, the forces underlying it, and the bases upon which political community and an end to the war might be achieved.

Field research was conducted in South Vietnam primarily from August 1969 to January 1970, but this book's origin lies in an earlier visit made during the summer of 1967. At that time Vietnam was preparing for the election of a President and National Assembly of its Second Republic. Interviews with political leaders and candidates at that time encouraged me to return and assess the significance of the process begun and of the institutions established in 1967. The data presented in this book were derived from materials made available by the Department of State's Vietnam Working Group, the American Embassy, the United States Agency for International Development Mission in Saigon, the Government of Vietnam's Ministry of Interior, the Upper and Lower Houses of the National Assembly, and religious and political organizations throughout Vietnam. In addition, 280 interviews were conducted with Vietnamese political leaders and government officials, and in depth discussions held with 60 deputies of the Lower House of diverse experiences, ideologies, and activities.

The purpose of the interviews was to assess the impact that the functioning of the Lower House had upon political organizations in Vietnam, and this required that the comments made by the deputies be compared with those of the political leaders in their constituencies. Since opportunities to witness interaction between these two sets of individuals were limited, each deputy was interviewed at least twice so that the discussion could reflect the impressions derived from visits to their constituencies, or, in the case of those deputies seen only once, the interview was conducted after a visit to their constituencies. Deputies and political leaders spoke freely, though anonymously. Free exchange was further encouraged by the presence of my Vietnamese research assistant; neither he nor I wished or sought to be privy to confidential information. To be sure, political interviewing has its limitations as one study of this research tool has pointed out: "Every conversation has its own balance of revelation and concealment of thoughts and intentions: only under very unusual circumstances is talk so completely expository that every word can be taken at face value."* Nowhere is this truer than in Vietnam where American scholars are too easily mistaken for government officials and frequently provided with data and opinions that reflect individual goals and ambitions rather than present realities. For this reason, not all deputies of the Lower House were interviewed. Given the limits of time, I sought to maximize the opportunity to corroborate the material derived from the interviews.

Finally, it must be noted that this book, while relying to some extent upon theories and concepts derived from the study of comparative politics, is not comparative in scope. Examples of developments and phenomena in other polities are presented where they facilitate description and explana-

*Mark Benney and Everett C. Hughes, "Of Sociology and the Interview," *American Journal of Sociology,* 62 (Sept. 1956), 137. See also Raymond Gordon, "Dimensions of the Depth Interview," *ibid.,* pp. 158–164; and Myron Weiner, "Political Interviewing," in Robert Ward, ed., *Studying Politics Abroad: Field Research in the Developing Areas* (Boston, Little Brown, 1964). pp. 103–133.

tion of Vietnamese politics and institutions. Basically, *Politics in War* is a study of what one scholar has termed "the most fundamental aspect of political modernization; namely, the participation in politics beyond the village or town level of social groups throughout the society and the development of new political institutions . . . to organize that participation."† Essential to sustaining political modernization under conditions of internal war is the capacity to expand participation and to create effective political institutions that can pace and regulate the transformations of society, economy, and politics generated by such wars. By referring to the case of South Vietnam, this study investigates the hypothesis that legislatures at the microlevel of politics can substitute for the political community lacking in the society at large. In addition to implications this study may have for the analysis of political modernization in general, it is also intended to suggest a perspective on legislatures that has been notably absent in contemporary approaches to those institutions in developing polities.

Research, I have found, involves the accumulation of immense personal and intellectual debts. Great teachers are rare, and I was fortunate to find at Harvard both a great teacher and a friend in Samuel P. Huntington, whose creative scholarship and inspiring dedication to the profession had a profound influence on my work, this study, and my decision to pursue an academic career. Throughout my months in Saigon and for almost a year thereafter, I benefited greatly from the dedication and scholarship of my colleague, Nguyen van Hien. Mr. Hien, now at Princeton University, provided an understanding of Vietnamese life and added depth to my interviews that made the present analysis possible. Frederick S. Carr, Jr., a former student at Harvard, undertook to edit the entire manuscript. For more than six months he eased me through substantive and stylistic changes that no author really has the objectivity to make alone. Mr. Carr helped me understand the underlying dynamics of Vietnamese politics by his persistent questioning of assumptions and encouraged me to write for a broader audience than the Vietnam experts who had encouraged my earlier work. That I was able to do so, is largely the result of the skill my editor at the Press, Rita Howe, contributed during the final stages of preparing the manuscript.

I was fortunate also in the early stages of research to have the advice of

†Samuel P. Huntington, *Political Order in Changing Societies* (New Haven, Conn., Yale University Press, 1968), p. 36.

John Donnell, John Montgomery, Ithiel Pool, Milton Sacks, Charles Sweet, and Myron Weiner. Special thanks are due to Samuel Popkin who proved to be a wise advocate in suggesting that I resist the temptation to do only a study of Vietnamese elites. My research and the freedom to undertake it were supported by a grant from the Asia Society's Southeast Asia Development Advisory Group. The late Kenneth T. Young, John Quinn, and Jane Levitt of that institution were extremely helpful in facilitating arrangements for field work, as were James Rosenthal and Richard Teare of the Vietnam Working Group of the Department of State; Karl Bode and Philip Sperling of the Agency for International Development; Harry Ellis, William Steckle, and Monica Boyle of the American Mission in Saigon. I also benefited from the cooperation of the American Embassy in Saigon and gratefully acknowledge the support of Ambassador Ellsworth Bunker, Laurence Pickering, Lyall Breckon, and the Provincial Reporting Unit of the Political Section. Assistance from the Francis A. Harrington Public Affairs Fund at Clark University greatly facilitated the revision process and made publication of this volume possible.

Needless to say, without the cooperation of the deputies of the Lower House my research would not have been possible. I was greatly aided by the kindnesses that Le cong Thanh, the Administrator-General of the House, and Congressmen Dinh van De, Khieu thien Ke, and Ho ngoc Nhuan, in particular, showed to my wife and myself. In thanking these kind and wise gentlemen, I hope that all my colleagues there will understand that I am speaking to them as well. Nguyen-Khoa Phon-An of the Center for Vietnamese Studies in Saigon was also an important contributor to the ease with which we were able to adjust to life in Saigon and begin work. Miss Le quan Hoa added her talents and her charm to the difficult task of arranging interviews and organized the documents used in this study. In Cambridge, my work on the French colonial period was aided by the graceful pen of Maida Uhlig, who helped render my French translations into readable prose. Nancy Belt labored over my enigmatic first draft, and Pamela Abbey at Clark served as chief of staff in shepherding the manuscript through what must have seemed endless revisions and changes. Janet Levine prepared the entire manuscript for publication, making valuable suggestions as I completed the revision process. Ann Ringle bore the brunt of my inconstancy and typed the manuscript perfectly twice. As a close personal friend, Mrs. Ringle encouraged me to publish the manuscript when she first read it, and her labors made this possible.

John C. Wood worked with me in Vietnam. He was a brilliant young scholar and for almost a year applied his talents to an investigation of the terrible events at My Lai. He spoke Vietnamese with an empathy few Americans in those times possessed. He was kind and gentle in our interviews in central Vietnam when I was not, and he died, I think, knowing more about the meaning of politics to the people there than I could ever hope to. In dedicating this book to his memory, I have instructed the Press to assign all royalties to the Center for Plastic and Reconstructive Surgery (Barsky Unit) in Saigon for their work with the children of Vietnam who have known only the war and not the promise of its politics.

Wellesley, Massachusetts
6 October 1972

Contents

Tables

Diagrams

Politics in War

At the eastern corner of Saigon's Lam Son Square stands a French colonial opera house that was converted into a meeting place for the National Assembly in 1962. In the square's center, a statue of two soldiers lunging forward symbolizes the aggressive spirit of the Vietnamese army. The two structures interact in an ironic way: the object of the soldiers' menacing charge is the meekly defended National Assembly building.[1] The image thus created dramatically illustrates the tension between the bases of civilian politics and military power in the polity, and the defenselessness of the former in the absence of any sense of community between the two.

In its politics, Vietnam is by no means unique. Of the eighty or so societies that by the 1950's and 1960's came to be regarded as developing countries, most are characterized by governments of the few that are incompatible with the community of the many. With rare exceptions, efforts to develop effective governing institutions have resulted in frustration and political decay,[2] producing, instead, institutionally elaborate but fundamentally weak republics. Increasingly, regimes are buttressed by coercion, rather than participation, of the masses in politics. Such polities lack effective institutions of government that facilitate the creation of political community. In Vietnam the tension between military and civil politics, so strikingly portrayed in Lam Son Square, reflects not only the conflict between political organizations but also the lack of any means to regulate conflict between the government and the governed. In Vietnam, as elsewhere, the creation of institutions designed to foster political community remains the paramount problem of politics in the 1970's.

Political Community as a Political Variable

The political community achieved by a society depends on the level of political participation and the scope of political institutions. Participation refers to both the numbers and types of people involved in politics, ranging from the elite to the middle classes and to the population at large, as well as to the impact that such involvement has on the functioning of government. Societies in which politics is controlled by an elite do not

1

possess a high degree of political community. In societies where the masses are politically mobilized, but where such mobilization has little impact upon the decisions of government, the level of political community is also low. Political community requires that the expansion of political participation be accompanied by a broadening of the scope of political institutions to accommodate the interests the new participants represent.

Political community is, thus, an acquired characteristic of political systems; for regimes to develop it, they must create power that can be shared with those who seek to participate in politics. To create power, regimes must mobilize social forces and organize their participation in a process that affects decisions of the government. Most developing polities today do not lack either conscious political participants or political institutions; rather, they lack enough power for the two to share. In South Vietnam those who control power also control participation and, to date, there has been little interest in creating more power. The activities of Vietnamese governing institutions have been segmented and the scope of these institutions has been narrowly perceived. The power of governing institutions rests not upon the ability to mobilize social forces, but upon the ability to displace elites.

In the precolonial era the creation of power was restricted by the Confucian social order and the traditional autonomy of the village. By prescribing the place of individuals and institutions within a hierarchy, Confucianism based any connection between elite and government and between government and the masses not on participation in the court system, but on respect and obedience owed the court.[3] Rulership was also influenced by village autonomy; it was specified that the writ of the emperor stopped at the village gate. Only the link between the village elite and the court mandarins was essential for government.[4]

During the colonial period this division between elite and mass was preserved, and it stimulated intraelite conflict over the limited government authority permitted by the French colonial administration. With the coming of independence in the South, this division was preserved by the social forces mobilized in war, forces which sought to conserve power gained by limiting the amount of power that could be created. In the postindependence era, the most effective way of limiting power has been to restrict both the mobilization and the participation of the mass in politics at the national level. Limiting participation and restricting the mobilization of the masses has strengthened the army at the expense of other social forces.

Indeed, South Vietnam is an almost classic example of a praetorian polity. As one central Vietnamese political leader observed in 1969, "the present regime presents [the image of] a centralized government, filled with power, but cowardly, incapable, confused and closed, under an administration of decrees and *arrêtes*, but in reality, an administration of money."[5] If the institutions of a praetorian society are weak, so also are most of its political forces. No general consensus exists within such polities about the existing distribution of power or, more importantly, the legitimacy of the means by which that distribution has been determined. While institutions lack the ability to create a sense of community among politicized social forces, political organizations lack the power to create a community of interest among themselves. Family dictatorships can give way to military ones, religious elite domination to secular elite domination, but the political structure of the society remains essentially the same. Whatever power exists is fragmented into small quantities held by many groups, none powerful enough to stabilize a set of national political institutions. Regimes govern not because they are strong, but because opposition to them is weak. Alternatives to government by a powerful minority do not exist, and power, which exists in both active and latent forms, cannot be cumulated to change the nature of politics or government.

Praetorian political systems can, of course, be transformed into participatory ones, although the opportunities for this are fleeting. Essentially, "escape from praetorianism requires both the coalescence of urban and rural interests and the creation of new political institutions."[6] Replacement of a succession of military juntas by an elected, constitutional republic in 1967 ended the instability that had plagued South Vietnam ever since the fall of the Diem government, but it did not increase the amount of power that existed in the polity or change the way Vietnam was governed. Only political forces independent of the regime appeared, by the end of the 1960's, to be engaged in an effort to discover the bases of political community. My purpose here is to describe what this experience meant to nationalist political leaders and to analyze their effort to organize political participation and create political power by focusing on the development of the Lower House of the National Assembly.

This study is also designed to provide a basis for understanding the requisites for peace in Vietnam. A political solution to the war will depend upon the development of political community, and the war will only end when communist and noncommunist forces can compete politically. An understanding of current politics is essential in assessing the kind of solution that nationalist political forces can facilitate and support.[7] The period from 1967 to the end of 1969 was one of experimentation with political relationships. Nationalist political forces began to discover ways they might participate within the framework of the 1967 Constitution and thereby create a community of interest between the forces they represented and the government. As one of its members suggested in an interview, the House "must be judged on the basis of what we have learned about politics and how this is translated into our political activities." This book describes the lessons learned about politics and, particularly, about creating power by Lower House deputies and seeks to establish that politics, rather than the war, should be the principal focus for research on Vietnam. The war represents a direct result of the failure to achieve political community at an earlier time between the nationalists and the communists. Its resolution will depend upon whether such a community can be constructed in the future.

Most social science research on Vietnam, and the body of existing research is not large,[8] is issue oriented. Samuel Huntington has noted: "Because of the governmental concern, most of the recent writing on Vietnam has been directed to the reporting of current history and analysis of immediate policy problems."[9] To Americans, the central feature of our involvement in Vietnam has been the war, and research has largely been concerned with its strategies, tactics, and effects. Such approaches, however, fundamentally obscure both the significance of the conflict and the Vietnamese view of it.

For their part, Vietnamese view the war in a symbolic rather than a strategic sense,[10] and those who speak openly about the need for peace do so by suggesting that reconciliation and not victory is essential. One Vietnamese friend described the predominant view:

> There is a game we play in Vietnam that is a contest of strength between equals. It is like your game of Indian arm wrestling except that the opponents oppose each other at the wrists rather than with their hands joined. Between the players' wrists is placed a stone. Thus each party is made to suffer. The one defeated is thus not necessarily the one whose arm is pressed down on the table but the one who can no longer stand the suffering of the combat.

Such a concept of the war is also allegorical. The two opponents are Vietnamese nationalists and communists, and the stone between their wrists represents the intervention of foreign powers. If the "stone" were removed, the opponents might clasp hands to continue the struggle, and the suffering on both sides would be reduced as conflict shifted from the military to the political arena. With the struggle thus transformed, the creation of political community would be vital to achieving and sustaining a political settlement.[11]

The impact of the war has, of course, been great. "Vietnamese society as a whole has undergone a change which can best be described as the militarization of the population. The public bureaucracy, particularly at the local levels, has been shaped into a military machine, and a massive effort is now underway to convert most of Vietnam's hamlets into armed bastions. . . "[12] As the intensity of the war increased, so also did its impact on society. The traditional isolation and autonomy of the village have been eroded as villages have become dependent upon the government for security, economic assistance, and emergency relief.[13] The war has also polarized the population, but it has not, by and large, resulted in their political mobilization. Such mobilization is a function of politics not warfare;[14] it requires the political community that Vietnam lacks.

The Legislature as a Micropolitical Community

A legislature is both a technique of government and a process of politics. Legislative institutions may, in fact, be the emergent microcosm of a society's politics. Drawn from the whole of society or even only a segment of it, the legislative arena permits experimentation and innovation at the microlevel of society that may be impossible or impractical at the macrolevel. Historically, the genesis of government has not coincided with the appearance of legislatures as political devices. Machiavelli observed that the founding of a state must be the work of one man alone, an individual who, having gained power, finds it difficult to share. In most polities whose systems of government now include a legislative body, legislatures were the products of social and political conflict. In rare cases, the development of a legislature was a function of social organization rather than of social conflict. The Greek *polis*, for example, was governed by a legislative-type assembly simply because it proved a rational means of governing a small homogeneous population.[15] In other, much larger polities, perhaps the closest forerunner to a legislature was the royal or dynastic advisory council, which aided the ruler in the formulation and conduct of policy. Strong rulers dominated these advisory councils and used them for the co-optation of individuals and social forces; weak rulers were dominated by the councils which in turn became centers of organized political activity.

Viewing a legislature as a political arena in microcosm rather than as a particular cultural value or institution permits it to be studied in a variety of settings. In Vietnam, although the legislature appeared during the period of French colonial domination it is regarded as part of an indigenous and older cultural tradition.[16] Even if the creation of legislatures appears inseparable from the influence of colonialism or imperialism, however, the tenure of legislatures depends upon their remaining viable and rational political arenas where political conflicts are satisfactorily regulated. Legislatures are not inherently "democratic" or liberal institutions. They can exist as instruments of repression or function to control or forestall the expansion of political participation or political power, as is the case in North Vietnam, North Korea, the Soviet Union, Brazil, Ceylon, Ghana, and India in the 1950's.

The effectiveness of any legislature as a political arena is related to its ability to perform political functions and to influence the broader institutional and political system. In a praetorian polity the organization of political participation is crucial to the legislature's survival if such survival requires the creation of political power. In the Philippines, for example, the legislature created in the wake of the struggle for independence fostered the development of political parties as a means of expanding political participation and creating power. But the parties emerged as the dominant political institution, and the legislative body never developed the capacity to regulate the intense political conflicts that have divided Philippine society ever since. Because legislators increasingly had to depend upon the President rather than their constituents for support, political power is now measured in terms of personal influence, not the ability to organize popular participation.

The decline in the political functions of legislatures has often paralleled the rise of the modern executive. In the West, the challenge to absolutism marked the period of greatest political activity within the framework of legislative assemblies. But the emerging political forces made little lasting or specific commitment to the legislature as a regulator of political conflict. Indeed, if strong executives have come to overshadow the governing functions of legislatures, so also have strong party systems tended to displace the political functions of legislatures.[17] In order to survive in praetorian polities lacking a strong party system, therefore, legislatures must behave as if they were political organizations rather than constitutional institutions.

The three distinct processes relevant to the study of legislative politics, therefore, are: the founding or creation of the legislature, its organization as a micropolitical community, and its functioning as a political arena. Aside from those rare cases where a legislature has appeared as a natural consequence of a particular pattern of social or political organization, most legislatures have been founded as the by-product of a particular social conflict. The political forces which demanded the creation of such consultative decision-making bodies constituted a challenge to political order. In many postcolonial societies, in contrast, the legislature has often been imposed by the colonial power to preserve a facade of democracy while maintaining control over the political process. In Indonesia, for example, the Dutch used the legislature to provide a semblance of popular participation while insuring continued dominance over Indonesian politicians. The division of the republic into sixteen states of unequal population, but each with equal representation in the legislature of 1949, "testified to the artificial nature of the federal system which the Dutch had been sponsoring and made clear that in constructing it they had been more concerned with promoting a strategy of divide and rule, calculated to eventuate in a political order which they could indirectly control . . ."[18] Indeed, the indirect control characteristic of most postcolonial legislatures are reflected in the legislative institutions established during colonial rule. "The colonial legislature had two main functions. The first was to provide a sounding-board of opinion; to assist the government to be informed of the main grievances and aspirations of the different communities. The second function was that of a safety-valve: to provide a platform upon which westernized *evolues* could work out their passions and plans, without actually starting an insurrection."[19] And, in the case of those independent polities where legislatures were created in the wake of changes in the governmental systems, the legislature represented a compromise or co-optative institution through which those newly acquiring power sought to legitimize their rule and the opposition to it. The founding of legislatures in most developing societies, thus, is often an experiment in political control, or, in the expansion of political participation, it is designed to serve the interests of those whose position the legislature was created to legitimize.

The political organization of legislatures refers to the process by which political and governmental functions are acquired.[20] For a legislature, its initial political activities and organization are crucial to its ultimate emergence as an institution of government and politics. It must alter the political process before it can alter the form of government under which it exists. In most developing polities, however, the acquisition of governmental functions by a legislature depends upon the individual political activities of its members rather than upon the specific prescription of functions outlined in a constitutional document. Before governmental power can be divided between an executive and a legislative body, sufficient power must be created to make such a division something less than an attempt on the part of either to conduct a constitutional coup. Intense competition between the executive and the legislature over implementing a separation of power reflects that there is only a limited amount of political power to be separated. This has led one scholar to conclude that "the doctrine of the separation of powers . . . has . . . uniformly failed to provide an adequate basis for an effective, stable political system."[21] Instead, creation of power is the fundamental imperative for newly established legislatures, and this requires that the political activity and commitments of its members be linked to the development of the institution as a whole.

While most legislatures acquire certain initial political functions, they frequently fail to achieve tenure in the political system. They can be dissolved at will,[22] or they become an institutional facade behind which the strongest party or the executive claims legitimacy. They are not, however, valued themselves as an institution. The failure to transform the procedures and values of its micropolitical aspects to politics at large produces legislatures which do not achieve the institutionalization—the "process by which organizations and procedures acquire value and stability"[23]—required for their effective functioning or continued existence. The founding of a legislature can thus be distinguished from the process through which it acquires political functions and the process through which it comes to reflect certain stable and recurring patterns of political behavior.

The founding and functioning of legislatures have been popular subjects of comparative political studies, but little attention has been paid to the political organization of legislatures.[24] We know a great deal about why legislatures were created in developing societies and about what they have become, but relatively little about the process by which they succeeded or failed to achieve political tenure. As a result, we have many hypotheses about why legislatures have developed in a particular way, but the dearth of data on their initial political organization makes the proving of any hypothesis developed in such a *post hoc* fashion difficult. Moreover, research on legislatures in developing countries in the past has tended to be based on views of what legislative bodies ought to be rather than their role in modern politics.[25] Noting the diversity of the research extant on legislative bodies, one scholar observed: "It has become more-or-less conventional to characterize legislative behavior research as involving three kinds of studies. One involves research on legislative recruitment, which usually means analyses of legislators' social and political attributes. A second involves research on legislators' motivations and roles, though the corpus of research of this kind is rather small. Finally, research may focus on legislative decision-making, and the major type of work in this category has involved analyses of legislative roll-call voting behavior."[26] What is lacking, however, is a fourth dimension: the study of a legislature's political organization, or its functioning as a micropolitical community. My description of the South Vietnamese Lower House is thus designed as a case study within which the diversity of concepts and hypotheses so far advanced in the comparative study of legislatures can be integrated.

The achievement of political community is rare. Lacking opportunities to develop political community at the microlevel, polities most certainly do not achieve it at the macrolevel. While the legislature may function as a potential link between these two levels of politics, the importance of the legislature as a vehicle for the creation of political community has been overshadowed by the preeminent role of the executive. A study of representative institutions in forty-one countries by the Inter-Parliamentary Union concluded, for example, with the observation: "The initiative in legislative and financial matters has to some extent slipped out of its [Parliament's] grasp; the practice of delegating powers has made for the curtailment of its role in the realm of law. But concurrently, the prerogatives of Parliament have shifted in the direction of control of government activity. The government initiates and directs; Parliament controls, approves, disapproves, and, now and then, inspires."[27] Indeed, one observer suggested, "The rise and predominance of the executive appears to be a leading characteristic of modern political organization."[28] In countries with established traditions that provide the population with adequate safeguards against encroachments on their personal and political liberties, legislative bodies have to some extent prevented strong presidents from turning into autocratic executives. Both institutions exist within a consensual framework that regulates and legitimates the domination of the few over the community of the many. Predominant executives, however, are not found in modern democracies alone. Of the roughly eighty countries today considered underdeveloped, all but three have parliaments. In more than 25 percent of these countries, however, the legislative body has been dissolved at least once since independence and roughly the same proportion (not including communist states) had members either entirely appointed by the executive or who all belonged to one progovernment party.[29] The developing nations not only tend to be characterized by weak parliaments but also by weak, narrowly based executives. The source of such weakness is the same for both institutions: in their process of government domination by the few is not based on acceptance by the community of the many. Such a functioning political community does not exist.

Government versus Politics: Traditional Political Institutions and the Absence of Political Community in Vietnam

Vietnam's national political institutions reflect the narrow base of political power with which the elite governs. Successive ruling groups have sought to remain in power by a strategy of divide and rule.[1] In the absence of institutions able to control and regulate conflict, political organizations in Vietnam have not been mobilized into a national political community, and this lack of political integration stems from the fundamental and carefully nurtured view that national politics is inherently unstable whereas local politics is not.

When Vietnamese observe that their country is not yet ready for democracy, they imply not only that the electorate is uneducated and lacks a national consciousness, but also that the ruling elite does not value or, consequently, promote the level of political participation that democracy requires. The failure of the Diem government, of the juntas which succeeded him, and of the present Thieu goverment has been, according to this view, that they have not linked their own survival to the political mobilization of the population.[2] Placed in power by the military, Vietnamese governments have, since 1963, become increasingly preoccupied with staying in power by appeasing the military rather than by mobilizing the population. Such a situation appears inherently unstable to the Vietnamese because too many are competing for too little power. Vietnamese village life and politics, in contrast, are viewed with a sense of cultural pride; the village is seen as the only stable system of government that can be identified for the middle and peasant classes.[3] And from the village came a revolutionary movement admired and imitated around the globe. Throughout most of the 1960's in Vietnam, the success of the communists contrasted sharply with the failure of ruling elites to base national government upon developing a sense of community among political organizations. While the communists were to inherit Lenin's conception of the party, the noncommunists could look to no national political institution for a model with similar capacities for political mobilization.

Legislative Traditions in Precolonial
and Colonial Vietnam

In Vietnam legislative-type assemblies served the dominant political forces of the society, rather than operating as independent institutions designed to serve the population and mediate between its political forces. In the precolonial era, quasi-legislative village councils served the administrative hierarchy of government. These councils appeared in 1461, shortly after popularly elected village chiefs replaced court-appointed communal mandarins. The members of the village council were the leaders of the village; the "voting" which took place represented an affirmation of the elite structure of village leadership rather than the results of a competitive system. "In the rustic communities of Vietnam a representative body was certainly useful but its object was not an equalitarian vote. Rather, it expressed the hierarchical structure of the society. Age, literary accomplishments, and—to a lesser degree—the accumulation of wealth provided the basis of the hierarchy."[4] These standards stressed ability to represent the village as a corporate entity to the court, not the population to the emperor or his mandarins.[5] Often, in fact, there was little difference in background between the village council member or the village chief and the officials of the court. As one early French scholar noted: "There were many successful mandarinate service examination candidates who, instead of working for the court went back to their respective villages and towns, where, together with retired court officials, they formed an informal local elite group. This group was very important in that while it represented the local people and the communities dealing with the court, it also helped the court to reach the people. (Nominees from among this group were very often elected by the local people to serve on village councils.)"[6] The village council and the process of politics underlying it served to identify the local elite and link them to a governmental system rather than to link the population to the government.

In fact village councils compensated the court for its failure to develop a national system of government extending to the local level by providing local counterparts for provincial administrative services. Village councils, then, had a place in the court system but not in the court itself. At the top existed the emperor and his ministers of state who convened into a national decision-making body, the *Noi Cac* (Supreme Council). In practice, the *Noi Cac* reflected the interests of the emperor and the court rather than the interests of the village council or the population.[7] The institution of a nominally representative assembly that linked the population directly to the government at the national level came only as the result of French colonialism.

The traditional Vietnamese village and its governmental obligations were described as:

> not based on authority and will, but on the recognition of universal harmony. In other words, the Vietnamese village was neither democratic nor autocratic, neither autonomous nor dictatorially controlled. The distinctions were irrelevant, even alien to the traditional system. Thus even in the fifteenth century, when the *xa* seems to have been subject to the traditional maximum of supervision from above, it would be wrong to assume that the nature of the supervision was precisely the same as what the Westerner means when he uses the word "control." The emperor made demands, and it was for the villagers to carry them out. But his guarantee that they would do so rested more on their sense of obligation than on an authoritarian system of coercion.[8]

Generally, the village also played its part in the court system because it enabled the population's obligations owed the emperor to be transferred to those he designated to represent his person in the provinces. The French, however, altered this built-in legitimacy when they introduced a system of local and national consultative councils and separated these bodies from the court's governmental system. They thus effectively circumscribed the executive and administrative functions of the councils. As the position of the court in the councils declined, so also did its ability to command the villages to obey. Coercion had to be substituted.

Province councils were established in each of the three states of colonial Vietnam during the latter part of the nineteenth century and the first quarter of the twentieth century. Members were chosen by the electorate from a group made up of active and retired chiefs and deputy chiefs of hamlets nominated by the French resident superior. The French viewed these councils as a device that would foster greater collaboration between their officials and local Vietnamese elites and as an institution that would co-opt influential Vietnamese to support the French administration.[9] Reasoning that in precolonial days what was essentially an elite was elected to village councils, the French believed such people were the natural leaders of the population: "The province councils are composed of notables which constitute, in relation to the simple populace, an elite which is in no way estranged from the latter, who rise from the latter directly, and who do not assume in their district the often distant superiority of the mandarins."[10] Through their control of the nomination process, consequently, the French endeavored to assure that the local gentry most sympathetic with French rule would be elected to the province council. Those critical of French rule were seldom if ever elected; instead, they led the early uprisings against the French.

Rather than deal with the government for the village as precolonial councils had, the French-supported councils had only advisory duties.[11] Members were elected for terms of three to four years, and the councils sat in a short closed session twice a year. The resident superior was required to submit the province budget each year for the council's vote of approval and it was also required to vote on any public works projects or proposed changes in province or canton boundaries. Similar functions were ascribed to municipal councils established for Saigon-Cholon in 1877-1879, Hanoi-Haiphong in 1891, and DaNang in 1908. Discussion of political issues was strictly forbidden.[12]

The colonial provincial and municipal councils, which preserved the division between elite and mass embodied in the precolonial village council system, deepened this same division at the province level. Election to the provincial councils depended not upon ability to secure popular votes, as the village council system had, but rather upon the ability of one local elite to secure the votes of other local elites and, of course, the support of the French administrators. The French sought to rule by dividing the society against itself and by "assimilating" those Vietnamese who would support the administration to effect, as one scholar of the period observed, "the destruction of existing native institutions and their replacement by those prevalent in France."[13] The emerging legislative system came increasingly to be based not on the strengths of the village council tradition but upon the weaknesses of a foreign system.[14]

At the national level the French created an institution to parallel the provincial councils. Each of the three states of Vietnam had a consultative national body representing the Vietnamese elite. But in only one case, that of the Colonial Council of Cochin-China, could the council actually legislate. The Colonial Council of Cochin-China, established by decree in 1880, was administered directly by the French governor-general. He set the agenda for and fixed the length of sessions, inaugurated them, and nullified any decisions at will. Only six Vietnamese were members of the council, elected by about twelve thousand eligible voters.[15] Twice that number of Frenchmen were members, six of whom were elected by French citizens (which could include ethnic Vietnamese of French citizenship, although such Vietnamese could not run for office) and six were appointed by the governor from among the membership of the Chambers of Commerce and Agriculture in Saigon.[16] Since the electorate itself was an elite, membership on the colonial councils precluded the need for such elites to relate to any portion of the Vietnamese peasant population.

The jurisdiction of the colonial council stressed its deliberative nature rather than its limited ability to make laws.[17] All of the council's resolutions were subject to the review of the governor-general and could be overturned or ignored by him; council procedure did not require that vetoed legislation be returned for reconsideration. The jurisdiction of the council, moreover, was determined by the governor-general and provided the source of his power to nullify council resolutions: "The governor of Cochin-China in Privy Council can nullify the resolutions of the Colonial Council when these resolutions do not come within the jurisdiction of the Council."[18] The strong arm of the governor-general, reaching into the very functioning of the council, met with no resistance from the council members.[19] "Disadvantaged by the language [French was the required language of the deliberations] and by a situation of social inferiority vis. that of their European colleagues, the native members could hardly seriously resist the drafting of the orders of the day by voting against the Frenchmen. And if it happened that some of the native members, conscious of their role as representatives of the people, formed an opposition party, they would fear sanctions against them or [they would be] bribed."[20] Indeed, any statements that the members wished to make on their own initiative were required to be submitted in advance to the president of the council who would, in turn, submit them to the governor-general. The result of these restrictions pleased the French, who viewed the council as the beginnings of the rudimentary democracy that they sought to impose on Vietnam. In their view the council lacked "a spirit of particularism which would have ... caused the delegates to focus upon only the interests of the canton or the village; rather, the subjects discussed, the solutions foreseen and proposed, inspired the needs of collectivity and marked thus a happy adoption of the institution that the French administration wished to encourage."[21]

Of all the councils in Indo-China the Colonial Council of Cochin-China proved the most troublesome for the French. Although never a significant source of direct political opposition,[22] the council, in 1917, aided the rise of the Constitutional party that flourished in the 1920's. The party (one of whose executive committee members was a deputy of the council) sought to work for political reforms through the French system rather than in opposition to it. As such, it was only one of a number of quasi-opposition organizations that were publicly constituted and sought to mobilize support for candidates in local elections as well as in the election of the French representative of the colony who sat in the French Assembly; as such, the Constitutionalists were, between 1917 and 1924, "virtually the only organized political group in Cochin-China, at a time when opposition of any more extreme kind would have been rigorously suppressed."[23] Nonetheless their membership and support were limited primarily to the Saigon metropolitan area, and they were unable to link their activities even clandestinely to those undertaken by more extreme opponents of French rule. Perhaps they were not inclined to work outside the system since they were part of its elite: "The gulf between the moderation of the Constitutionalists and the extremism of the other groups tended very often to coincide with the gulf between the town and the country."[24]

The failure of the Constitutionalists serves to underscore the significance of the legislative bodies created by the French, which perpetuated the division between elite and mass through restricted franchise and turned the elite in urban areas against those in rural areas through co-optation of the former. As one contemporary Vietnamese observer has noted, most Vietnamese who gained election to the council were French citizens; thus, "one sees immediately that those who are able to best defend the interests of the uneducated masses are excluded from the representative assembly of Cochin-China."[25] Indeed, those elected appeared to Vietnamese and Frenchmen alike as sons of France, not Vietnam. A government report on elections in 1914, for example, suggests that "Numerous candidates have been elected in the first round of balloting by very huge majorities, some even unanimously; these representatives are serious and honest men of moral renown, with an open mind to progressive ideas and devoted to the French cause . . . "[26] What potential the council might have had to bridge the resulting gulf remained latent. As a political institution then the colonial council had virtually no significance as a source of opposition to French rule.

French troubles with the council concerned not its political influence but its corruption. Particularly after the turn of the century the public reputation of the council was widely challenged by the French and the Vietnamese press as well as by a series of short-lived pamphleteers.[27] And one contemporary critique of the functioning of the council in this period viewed the institutions as so corrupt and its members of such poor quality that even extensive changes in suffrage would not have reformed the council to French Satisfaction.[28] During the first decade of its existence, six specific reforms were directed at the council in the form of procedural and jurisdictional changes aimed at altering the practices and reducing the powers used by the councillors for graft and profiteering. More than twice that number of reforms were promulgated by the governor-general after 1910 for the same purposes. The vehemence and consistency with which the popular press and other journals denounced the council, however, suggests that these reforms had little impact. The French administration failed to root out the corruption in the council largely because it was intimately linked to the corruption of the colonial regime itself. André Malraux who in the 1920's published a series of anticolonial newspapers in Saigon wrote:

> The elected bodies of Cochin-China . . . have been formed under conditions of flagrant illegality; their leaders, whom the Governor holds by the hand like Children, are without authority. The press is dominated by the same Governor in the same way.
> If Indo-China is—according to M. Daladier's expression—a "private preserve," then Cochin-China is one for the Governor himself and for his friends, contrary to all law.[29]

Devoid of any political function and reflecting only the dynamics of divisions within the elite, the colonial and consultative councils of French Indo-China became instruments of colonial policy which, along with the civil and provincial services, sought to co-opt Vietnamese into supporting French domination. Only two options were available for politically mobilized Vietnamese: becoming a colonial mandarin or civil servant, which meant the acquisition of French citizenship, religion, and culture, or becoming a revolutionary.[30] The French institutions tended to keep the co-opted Vietnamese elite preoccupied with competition among themselves.

The Legislature and Independence

Independence did not change the political significance of legislative institutions as they were established both in the North and in the South. But the absence of change was not entirely a consequence of the hundred years of French domination. In creating national legislative bodies the

French merely preserved and built upon the gaps between and within elite and mass and between town and countryside that they had found in Vietnam. By changing the relationship of the village to the state decision-making process, the French altered the structure of national government rather than the political process of the village. As Ralph Smith has suggested, after considering the political process that existed before the French arrival, one need not "assume the existence of a colonial government as a prerequisite for conflicts between canton or district officials and the notables of villages. A great deal of political maneuvering must have gone on beneath the surface of formal village harmony."[31] Periodically the harmony of the Confucian social fabric was more a mask:

> Beneath the surface of Confucian order . . . there existed an underworld of secret societies and political revolt. Sometimes the opportunity for action was created by factions within the imperial court and bureaucracy. A crisis there might well be the signal for revolt in the country. In other cases the opportunity arose from the grievances of the peasantry, and a rebel leader might recruit a large following in a particular area, to create what amounted to a private army.[32]

It was this underlying tension in Vietnamese society that political institutions in both the colonial and the precolonial period failed to regulate. Such institutions represented not authoritative means to resolve political disputes but a means to rationalize the domination of a portion of the elite over the polity. To challenge the government was to challenge the elite that controlled it.

Even in present-day Vietnam the salience of elites in local and national politics is particularly manifest in Vietnamese voting behavior where, for the most part, those elected are elite members of the society who are expected to deal with other elites for the village. Representation has not yet become a form of popular participation but remains a process of elite competition and selection. In terms of the political behavior of Vietnamese institutions, therefore, it is difficult to determine whether the political process which succeeded the colonial administration, equally as repressive and elite-oriented in the South as in the North, represented in its legislative bodies the French influence on political behavior, or reflected an indigenous preference for elite rule. Indeed, while the need for mass bases of support was a product of the anticolonial struggle, it was only an extension of struggles within the elite aimed at replacing the leadership of one class with the leadership of another. Thus the result of the anticolonial struggle was not a particularly new form of government but rather a division of the territory into two political entities: one retained the Francophile elites, and one replaced them.

During the anticolonial struggle the two legislative bodies established in Vietnam reflected the bases of the two governments that emerged in the wake of the Japanese surrender. In January 1946 the Democratic Republic of Vietnam held elections for its own Vietnam National Assembly. Two features of the election, however, suggest that it was not a popular referendum on the legitimacy of the government but rather a *pro forma* ratification of its hegemony. First, parties in opposition to the Viet Minh were assigned a fixed number of seats before the election took place, a much smaller number than were assigned to the Viet Minh. Second, the reported electoral turnout of 73 percent of the voting populace and 91 percent of those registered was considered rather high for a country's first efforts at conducting an election based upon universal suffrage. It was concluded at the time that "the National Assembly itself could hardly be discounted as a representative body for the Vietnamese. Its membership reflected all political currents and tendencies, from the conservative mandarinate to the extreme left."[33] As subsequent developments made clear, the assembly was constrained by what "representation" meant in the early days of the DRV.

The National Assembly determined the composition of the government and thereby weakened groups which opposed the Viet Minh. This was evidenced by "the ubiquitous police agents of the government [who] kept a close check on some of the dissidents and a few members disappeared after the convocation. Police agents conducted several house searches and contributed in some measure to a feeling that it was dangerous to oppose the government too strongly."[34] The Assembly, elected for a three-year term initially, remained in office for ten years and met only twice during that period. In the process it changed from an institution which included members of the entire political spectrum in the North to one which, by 1956, represented only the interest of the Viet Minh (subsequently the *Lao Dong* party) and served subsequently to ratify its policies. The nominal opposition elements elected had all but disappeared from the proceedings by the end of the second session.[35] Ironically, the National Assembly preserved the tradition of dependence upon the executive from the colonial era. A typical meeting of North Vietnam's legislature in 1965 lasted only two days. The assembly listened to speeches by Ho and Pham van Dong, unanimously endorsed their content, and passed a single resolution calling on other legislative bodies of the world to condemn US imperialism.[36] To date, the formalistic, ceremonial functions of the legislature in the North have not changed.

During the struggle for independence in the South, the legislature was more intimately tied to the functioning of the government, but involved only a small segment of the political spectrum. In February 1946, the governor-general of Cochin-China appointed four Frenchmen and eight Vietnamese to an advisory consultative council, modeled on the colonial council that had existed before the war. All members of the new council were appointed by the French governor and most, despite their ethnic background, were French citizens. In June, the council proclaimed the Republic of Cochin-China, and its functions were expanded to include the selection of a government from among its membership. No elections were to take place. The French contended that the lack of security in the countryside would have prevented fair elections from being held. While North Vietnam had replaced the consultative colonial council of the French with one that the party could dominate, South Vietnam, until the withdrawal of the French in 1954, maintained essentially the same colonial bodies that had existed before the war. After 1954, the legislative bodies which emerged in both countries remained under the firm control of the leaders of each government. Neither achieved the degree of political organization or acquired the political functions that would permit development into an independent institution of government. Diem, like the French before him and like the party that controlled the government in the North, used the National Assembly to ratify his policies rather than to legislate them.

Early in 1955 the Diem government recognized the need for an elected assembly to add a more democratic flavor to the decisions of the regime. In April Diem declared, "The day that an assembly representing the nation holds session, I will gladly accept its judgment."[37] On the basis of interviews held with those delegated to prepare an election plan, however, it was clear that Diem also wanted such an assembly to reflect his personal political strength and that of his own political party. This required the creation of a legislature that would add the flavor of democratic procedures without the customary challenges to governmental policies that legislatures often provide. The character of the assembly required by the Diem government was perhaps best, if rather unwittingly, described in the editorial of a northern Catholic daily paper: "Though the foreign policy of the government is on the right track and its actions most timely [that is, in that it was shortly to oppose the referendum on reunification that was scheduled for 1956 by the Geneva agreements], the lack of an assembly to ratify decisions tends to make the people think the government is merely provisional."[38] The assembly desired, and the one that ultimately emerged, had the primary function of ratifying the policies of the Diem government and providing it with a semblance of legitimacy.

Diem convened three National Assemblies during his tenure in 1956, 1959, and 1963.[39] These assemblies were chosen by all Vietnamese citizens eighteen and older whose names appeared on the police registration lists. In each election no less than 85 percent of those registered (some six to seven million persons) voted. All Vietnamese citizens twenty-five and older with six months of continuous residence in Vietnam who had completed their military service obligations were eligible to be candidates in the election. In 1956 there were 468, and in 1959, 441 candidates for the 123 seats in the assembly. Rather than represent a variety of political organizations and groups, however, the candidates generally reflected those the government favored. "A fairly large number [of candidates] were selected and designated or asked to run by the inner leadership of the government party; others were approached by province chiefs and other officials. . . . Some candidates might have been attracted by the high salary and low work demands of membership in the National Assembly, or for whatever prestige was thought to accrue from being a deputy."[40] The results of the elections for the various National Assemblies produced an institution controlled by and responsive to President Diem.[41] The most powerful member of all three assemblies, for example, was thought to be Madame Ngo dinh Nhu,[42] the wife of Diem's brother. Though her husband, who controlled the police and security services, was also a member of the assemblies, he never participated in them himself. The control that Diem maintained over the functioning of the assemblies reflected his concept of the need for a strong progovernment party with the development of any opposition controlled and severely limited. Diem considered Vietnam distinct from more secure and developed regimes that could afford an organized opposition. He believed that, if South Vietnam were to survive the threat he perceived in the northern regime and avoid becoming a dictatorship in the process, strong, centralized direction and control were required. Parliamentary democracy was not, in his opinion, applicable to the needs of newly founded states. In a message to the National Assembly on 17 April 1956, shortly after it had been elected, Diem declared:

while this system [of parliamentary democracy in the West] in its application brought relative freedom to a minority, at the same time it diminished the effectiveness of the state, which became impotent to defend collective interests and to solve social problems. The events preceding the two world wars revealed these weaknesses more than ever before and in certain states led to the birth of fascism with its concentration of power under personal dictatorships. In the same pretext to organize effective power in the name of social justice, another reaction appeared in the form of communism under the so-called popular democracies. At the cost of heavy restrictions and the sacrifice of industrial freedoms, these systems have merely imposed dictatorships of political parties.

In finished societies, all the main elements are complete and the national government has only to arbitrate between them. In a new and primitive country the main elements of society must simultaneously be created and directed from the center. And government trying to accomplish this must operate more directly upon public opinion than it would . . . in a finished society.[43]

Such direct action from the center involved Diem in the creation of his own political party, the positioning of its members in governmental institutions[44] and particularly in the National Assembly, and the weakening of all political organizations that he could not trust. New political parties were forbidden by presidential decree, and established nationalist parties such as the *Dai Viet* and the *Vietnam Quoc Dan Dang* experienced difficulties in finding a place in the institutions of the new regime. "The Diem government has reacted to the older nationalist parties in one of two ways: it has either denied them authorization to function legally or it has selected one tractable faction to operate in the name of the party and furnished it with quotas of National Assembly seats, operating funds, and other perquisites."[45] Too many parties espousing too many opposing points of view, Diem believed, would weaken the fabric of government which, in turn, would weaken its ability to compete with the North.

Diem apparently realized that allowing political organizations free reign would threaten his family's hold over government. Rather than representing opinions critical of the government's policies, the existence of many groups would challenge the government itself. Dennis Duncanson, a British Foreign Office official at the time, explained Diem and Nhu's philosophy of political competition in the following way: "they were able to foresee that their rule would never encounter opposition over particular measures: any who opposed them would be outright rivals for power, not critics of policy, with no more right to rule arbitrarily, and probably less capacity, than themselves."[46] Both individuals and organizations were so viewed. In 1959 three opposition candidates representing a political association between Saigon intellectuals and disgruntled nationalists were elected despite considerable efforts on the part of the government—manipulating the polling and the counting of ballots—to defeat them. Only one of the three ever took his seat: one was disqualified, and the other incarcerated until the fall of the regime in 1963. One former deputy said during the course of an interview that most of the members felt the opposition speeches of the imprisoned deputy (Dr. Phan quang Dan, now Minister of State for External Relations in the Khiem cabinet) "were aiding the communists" and that the deputy should have been imprisoned not for his election but because of his suspected clandestine activities against the Diem government. "The times required that all the people support President Diem and that this would be the most effective way of combating the Communists. Thus, Dr. Dan's open participation on the floor of the Assembly would not lessen his threat to the Republic since he would not support President Diem." The deputy also suggested that the membership of the assembly agreed that to support the President was to support the Republic in the time of war. "We all felt it incumbent upon ourselves, therefore, to support Diem and not present our opposition on the floor of the Assembly. Instead we sought to communicate our criticisms privately to the President. Also, since the politics of the government were clearly declared we felt little efficacy would come out of handling particular issues in public debate." Supporting the President meant support not only of his policies but also of the Ngo family's political organization. In addition, an unstated but enforced embargo on deputies' political activities limited contact between the deputies and their constituencies. As Scigliano has noted, "the deputies do not have roots even in their own constituencies, and as one newspaper has pointed out and the average Vietnamese is well aware, a good many deputies had not, on the eve of the 1959 election campaign, returned to their districts since they were elected to the National Assembly in March 1956."[47] With the exception of the three opposition candidates referred to above, only those who favored the Diem government were able to win elections. The Ngo family's attitude toward political competition and their fear of it led, consequently, to the emergence of a National Assembly controlled by a single, progovernment party of which Diem's brother was the chairman.

In the National Assembly elected in March 1956 as well as in that elected in August 1959, five basic political organizations were represented

(Table 2-1). In both cases, however, the political affiliations of the deputies elected were largely with the splinter groups or hastily organized fronts of the main government party, the National Revolutionary Movement. The diversity of Vietnam's political organizations was not reflected in the political affiliations of those elected to the assembly. As the 1956 assembly characterized itself shortly after its organization "with the political status of Free Vietnam, the new Congress cannot be divided into proleft, proright, or moderate tendencies: thus, the divisions as [reflected in the political affiliations of the membership] does [*sic*] not mean a deep conflict of tendency."[48] With the National Revolutionary movement and later the *Can Lao* party[49] forming the main springs of political action in the assembly, two blocs were organized, but they functioned without substantial differences of opinion.

> The artificial character of the government parties is seen in their role in the National Assembly. In the first place, the legislative elections were quite carefully manipulated by the government to produce mostly safe deputies, and there has not yet developed any close relationships between the deputies as a whole and their constituencies. Secondly, the bulk of government policy-making is done through the executive branch and that which is carried out in the National Assembly is done under strong executive influence. The deputies are organized into blocs, called simply "majority" and "minority" during the first National Assembly. At the time they were organized, many deputies were evidently confused as to the purpose of the blocs, and there was not much in fact to distinguish them in programmatic terms.[50]

When the first debate on the internal organization of the assembly turned to the question of the nature of the blocs, the meeting was summarily adjourned "because of the extremely delicate character of the matter."[51] When debate was resumed, it was explained that some deputies had simply wished to have two blocs, and it was subsequently decided that all deputies could choose between belonging to one or the other or abstaining from participation in either. The adjournment of the assembly when the two bloc system was challenged, some of the members felt, reflected the fact that to challenge the conception of the bloc system would have been tantamount to challenging the wishes of Diem.[52]

By the beginning of the 1959 assembly the blocs had been named, and each had promulgated a "policy" stand. Approximately eighty deputies belonged to a Personalist Community Block (*Khoi Cong-Dong Nhan-Vi*), including all deputies who were members of the National Revolutionary

Table 2-1   Declared political affiliations of National
Assembly deputies, 1956 and 1959

Affiliation	1956[a]	1959[a]
National Revolutionary Movement		
(Phong Trao Cach-Mang Quoc-Gia)	61	78
Citizen's Assembly		
(Tap-Doan Cong-Dan)[b]	25	–
Revolutionary Labor party		
(Can-Lao Nhan-Vi)[c]	15	2
Movement to Win and Preserve Freedom		
(Phong Trao Tranh-Thu Tu-Do)	8	–
Dai-Viet Progressive party		
(Dai-Viet Cap-Tien)	1	–
Declared Independents	11	28
Hoa Hao Social Democratic party		
(Dan Xa Dang Hoa Hao)	–	3
Vietnam Socialist party		
(Xa-Hoi)	–	4
Vietnam National Restoration party		
(Vietnam Phuc Quoc Hoi)	–	2
Miscellaneous labor unions	–	3

Sources: Secretary of State for Information, Republic of Vietnam, *The Constitution of the Republic of Vietnam* (Saigon, 1956), p. 13; Quoc Hoi Vietnam [Congress of Vietnam], *Nien-Gaim Quoc-Hoi Viet-Nam* [The Legislative Congress of Vietnam] (Saigon, 1956), p. 41; Embassy of Vietnam, *News from Vietnam,* 5 (16 October 1959), pp. 2–3; Quoc Hoi Vietnam [Congress of Vietnam], *Nien-Giam Quoc-Hoi Vietnam: Quoc-Hoi Lap-Phap Phap Nhiem Khoa Hai | Legislative Congress of Vietnam,* Term II] (Saigon, 1959), p. 16.

[a]Two deputies were not permitted to take their seats in 1956, due to election violations which resulted in a Congress of 121 rather than 123 deputies. In 1959, two deputies were barred from the assembly for political reasons.

[b]Merged with the NRM in July 1958.

[c]Most *Can Lao* deputies preferred membership in the NRM when the former began to be organized as a party for government civil servants. See the discussion of the National Revolutionary Movement in John T. Dorsey, Jr., "The Bureaucracy and Political Development in Vietnam," in Joseph La Palombara, ed., *Bureaucracy and Political Development* (Princeton, N. J., Princeton University Press, 1963); and Robert Scigliano, *South Vietnam: Nation Under Stress* (Boston, 1964).

Movement. Approximately thirty deputies formed the membership of the Socialist Union Bloc (*Khoi Lien-Minh Xa-Hoi*), including the deputies affiliated with the Socialist Humanist (*Can Lao*) party. The program of the Personalist Bloc was based upon the philosophy of personalism to which Diem was attracted,[53] and it included the denunciation of communism, support for an independent and unified Vietnam, the elimination of inequality, "complete personal freedom," elected government, "the liberation of mankind from materialism," the assurance of the population's right to well-being. In short, the bloc supported "a personal revolution in morality and culture to improve the community and a communal revolution to enhance personalism."[54] Though less pedantic in summarizing its philosophy, the Socialist Humanist Bloc supported the same goals as the Personalist Bloc. Rather than reflect any political differences, of course, the blocs of the assembly functioned as facades behind which the government controlled deliberations.

The functioning and deliberations of the assemblies reflected their domination by the executive. Lacking a political organization responsive to Vietnam's diverse political forces, the assembly lacked the initiative to propose legislation, and throughout its existence the President constituted the primary source of legislation. To the observation that "The National Assembly is a pitiful parody of parliament, not only a rubber stamp, but one which is self-inking,"[55] Scigliano added: "No bill has been modified to any important extent in the National Assembly and little serious debate has issued from it."[56] Indeed, the most significant legislation passed, in contrast to its rather mundane output of ratifications of international treaties and domestic statutes, were those proposed and managed by members of the Ngo family. In 1959 and in 1962 Madame Nhu submitted two bills concerned with family law and with the protection of morality which reflected the regime's martinet tendencies in matters of public morals.[57] "A number of deputies arose to argue against its passage. . . . After they had completed their speeches, however, Madame Nhu is reported to have told them that she had listened patiently to their arguments and some of them might be impressive but now she wanted the bill passed. It was thereupon passed, with even the former dissenters voting for it."[58] Such overt pressure from the executive was, however, rare in the assembly's deliberations; it was seldom necessary. Diem formed the political, administrative, and legislative power center of a governmental system in which the assembly held essentially an advisory position. The President could attend its sessions, speak before them, confer with its officers on the agenda, veto entire bills or items of them which could be overridden only by an impossible three-fourths vote. During the entire life of the first assembly and a portion of the second, moreover, the President was granted broad emergency powers that, according to Article 98 of the constitution, enabled him to decree "a temporary suspension of the rights of freedom of circulation and residence, of speech and the press, of assembly and association, and of formation of labor unions and of striking, to meet the legitimate demands of public security and order and of national defense."[59] The constitutional prescriptions for a separation of powers, consequently, reflected a goal of political order rather than a true separation. Such a separation "does not, and cannot mean a rigid and mechanical partition of power. 'Separation,' as expressed through the intention of the Constituent Assembly and in the constitution itself, means rather the harmonious balance of the legislative, executive, and judicial functions in a way designed to meet the needs of Vietnamese democracy and to assure its peaceful development in the future."[60] A true separation of power would have required that sufficient power be in the preserve of the National Assembly, and neither the constitution nor the political organization of the legislature functioned to provide such power. The notion of "harmonious balance" consequently rested upon the goodwill of each branch toward the other and hardly provided the basis for a system of checks and balances. Indeed, as Duncanson observed, "Separation of powers was made much of; however the legislative power was delegated to the executive when the National Assembly was not sitting (that is, most of the year). . . . The President enjoyed full executive powers . . . but without most of the checks and balances . . . [and] it is in fact hard to think of any power his constitution did not confer on President Diem. He could legislate without the Assembly, but not the Assembly without him."[61] The constitution, drafted by a committee chosen by Diem, reflected the President's own philosophy of administration, his belief that Vietnam needed a strong executive. Rather than weaken his powers or suggest that they should be shared with another branch, therefore, the constitution acted to preserve in principle what Diem preserved in fact by repressing political opposition to his regime.

The activities of the first assembly clearly reflected the limitations on its legislative powers. While able to vote the national budget, the assembly lacked an independent source of information about government expenditures, expertise in analyzing the budgetary process, authority to discuss the allocation of funds from the United States Agency for International Development, and, in light of the requirement that for any proposed expenditure suggested by the assembly it must also suggest an adequate source of revenue, it lacked authority over appropriations.[62] The budgets passed each consecutive year with no changes in substance and with no recorded opposition.[63] The assembly also passed without serious challenge the draft of the constitution submitted by Diem. Aside from the constitution and the budgets, most of the legislative output of the assembly was either of a ceremonial nature or consisted of rather technical laws that supplemented the administrative regulations of government ministries.[64] On balance, the first assembly produced few laws in comparison to the decrees issued by the executive, and what laws it did vote on were without exception submitted either formally or informally by the executive.[65]

While, on balance, the second National Assembly did not differ substantially in character of output from that of the first, for a brief period in 1960-61 it did show signs of a greater awareness of both a need for power and of the need to criticize the Diem regime. "Numerous deputies are torn between the long range ideal of democratization of Vietnamese political processes to which all Vietnamese give at least lip service and the more immediate considerations of their own comfortable status and perquisites, together with their vague anxiety about the old bogey of the assumed low level of the masses' political understanding. Even so, it appears that probably most deputies, although timid when first entering the Assembly, and still generally subservient to the Executive, have come to believe that the National Assembly should have more power, particularly in view of the need to temper the capricious authoritarianism of the Ngo regime."[66] The steadily increasing fear of the Ngo family of any political organization or any criticism that emerged in the wake of attempted coups against the regime, however, kept the assembly from becoming anything more than an appendage of the executive. Although the sentiments of the deputies never resulted in a direct break with the Diem government or significant opposition to its programs, the customary debate over the budget, for example, resulted in so much criticism of the executive that the minutes were classified and did not appear in the published record of the sessions.[67] Other deputies used the assembly as a forum in which to denounce corrupt government officials in the 1960 and 1961 session, and Donnell reported that at least one province chief was dismissed from office.[68] Those deputies who managed to get elected as representatives of some of the religious and secular secret political organizations used the assembly as a means to attract attention to themselves and their grievances. Scigliano noted that these deputies, probably less than six,

> had no illusions about the role of the National Assembly, though they were hopeful that the legislature might be converted over the years into an agency independent of executive domination. Most important of all, perhaps, was the fact that membership in the National Assembly would

provide access to the population. These people have not forgotten the popular strength which a few anti-colonialist Vietnamese had built from within the Colonial Council of Cochin-China in the 1930's, and they viewed the National Council, with its parliamentary immunities and the coverage of its activities by the press as a forum opening to similar opportunities.[69]

The increase in police and security forces after the abortive coup in 1960 and the imprisonment of leading opposition figures heightened fears of retribution among dissenting deputies and forced their activities underground. Limited press coverage of the assembly by both cautious and bold opposition daily papers after 1961 documents the sharp decline in the discussion of political issues and in the criticism of the Diem regime. Propagandistic use of the National Assembly by political organizations, while never great, ceased to be an element of their strategy after 1961.

During the period of greatest legislative concern with lack of power, most deputies sought to divorce any political motive from their statements, and many declared over and over again their support for President Diem. The increasing pressure of public opinion for fairly limited demands disturbed the great majority of the deputies, and they responded to the pressure. "In the fall of 1960 National Assembly members explored means of increasing their power in the determination of policy dealing with the deteriorating security situation. They were rankling at the unfairness of a situation in which they were blamed by their constituents and the public at large for not doing anything about security but in which they actually had no voice in security policy."[70] Little more than presidential recognition of the needs of security as expressed by the deputies resulted from these efforts, reflecting the Diem government's inability to cope with Viet Cong mobile warfare, then beginning in the Mekong Delta and elsewhere. A second effort on the part of the National Assembly to have a more decisive impact on government policy making occurred in May 1961. During his April campaign Diem agreed to the assembly's request that cabinet ministers be subject to interpellation. The assembly's officers with almost unanimous support from the membership linked this demand to several others in the form of a memorandum for the President. In addition, the memorandum contained criticism of the government directed at its programs and some of its personnel in the provinces, noted the need for more contact between the President and the body's officers, suggested that assembly deputies be included in the membership of committees convened to investigate official corruption and ineptness, and concluded by calling for a statute to define the status and the authority of deputies vis-à-vis other government officials.[71] More than a year later, in September 1962, the assembly finally won the right to interpellate cabinet officials, but none of its other suggestions were accepted by the President. Thus ended the institution's only major bid to increase the powers and authority attached to its role in the governmental system.

The second assembly ended in the summer of 1963 when elections were held for the third term. This was a time of unrest and demonstrations against the Ngo regime culminating in the coup d'etat and the assassination of President Diem and Ngo dinh Nhu. In the wake of the coup, legislative functions of the government were based largely upon the decreemaking powers of successive juntas and the variety of advisory councils they organized between 1963 and 1967. Four days after the coup a provisional charter centralized the legislative and executive powers of the government in the Military Revolutionary Committee composed of the coup leaders and charged with designating the composition of a provisional government. With the exception of defense, budgetary, and fiscal matters (which remained within the authority of the committee), the provisional government was to assume all legislative and executive functions. On 6 November the committee established a Council of Sages that the provisional government was required to consult on all questions involving the disposition of private property, personal liberties, and any other matter brought before it by the government. This body consisted of forty to eighty persons appointed by the chairmen of the committee to meet in four closed sessions per year until a new National Assembly could be organized. The council was allowed to request the participation (that is, interpellation) of cabinet members in the course of its debates. In August of the following year General Nguyen Khanh resigned as chairman of the committee, a new head of government was to be selected, and the remaining members of the committee were to "return to the actual military leadership of the Republic of Vietnam's forces in order to fight against Communism, Neutrality, Colonialism, and other forms of dictatorship."[72]

The Military Revolutionary Committee, however, failed to agree on a new chief of state and appointed instead a Provisional Steering Committee and an Acting Premier. From August to September 1964 the fragile Provisional Committee was faced with one attempted coup, student demonstrations against one of its members (General Khanh), and the rebellion of the Montagnards in central Vietnam. As a partial response to the growing political unrest the Provisional Committee declared on 8

September that a Nationl Supreme Council "entirely independent of the Executive"[73] would be organized to convene a National Assembly, draft a constitution, and implement the institutions it would suggest in the constitution. The Supreme Council was to be "composed of 10-20 members selected from representatives of religions, venerable personalities, and really revolutionary components of the nation."[74] The Provisional Committee promised to dissolve itself once the constitution and its institutions were established. The provisional charter drafted by this council, however, was all that remained when the Provisional Committee itself fell victim to a coup in December 1964 and was succeeded by a High National Council with full legislative and executive powers. The new council in turn had a short-lived existence and was dissolved on 20 December by the Armed Forces Council which declared that

> the High National Council is being abused by counterrevolutionary elements who are acting against the spirit of national unity to the detriment of the highest interests of the nation in violation of the Provisional Constitution, thus hampering the reorganization of the armed forces and weakening the anti-communist potential.[75]

In February 1965 the Armed Forces Council, under the leadership of General Nguyen Khanh, established a National Legislative Council composed of those selected "after consultation with various political and religious groups"[76] and organized along the lines of and in accordance with the High National Council of 1964.

The new council had twenty-six members, only six of whom were military officers. It met only sporadically and was dissolved with the fall of Khanh from power. From the spring of 1965 until June 1966 the Armed Forces Council unilaterally determined the composition of the government and acted as a legislative and advisory body. Composed of all generals on active duty within the republic and any field grade officers who held commands normally filled by a general, the Armed Forces Council regulated defense and military affairs and advised "the government on necessary measures to solve serious problems arising from the changing situation[77] and consequent requirements of the war and of the economy." In June 1966 the succession of temporary legislative-consultative bodies ended with the establishment of a Council of the People and the Army. This Council was designed to advise the National Leadership Committee, drawn from the executive committee of the Armed Forces Council, in all political, cultural, social, and economic matters. It was composed of eighty members; three-quarters were "civilians representing various social strata [and] nationalist trends."[78] The primary function of the council, however, was to pass on the national budget. The Council of the People and the Army was dissolved with the election of the Constituent Assembly in September 1966.

The Legislature and Political
Organization in Vietnam

Until the formation of the Second Republic by the 1966-67 elections, legislative institutions were adjuncts to ruling elites rather than independent, effective processes of government or politics. The governments organized by the French and later by Diem used legislative councils and assemblies in an effort to legitimate their rule both within Vietnam as well as in the larger community of Asian and Western nations. But the domination by first a cultural and then a religious minority did not permit the legislature to acquire the political organization required for effectiveness. The legislatures did not achieve any significant independence from the executive branch of government, and they failed to mobilize the population in support of particular regimes or to mediate political conflicts between the government and religious and political forces. Reflecting the interests of an urban elite rather than one associated with and responsive to the needs of the rural areas, successive legislatures served to contain competition among the elite for positions in government rather than providing incentives for the elites to foster political mobilization as a means to achieve power.

The legislature's subservience to the executive both during the period of colonial domination and during the Diem era was determined in part by the purpose for which particular legislative bodies were founded. The French colonial councils were founded to co-opt ethnic Vietnamese to support government policies and foster democratic institutional development in the colony. The dependence of the councils upon the French governor-general was assured by the government's authority to directly influence deliberations and restrict the scope of their activities. The National Assemblies founded during the Diem era, similarly, reflected the regime's desire to co-opt promising young politicians to assure that no significant opposition to the government would develop. The assemblies aided the development of executive power with liberal grants of emergency authority while the separation of powers between executive and legislature (based on the expectation that harmony would naturally result) virtually precluded the development of a policymaking role for the legislature. Given little power initially under the 1956 Constitution, provided with no means of gathering information to make independent judgments, and restrained from developing a role on its own by the Ngo family's attitude toward political competition, the assemblies could do little more than respond to the wishes of the President. While some deputies viewed the assemblies as an important forum where public grievances could be aired, fear of retribution, both individual and organizational, prevented the use of the legislature in any significant way for the purpose of political mobilization. Indeed, only after the fall of Diem did legislative bodies established by the juntas seek to include members of some political and religious organizations to demonstrate that the legitimacy of the government was based on representation of the population.

The failure of the legislature to emerge as an independent institution of government stemmed from its inability to function as a political organization. In summarizing the salient features of Vietnam's legislative tradition, one Lower House deputy observed that it

> stems from the pre-French autonomy of the villages where any decision taken by a village leader would be made only after the people were consulted by means of the village council. Thus our tradition is one of consultation rather than legislation. For the purposes of consultation it was only necessary to know who the local elite were since they could speak for the population. Thus our tradition only encouraged the organization of the elite. But to legislate would have required the organization of the population so that the deputies would know the needs of the people and be able to demonstrate to those who controlled the government that they represented actual political forces whose voices could not be ignored.

The transformation of a legislative institution from one that functioned as an agent of consultation and ratification to one that could influence the policies and actions of the government required a level of political power that simply did not exist in South Vietnam. The diversity of the society's political life and the lack of integration and opportunities for participation in national political institutions, moreover, indicated that no basis existed upon which such power could be created either by the government or political organizations. The mass of the noncommunist population had not been mobilized into politics in the past, and the 1966-67 elections clearly demonstrated that such a development was not imminent.

The impact of elections on political participation depends upon the level of competition permitted in and fostered by the political system. Although elections may stimulate political organizations to increase their membership or expand the scope of their activities, they do not necessarily result in the creation of new forms of political mobilization. More often elections reflect the weaknesses of existing parties or other organizations. As Samuel Huntington has observed,

> Elections and parliaments are instruments of representation; parties are instruments of mobilization. Parliaments or other types of elected councils are hence quite compatible with a relatively static traditional society. The strength of the dominant groups in the social structure is reproduced within the parliament. The existence of an elected assembly is, in itself, an indication of neither the modernity of a political system nor of its susceptibility to modernization. The same is true of elections. Elections without parties reproduce the status quo; they are a conservative device which gives a semblance of popular legitimacy to traditional structures and traditional leadership.[1]

Elections in most developing polities are designed to serve the interests of the ruling elite. Should elections stimulate the development of political organizations capable of challenging the rule of the elite, however, the elected bodies are frequently dissolved unless the newly created organizations are either powerful enough to gain control of the government or are willing to support the continuing rule of a particular elite. There are few cases similar to the Philippines where the incumbent government can be voted out of office. There are even fewer cases of incumbent governments peacefully accepting the results of such a vote, as has also been true in the Philippines. Rather, in most developing polities the tenure of elected bodies depends upon their ability to tread, if so inclined, the thin line between opposition to government policy and opposition to the government itself. As a result, election systems in developing polities are rarely sources of stimuli for political mobilization apart from the efforts permitted and monopolized by the dominant group. Elected assemblies also rarely function as institutions which mobilize political opposition.

1776745

Legislatures generally fail to develop a life of their own apart from those who control the government. They seldom acquire the political power required to function as an agent promoting the assimilation of new social forces. Successive elections held within a system that effectively limits and controls the organization and participation of social forces in politics, moreover, tends to result in a tapering off of voter turnout and a general decline in citizen interest. The number of voters may initially increase, but it subsequently declines because the novelty of the franchise cannot indefinitely substitute for political mobilization. Sustaining high levels of voter participation apparently requires a level of political competition[2] that most regimes in developing polities are unwilling or unable to permit. Levels of voter turnout greater than 70 percent appear directly correlated to the existence of an established one-party system during the 1950's and 1960's; this level was reached in only ten polities that would be classified as developing. The median vote in forty-four other developing polities was only 37 percent.[3] The high levels of turnout sustained in some developing polities appear to stem from either effective government control of the election process or the existence of only a single party for which the population must vote.

Elections in which many parties compete may not result in significant efforts at political mobilization, either. Elections of 1966 and 1967 in South Vietnam under a plurality system maximized pressure on political organizations to concentrate upon winning only a small percentage of the total vote. Such elections may provide each group with at least one representative in an elected body, but this more often reflects the nature of the electoral system than the mobilization skill of any one group. In 1967, for example, governmental support coupled to the highly organized nature of Catholic parties resulted in consistent overrepresentation; they had more seats than their members in the total population would warrant. Other groups were also "overrepresented," not as a result of political mobilization but because of the nature of the electoral system. Political mobilization is directly correlated with the failure to achieve any seats or the ability to achieve more seats than sheer numbers would warrant in an elected body.[4] Between these two outcomes success in a fragmented and essentially weak party system depends upon the amount of competition that exists within electoral districts. Competition, in the sense in which it will be used here, denotes a strategy of campaigning rather than mobilization: narrowly based parties tend to focus upon achieving narrowly based victories, limiting mobilization efforts to that level required for election within particular districts. In Vietnam, the higher the level of competition as defined by the number of candidates seeking a particular position, the lower the level of political mobilization since fewer votes are needed for election. The elections which established the Second Republic in Vietnam, consequently, were characterized by their high level of competition and their low level of political mobilization.[5]

The Electoral Process in
South Vietnam

The electoral process, like the legislative process, has generally served to confirm the government leadership and ratify its policies rather than to determine leadership or policies. Local elections, similarly, have ratified the distribution of power in the province or village rather than altered it. As a result, the agreements reached to hold elections have been more significant than the actual process of casting ballots, and the governing elite has viewed control of the organization and administration of elections as crucial to the outcome. While all political parties and organizations were permitted to run in the elections of 1966-67 except the Viet Cong[6] and most groups did participate, this tolerance has been closely linked to the GVN's confidence in its ability to secure progovernment majorities. One high government official observed: "We were concerned at first that by permitting all groups to participate we would lose our control over the Assembly. But as we analyzed the situation we were convinced that we would win. The participation of many groups in politics and in elections is all right as long as it serves the government and our stability in the anticommunist struggle is not thus threatened and our freedom to act is not impaired." The attitude of the government toward elections was more succinctly summarized by another high official: "If we can pick our candidates and through the election law [that is, the plurality system] also pick those who will win, then the risks of holding the elections are within the bounds of what we can afford."

Indeed, the frequency with which elections have been held in South Vietnam since independence, almost two per year, suggests that the government's control over their organization[7] has remained rather constant. Elections in South Vietnam have not been characterized by an increasing level of political mobilization or an increasingly competitive political system, but rather by a more finely developed process of organizing and running elections whereby successive governing elites could control them. Indeed, the absence of competition and strife following the enfranchisement of the mass of the South Vietnamese population in the 1950's of the kind that Sartori had in mind when he noted the strong positive correlation between the "maximization of suffrage" and "long periods of considerable strain and turmoil" in the West[8] indicates how little impact elections had on the Vietnamese political system.

The facade of democratic procedures and legitimacy which elections provide has been important to South Vietnamese governments as contrast with the regime in the North. During campaigns, posters exhort the population to vote as a means of fighting the "Communist Dictatorship," as part of a citizen's "national duty." Scigliano observed posters in 1959 which declared that "Every ballot is a shell through the Vietnamese Communist flag."[9] Variants on this theme appeared during the 1967 elections for the President and the National Assembly. In some elections more posters exhorted the population to vote than to vote for a specific candidate.[10] Such an orientation seeks to project an image of partici-patory democracy.

While they are important to the image of government, elections in South Vietnam do not constitute a process of government. The voting and campaigning which take place resemble a ritual more than a decisive process. In 1967, for example, candidates appeared before the population in organized debates, made short presentations followed by synchronous applause, and occasionally were asked to answer a few general questions. The level of communication in these encounters was quite low, and some voters suggested that they derived greater enjoyment from the atmosphere of gathering in a crowd, listening to band music, and purchasing a treat from sidewalk vendors as diversion from the drudgery of rural life. Voting appeared equally ritualistic. In the presidential and Upper House elections, for example, voters entered a schoolroom and were given eleven ballots for presidential and forty-eight ballots for Upper House slates. They then stood in line to enter a curtained voting booth to choose one presidential ticket and six Upper House lists. After stuffing the ballots into separate envelopes, they emerged from the booth, approached the ballot box holding the envelopes high above their heads, deposited them with a great flourish, and proceeded to have their identity cards clipped at one corner as a sign that they had voted. By midday a certain rhythm had developed in the polling places that resembled a Kabuki play, only at a much livelier tempo.

Elections in South Vietnam have traditionally been part of the process of autocratic government rather than an alternative to it. Neither the balloting nor the functioning of the elected bodies has served to mediate political conflicts and divisions; instead, both have functioned to keep such conflicts largely outside the formal government structure and decisionmaking process. The real source of power in Vietnamese governments in the past lay in personal political alliances. Even leadership committees organized in the period of the juntas (1963-1967), though aimed at representing both civilian and military interests, were subordinate to the personal power of the head of state and allegiance owed him by senior army generals. The National Directory of Premier Nguyen cao Ky, for example, included ten civilians both to "balance" its military members (that is, Ky, Thieu, the Defense Minister, the four corps commanders, and the commander of forces in the Capital Military Zone) and to represent religious and occupational groups. There were, however, no Buddhists on the civilian side of the Directory, and Hoa Hao and Cao Dai representatives were classified as "retired religious leaders."

The war and foreign pressures for governmental reform have emphasized the need for change, but top-level civilian and military officials have changed little in character.[11] Though the mood of the times can be seen in the rhetorical emphasis on reform, Vietnam's power brokers have seemed hardly so inclined. Neither overall reform nor "social revolution" has materialized. The war and subsequent pressure for development have increased the demand for what the Saigon elite has been unwilling or, perhaps, unable to provide: meaningful opportunity for participation by dissidents and freedom for political organizations to foster the political mobilization of the population. South Vietnam does not lack alternatives to its present government; rather, it lacks political alternatives to influencing governmental decision making through coups d'etat or such desperate acts as the immolation of religious figures. And the decisions which led to the election of a Constituent Assembly in 1966, the drafting of the 1967 Constitution and the creation of the Second Republic by elections held later that year were precipitated by a search for political alternatives to continued instability within the GVN.

"Struggle Six": Elections as
a Political Demand

The round of elections that began in September 1966 for the Constituent Assembly and ended a little more than a year later with the election of deputies to the Lower House of the National Assembly were viewed by those who had precipitated them and by those who had organized them as an expedient political alternative to the instability of government by military junta. The government of Nguyen cao Ky had committed itself to organizing elections and preparing a constitution at a meeting held with President Johnson in Honolulu in February 1966. The Ky government pledged "to formulate a democratic constitution in the months ahead, including an electoral law; to take that constitution to our people for discussion and modification; to create, on the basis of elections rooted in that constitution, an elected government."[12] Ky's return from the Honolulu meeting, however, brought little subsequent progress in either drafting a constitution or preparations for holding elections. Instead, Ky continued to focus on the problem of consolidating his support within the coalition of generals in the National Leadership Committee (the Directory).

On 8 March, Ky called for the resignation of General Nguyen canh Thi, the popular commander of the I Corps region and one of Ky's rivals within the Directory. The popular base that Thi had developed during his tenure in I Corps, however, had made him a powerful opponent. Within two days of the resignation order, riots and demonstrations (led by militant Buddhists calling for the reinstatement of General Thi and the ouster of the Ky government), broke out in DaNang (the administrative capital of I Corps), Hue, and other major urban centers. During the course of the sporadic riots of the following weeks the American Library in Hue was burned by protesting students, a number of other anti-American demonstrations were held to protest the American ambassador's open support of the Ky government and the use of American aircraft to transport government troops to DaNang to quell the disturbances. Divisions of South Vietnamese troops ruled the most troublesome cities under martial law and occupied Buddhist pagodas, and security agencies arrested as many of the leaders of the struggle movement as they could find.

The action of the government in response to the rioting reflected Ky's initial assessment of its significance. He regarded it basically as a movement aimed at demonstrating support for General Thi and forcing his reinstatement as commander of I Corps. As such, it constituted a serious challenge to the stability of his government. He responded to the threat posed in military terms since it was not unlike an earlier campaign against the government of General Nguyen Khanh to organize new provincial and local governments replacing those appointed by Saigon. In DaNang, for example, the civilian mayor had openly declared opposition to Ky's move and had ordered a strike of government officials with the effect that the government, schools, offices and most businesses ceased their operations. At a press conference Ky declared: "Either the government will fall or the mayor of DaNang will be shot. As far as the government is concerned, DaNang is already controlled by the Communists and the government will organize operations to . . . liberate DaNang."[13] In early April two battalions of South Vietnamese marines occupied DaNang. Ky, aside from viewing the demonstrations as aimed at pitting the basis of his support against that of General Thi, was also convinced that the disturbances were the direct result of communist agitators who realized an opportunity to weaken the GVN. Although Ky's view of the significance of the movement was altered after a trip to DaNang, he apparently retained his conviction that communist-inspired agitators had been largely responsible for the crisis. In a letter transmitted by government radio on 30 June 1966, responding to a broadcast questioning government policy paid for by the leader of the Buddhist Institute for the Propagation of the Faith (*Vien Hao Dao*), Ky stated, "I think that all the actions by a number of Buddhists during the past few months obviously resulted from the misunderstanding which was sown by a minority of inciters."

The evolution of the crisis from one requiring the restoration of public order to one involving a question of the government's attitude toward the promised elections reflected the evolution of Buddhist demands from those concerned primarily with the return of General Thi to those concerned with the question of their future political participation. Buddhist participation in South Vietnamese politics in the past had largely been limited to the organization of demonstrations that were short-lived and had failed to produce an effectively organized Buddhist political party. "Struggle Six" (as the Buddhists termed it) was part of a series of six movements occurring between 1963 and 1966, the earlier five being against the Diem, Nguyen Khanh, Tran van Huong, and early Nguyen cao Ky governments. The success of the movements depended upon Buddhist ability to mobilize mass sentiment in response to repressive action by the government. Speed and intensity were vital, but, as rapidly as the Buddhists organized, they had to disband because of the expected response of the police. This was certainly no enduring political organization with mass support. Rather, it was a series of isolated responses which the Vietnamese referred to as *phong trao* (movement), a term used to describe the dramatic but temporary surge of a tide or blowing of a wind. Part of the reason why the Buddhist political organization failed to develop lies also with the continuing debate among the priesthood over their role in political activities and over the proper response to imprisonment of many able secular, as well as religious, leaders. The demand for a constitution in Struggle Six, however, reflected the desire of the Buddhists to participate in the process of government rather than simply to change or overthrow it. While in the past Buddhist leaders had felt some success in their efforts to overthrow governments, they also sensed that no government could be overthrown unless the military leadership were willing to permit such an event. More realistic Buddhist leaders acknowledged that the Struggle Movements were probably mere incidents in recent history and that, as a group, they had little influence on government. Struggle politics had to be replaced by a more effective means of political participation, which some leaders believed might develop from a new constitutional system. The Buddhists did not, however, regard the April 1966 promise of a new constitution and elected government as a victory. They felt that Ky was not recognizing the right of Buddhists to participate in politics but was responding to the pressure of American diplomatic and public opinion roused by world reaction to the repression of Buddhists by the Diem regime in the fall of 1963.

It is unlikely that the American diplomatic community urged an election solution upon the Ky government. Despite the rhetoric of Honolulu, the United States did not subsequently push for immediate elections, believing that any elections during the war would be difficult if not impossible to hold and that they would divert needed governmental and administrative energies away from the task of winning the war. Elections were seen as a long-term goal to be achieved once the government had secured its position militarily. Once Ky had made his decision, however, American policy swung wholeheartedly behind the effort to make it as meaningful as possible.

It is more probable that Ky responded to pressures within the Directory to make a bargain with the Buddhists and thereby avert continued civil strife. The promise of elections was intended to stop Buddhist demonstrations and further activities in support of the return of General Thi. For the Buddhists, the promise of elections and a new constitution represented a tacitly made "bargain" at best since the decision was made without any significant communication between the Buddhists and the government. One leader of the movement reflected on these events by observing: "The struggle movement resulted in a constitution but not a promise about political participation made in consultation with the Buddhists. Government security forces were still trying to capture the leaders of the movement at the time Ky announced that elections would be held, and Ky promised a constitution as a device to quiet unrest and give the government a better image in world public opinion." The Buddhists approached the coming elections with caution, unsure if an opportunity for political participation was at hand.

The Buddhist demand for political participation included not only an electoral system in which they could nominate and control their representatives but also a call for an end to the repression and arrest of Buddhist leaders[14] by the government. What was sought was a policy of government nonintervention in Buddhist affairs. Concern with the effects of repression led Buddhist candidates to run for the Constituent Assembly strongly disavowing any affiliation with the religion's hierarchy so as not to endanger the organization. Many candidates were army officers who avoided imprisonment in the wake of Struggle Six by being in the army and maintaining a sympathetic but inactive posture with regard to the movement.[15] One leader of the movement suggested that in both the Constituent Assembly and the national elections of the following year they were denied participation "because most of our ablest spokesmen were still in prison or were disqualified from running by local security agencies."

Buddhist distrust of the government grew out of the contradiction between policy and rhetoric. On the one hand, the Ky government declared shortly after the struggle that

> With the unchanged policy of constantly and strictly respecting the freedom of faith, the government does not have and will never have the intention of occupying the Institute for the Execution of the Dharma [*Vien Hoa Dao*] or the pagodas throughout the country. If in the recent past security organs did resort to some necessary measures, this was beyond the government's will.
>
> ... The government has never advocated the policy of imprisonment of bonzes, nuns, Buddhists, and compatriots of various strata who were involved in the disturbances of recent months. The government has instructed its agencies to study all the cases quickly [of those who were arrested] in order to be able to free everyone, except for a number of individuals who have a Communist background or who have been taken advantage of by the Communists.[16]

Such rhetoric has continued in Vietnam while the arrest and repression of

Buddhists remains an equally constant feature of Vietnamese politics. Buddhist preoccupation with the repression issue reflects the deeply rooted suspicion of a non-Buddhist government and police that are in turn concerned at the apparent ease with which Buddhist demonstrations are infiltrated by the Viet Cong. Underlying the demands of Struggle Six for an elected government and a constitution, consequently, was a desire to participate in politics openly and without fear. As one leader observed: "What we hoped to gain in 1966 was not just a new constitution and new government institutions but a new political system in which we could participate as well." For Buddhists, the significance of the Constitution of 1967 depended upon the guarantees it included for freedom of political participation.

The constitution by itself was unlikely to assure unrestricted participation by Buddhists or any other groups in politics; rather, freedom of participation depended upon the vigor with which newly established organizations would seek to implement the rights provided by the constitution. Past Vietnamese constitutions had not created a new political order, but had provided a semblance of legality to one already established. Constitutional development in Vietnam has thus differed substantially from that of Western countries where there was a "distinctive political order which would protect [the people's] liberties."[17] Vietnamese constitutions, in contrast, functioned to "symbolize the legitimacy of the existing political system as well as to help obscure its essentially authoritarian character. In actual fact, coercive power has been the real determinant of political action."[18] And the free exercise of the rights prescribed by the various constitutions has depended upon and has been limited by what the dominant power holders would permit. While the Constitution of 1966 explicitly provided for executive dominance by such things as the granting of substantial emergency powers and prerogatives, that of 1967 reflected the likelihood that the executive would remain the dominant institution of government.

The principle of executive dominance in Vietnamese constitutions, in addition to certifying the power of the President based upon his dominance of politics, also seems to reflect a Vietnamese preference for government by such an institution. The Constituent Assembly debates and the deputies themselves evidenced a decided preference for a strong executive. The major controversy in the debates which occurred over the power of other institutions was not that deputies were given too little authority but too much. The deputies who maintained that the proposed constitution provided too little power to the legislature were small in number and based their arguments largely upon the grounds that additional powers were required to supplement those which should normally have grown from the inclusion of organized and effective parties in its deliberations. The arguments of these deputies were summarized in the following way: "I see that our country's status is one of many parties [which means that] the congress will have many unruly [that is, uncohesive] elements, and, if we give more power to the executive, then the relationship of the congress to the executive is just like eggs facing rocks."[19] The weakness of the congress lay in the weakness of the party system itself.

Progovernment deputies supported the creation of a strong executive out of loyalty to either Thieu or Ky since it was not clear which would emerge as a presidential candidate. The progovernment bloc which was formed, however, was loosely organized and received little direction from the executive as to how the constitution should be written. Deputies from this group, moreover, made no substantial contribution to the work of either the drafting committee or frequently participated in floor debates. Indeed, the drafting of the constitution fell largely to deputies who had been outspoken critics of current and past regimes, and the final product reflected the essential conservatism of those deputies toward limiting the powers of the President. Opposition deputies[20] sought to create a document that struck a compromise between unqualified executive dominance and a too-powerful legislature that might precipitate its own dissolution at the first opportunity. As one such deputy observed, "We wrote the constitution according to what the traffic would bear so as not to alienate the leadership of the government from the institutions we wished to set up. We had a long-range view in mind that would provide the country with what it needed now during the war as well as allow for the evolution of a government that in the future would be effective in peacetime also. We didn't want a constitution that would be offensive to the government now or one that would have to be changed in the postwar era." After reflecting upon the debates of the Constituent Assembly another deputy summarized the spirit in which the constitution was written:

One of the basic problems faced by the Constituent Assembly was the issue of coherency versus the adaptability of the constitution. Some deputies argued that the constitution should follow closely a particular model and not mix systems of government. It should be either parliamentary or presidential but not a combination of the two. I argued that the constitution should reflect the current needs and realities of Vietnam as well as the traditions of government and the culture. Thus what was needed most was a constitution which would be flexible and provide a framework under which a government particularly suited for Vietnam could develop. We need a strong government now while in the future we will need a strong legislature. The legacy of many years of dictatorship imbued in all deputies an abhorrence of this kind of government, but we also realized that to change from dictatorship requires evolution. Our institutions of government required claws, but these must be developed over time rather than all at once. Right now the claw of the legislature is the power to vote no-confidence in the government, but it will not become effective until we are organized enough to use it.

The costs and benefits of preserving the dominant position of the President were weighed in terms of present realities as well as future needs: "Thieu or Ky will not always be president but South Vietnam will always need a president."[21]

In essense the constitution that emerged in 1967 reflected a statement of intent and a compilation of the ideals of its drafters for a new government in Vietnam. "The Constitution must hold [within it] the continuation of our history, promoting traditional ideals of the people since ancient times. The Constitution also has to [suggest the way] to solve the political and social problems of the present time. And, at last, it must establish goals for the direction of progress of the nation in the future."[22] The constitution affirmed the principles of social welfare and political freedom and suggested the development of a noncommunist, sovereign state. The principles enunciated were straightforward and similar to those embodied in most of the world's constitutions.[23] The list of freedoms guaranteed was long and comprehensive, the relationship among the branches of the government specified but flexible, and the character and functions of national institutions well defined. While the process by which the document was created embodied the political demands of those who had struggled for it, such demands clearly would require continued political action to mobilize the support necessary to assure their realization.

The 1966-67 Elections and Political
Participation

Overview

In a little more than a year the Republic of Vietnam held five elections involving approximately 27,000 candidates for 14,000 public offices (see

Table 3-1). These elections represented the first attempt to measure the power of Vietnam's diverse political forces since the fall of President Diem in November 1963. The assassination of Diem brought a change of personnel in the Saigon government but little political stability to a country that had experienced thirteen changes of government leadership since July 1954 and that had no subsequent basis for the measurement of political power in the republic short of military coups and countercoups and the short-lived Buddhist Struggle Movements. Political groups and organizations, as well as the government itself, had no means to gauge their support. Military juntas, for example, asserted a legitimacy derived from the 1963 revolution, an act for which most citizens ought to be grateful. But the resistance the military encountered from the civilian bureaucracy, whose membership changed little after the fall of Diem, suggested that the act of revolution alone was not likely to engender loyalty to or political support for the new government. When the solidarity of the coalition of officers who led the coup deteriorated, the government's command of military loyalties was shown to be far from secure. Civilian political organizations, similarly, tended to assess their ability to mobilize the support of the population according to the length of their existence. Lacking any means to measure the dimension of the power vacuum created by the coup, juntas and civilian groups and parties operated in a milieu in which the claims and demands of all groups far exceeded their ability to actually influence the course of events and the policies of the governments between 1963 and 1967.

In the first ten months after the coup, three provisional constitutions stressing the primacy of military leadership had been promulgated and subsequently withdrawn. While the first experiment in civilianization occurred with the fourth provisional constitution of 20 October 1964, the provision for the orderly transfer of government contained in this charter (as provisional constitutions were called) was premature. Civilian leaders were not sufficiently organized to demonstrate that they had the support of the population, to provide a modicum of political participation for groups such as the Buddhists, or to develop an effective administrative apparatus to govern the countryside. Three civilian Prime Ministers later, on 19 June 1965, the government of Phan khac Suu fell to a group of military officers led by the now Vice President Nguyen cao Ky. The Ky government promulgated the republic's fifth provisional constitution, known as the Convention, which placed authority in an Armed Forces Congress until a permanent constitution could be drafted and a government elected.

Table 3-1 South Vietnam's 1966–67 electoral season

Election	Dates	Elected positions	Candidates	Candidate/position ratio	Percent of registered voters who voted
Constituent Assembly	11 September 1966	117	532	4/1	80.8
Village councils	2–30 April 1967	8,964	12,719	1.5/1	77
Hamlet chiefs and assistants	14 May–11 June 1967	4,983	11,643	2.5/1	78
Presidential	3 September 1967	2	22	11/1	83.8
Upper House	3 September 1967	60	480	8/1	83.8
Lower House	22 October 1967	137	1,206	9/1	73

The elections of 1966-67 were significant not for the government which emerged but for the test they provided for civilian political organizations to compete with what remained essentially a military junta. Many Vietnamese viewed the elections as a step forward in the construction of a more democratic regime, but not an indispensable one. Most Vietnamese interviewed echoed the sentiment of one political leader: "We would rather have seen reforms instituted in the old government institutions than merely the setting up of new ones." Such a view reflected the despair of most political leaders that the impact of the participation of many diverse and divided groups on the electoral process would promote reform. As one keen observer of the elections noted, "an adequate groundwork for representative government here has simply not been laid. This is true both of the countryside—where the revamped Revolutionary Development Program has so far had only scattered impact—and of the cities, where the intellectuals, the professional people, and the various religious elements, if they had been given more time and more encouragement, might conceivably have been able to get together and formulate some sort of logical party system before the voting took place."[24] For political participation to have improved the prospects for reform would have required an effective demonstration of widespread support for political groups, such support being directly connected to explicit reform proposals. The elections of 1966-67 indicated only how little support there was. Vice-President Ky assessed his own election as "a loss of time and money. They were a joke. They have served to install a regime that has nothing in common with the people—a useless, corrupt regime. We need a revolution. The laws we have protect the rich. We must make new laws that will give power to the poor."[25]

Participation in the election had little impact upon government policy, aside from proving that participation "by the members of an organization or the citizens of a society in political affairs is neither a necessary or a sufficient condition for rank-and-file influence on organization or government policy."[26] While the total number of votes cast against the military junta and its party exceeded those cast for it, the number of groups competing for votes was so large that each received only a small portion in comparison to the plurality that the military was able to muster, as much from their ability to control the election and its outcome as from failure of competing political groups to organize.

Vietnamese and American observers of the election process in South Vietnam have tended to concentrate their attention upon the degree of relative fairness in the elections and to place the blame for the outcome squarely upon the control exercised by the military in assuring victory for their candidates. While it has been a well-established finding of comparative studies that "electoral engineering," the control of districting, organization, and administration of elections is an important variable in assessing the outcome of elections,[27] electoral engineering is neither a necessary nor a sufficient condition to determining the outcome of the election. Of fundamental importance to the electoral process is the party system[28] which underlies it because "the effects of the electoral system cannot be assessed without assessing at the same time the properties of the party system as such, and particularly its manipulative properties."[29] Factions appear to be part of the prehistory of the formation of political parties and, at later stages, a consequence of divisive party conflicts. In either case a faction may be defined as "a portion of an electorate, political elite, or legislature whose adherents were engaged in parallel action or co-ordination of some consistency but limited durability in conflict with other portions."[30] In plurality systems characterized by the existence of many competing parties and organizations the case for the primacy of the party structure over the electoral system is convincingly demonstrated by Sartori who concludes, in fact, that "plurality systems have no influence (beyond the district) until the party system becomes structured in coincidence with, or in reaction to, the appearance of mass parties."[31] Multiparty political systems in which each party has a narrow base of support and little ability to mobilize the masses tend, even under majority systems, to produce outcomes that approximate the status quo. Participation in elections under these circumstances thus has little impact either on the control which the dominant group exerts over the political system (quite apart from its obvious ability to manipulate the electoral system) or on how a particular group gains and maintains its dominance. The analysis that follows concentrates on the multiparty system in Vietnam and the limits of political mobilization rather than on the control the government was able to exercise over the process. The three elections discussed are viewed as significant because they reflect the nature of political organizations in Vietnam and the magnitude of change required if they were to become effective instruments of political participation.

Competition versus Political Mobilization

For the first time in the elections of 1966-67 all political and social forces participated. Elections for the colonial councils under the French had been based upon a limited Vietnamese suffrage. The candidates were generally those sympathetic to the colonial regime or those whose criticism the French permitted.[32] Elections under Diem, while granting universal suffrage, were similarly controlled to exclude participants critical of or in opposition to the regime. The elections that inaugurated the Second Republic were theoretically open to all noncommunists, however. In the Constituent Assembly election, deputies were elected who had been disqualified or imprisoned as outspoken oppositionists under Diem, and, despite the militant Buddhist boycott of that election, the number of militant Buddhist sympathizers markedly increased in the Lower House. Six deputies disqualified for alleged communist sympathies when they registered for the Constituent Assembly election in 1966 were also elected.

The turnout did not appear directly related to either the activities of political organizations to mobilize the voters or to the level of competition for seats (see Table 3-2). In the ten provinces and cities most highly politicized

Table 3-2   Voting and competition in the 1967 elections

	Percent voting in presidential and Upper House election	Percent voting in Lower House election	Candidates/ position ratio for Lower House election
I CORPS			
Da Nang[a]	81	71	10:1
Hue[a]	82	66	6:1
Quang Tri	85	80	5:1
Quang Nam	88	82	6:1
Thua Thien	85	80	5:1
Quang Tin	93	91	4:1
Quang Ngai[a]	87	72	5:1
II CORPS			
Binh Dinh[a]	90	85	10:1
Phu Yen	87	81	10:1
Khanh Hoa[a]	88	80	10:1
Ninh Thuan	94	89	8:1
Binh Thuan	91	89	8:1
Kontum	89	75	5:1
Pleiku	82	75	5:1
Phu Bon	91	79	3:1
Darlac	87	81	6:1
Quang Duc	93	85	6:1
Tuyen Duc	88	77	7:1

Table 3-2 Voting and competition in the 1967 elections

	Percent voting in presidential and Upper House election	Percent voting in Lower House election	Candidates/ position ratio for Lower House election
Lam Dong	86	73	10:1
Dalat	81	61	17:1
Cam Ranh	90	83	10:1
III CORPS			
Phuoc Long	90	83	6:1
Long Khanh	85	73	15:1
Binh Tuy	88	82	13:1
Binh Long	86	78	9:1
Binh Duong	78	74	12:1
Bien Hoa[a]	80	68	8:1
Phuoc Tuy	88	79	8:1
Tay Ninh	86	80	6:1
Hau Nghia	80	72	7:1
Long An	85	81	10:1
Vung Tau	86	75	14:1
Con Son	94	75	–
Saigon[a]	76	58	15:1
Gia Dinh[a]	79	65	15:1
IV CORPS			
Dinh Tuong	84	69	11:1
Go Cong	92	85	9:1
Kien Tuong	89	79	1:1
Kien Phong	86	73	7:1
Kien Hoa	86	79	10:1
Vinh Binh	84	73	5:1
Vinh Long	83	74	7:1
Sa Dec	90	86	8:1
An Giang[a]	83	67	6:1
Chau Doc	90	87	4:1
Kien Giang	83	69	5:1
An Xuyen	85	73	11:1
Bac Lieu	82	69	7:1
Phong Dinh[a]	76	59	7:1
Ba Xuyen	84	72	8:1
Chuong Thien	93	75	7:1

Source: USAID, Vietnam, *Public Administration Bulletin, No. 41* (30 November 1967), and data supplied by Ministry of Interior.
[a]Denotes provinces in which two or more organized political groups competed with each other in the elections.

during the election, where two or more distinct political organizations competed, only three had higher than average voter turnouts; this number declined to two a month later in the Lower House elections. Five out of the ten constituencies had lower than average (9:1) candidate-to-position ratios in the Lower House election, suggesting a more capable organization except that the low ratios also correlated with lower turnouts. Even a heightening of competition between political groups did not appear to have much effect on mobilizing voter support. In the case of the Lower House election generally, the level of competitiveness as indicated by candidate-to-position ratios appeared to have had very little effect on voter turnout: in cases with a higher than average candidate-to-position ratio the average turnout was 73 percent compared with 71 percent for provinces with a lower than average ratio.[33] The highest voter turnout occurred in the least politicized provinces of the central highlands during the Upper House-presidential election, and it reflects the government's efforts to make sure it had won the Montagnard vote. It was reported that military vehicles were used to transport voters to the polls as had been done when Thieu and Ky made their appearance in some of the more densely populated cities. Turnout in the Highlands declined for the Lower House election (though still not below the average) probably because the government, assured of Montagnard support in any event, was less concerned with who won there.

The overall decline in voter turnout, greater than 10 percent between the two sets of elections, suggests that, despite potentially greater interest in the Lower House elections for most voters since they would be voting for provincial representatives on local issues, there was much less interest in and emphasis on voting in that election compared with the first two.[34] All persons voting in either election had to have their identity and voter registration cards appropriately marked and one corner clipped. The detached corners were then strung on counting wires to provide a means of checking the number of ballots against the number of persons who voted. The detached corner was especially significant to the voter since the identification cards would have to be shown to police and other government officials when persons claimed their rice rations or applied for government assistance. Many political leaders suggested that there was considerable pressure for the population to vote, and some officials made it clear that persons who did not have a card with a detached corner could expect difficulties in future dealings with both the police and other provincial officials. Similar remonstrances were not made in the case of the

Lower House election. Undoubtedly the desire to avoid such difficulties played an important part in promoting voter turnout, perhaps greater than the mobilization activities of those seeking election.

The elections provided few incentives to change the bases of political organizations. Most party leaders interviewed in 1967, for example, tended to view their principal opponents as either the leadership of another faction within the organization or another nationalist political organization. What was striking for the Western observer in particular was the lack of awareness that the principal opponent of all the nationalist groups was the Viet Cong and that it would have been to the mutual interest of all to demonstrate cohesion rather than division within the nationalist ranks.[35] Efforts to bridge the factionalism or avoid personality clashes were unsuccessful. Even alliances that were constructed for the elections with the specific hope of developing into new political organizations proved temporary as conflicts among the leaders led to the creation of competing factions.

Lacking goals beyond that of "getting elected," factions within the larger organizations could not unite in an effort to support political reform or changes in national priorities. The plurality system, coupled to the multiplicity of candidates, also encouraged the adoption of electoral strategies in which groups planned for victory through concerted efforts within certain districts, often the provincial capitals, rather than through large-scale mobilization. As a result, the average size of the vote received by those elected in 1966-67 rarely exceeded 20 or 25 percent. Finally, the need for more extensive bases of support for political organizations was not yet evident in 1967. Expecting rewards as the new government drew its cabinet from the ranks of loyal supporters, many people supported the junta in the presidential elections. Those opposed to the government, in contrast, were undecided as to what direction their activities should take or who should lead them. Both groups lacked the incentive and the organizational skill required to foster greater mobilization.

By 1967 most political organizations in South Vietnam were highly centralized around personalities and existed largely as central executive committees whose organization reached no further than the confines of a few urban and provincial areas. In the older nationalist parties in I Corps the membership remained merely a body of sympathizers, paying no dues and having virtually no links to the party leadership. These groups existed primarily in superstructure. The central executive committee functioned as a closely knit core handling all major issues of the organization. Such structures had neither opportunity nor resources to maintain or develop new bases of support outside their ranks. As one local leader of the *Vietnam Quoc Dan Dang* (VNQDD) observed:

> The membership of our organization consists mainly of the membership of our executive committees. To speak of the VNQDD in DaNang or Quang Ngai, for example, is to speak mainly of the few cadre who come regularly to the executive committee meetings. When they speak of our total membership they really refer to their recollection of it before the war when we had many dues-paying members and sympathizers. Since then we have been unable to collect dues or function as a political party because any organizing efforts would have resulted in the arrest of our leaders by the police. In my province, for example, I have about twenty cadres whom I see regularly, but we have not been able to go to the districts where we once were popular and really organize the people.

Candidates for election were in some cases designated by the organization's executive committees, but while their campaigns were aided by the work of party cadres, the votes they received were seldom due to the organization of the party. Voters cast their ballots for what could be considered a VNQDD candidate not because of party influence but because of their familiarity with the candidate or their sympathy with a VNQDD affiliation. Given the short period of time in which political organizations could prepare for the election, most identifiable groups were unable to effectively mobilize their supporters or to resurrect mobilization techniques dormant since the early years of the struggle against the French.

Most deputies' elections were aided by campaign organizations of cadres loyal to the candidate but not necessarily loyal to established political organizations. Less than 20 percent of all candidates held a declared political affiliation; the remainder ran as independents. The success of particular candidates depended primarily upon their local or national reputations. Organizational support aided the campaigns of popular candidates, but it was not strong enough to get lesser-known candidates elected without the support of established political figures. Campaign literature tended to emphasize candidates' backgrounds and professions more than their political affiliations.

In a sense the major issue of the Constituent Assembly election was not greater political participation for hitherto unrepresented groups but the nature of the constitution, and voters were exhorted to vote on the basis of a man's qualifications and principles (as demonstrated by past behavior) rather than his political affiliation. One campaign leaflet, which was widely copied, summarized the issue of the election by noting that the years of dictatorship were the result of a poorly written constitution. It went on to list the principles needed as:

> A constitution is to a nation like the rudder of a boat. . . . Realizing this, we, the Sunrise List run for the Constituent Assembly with the following plan:
> —To struggle for the Congress to have full authority to draft a constitution . . .
> —To insure a constitution in accordance with the United Nations Charter and the Declaration of Human Rights as well as the traditional culture of our people; bringing to every citizen freedoms and basic rights of politics, of economy, of culture, and of society, while clarifying citizens' obligations
> —To insure freedom of belief, freedom of organization and association, freedom of speech, of press and the right to opposition. But to strictly prohibit all organizations of dictatorship, of communism, of fascism . . .
> —To insure employment [to all] , a minimum salary, and free unions
> —To insure private ownership, especially to farmers, truly reflecting the principle of "one tills his own field" . . .

The debates of the Constituent Assembly give the impression that the deputies elected were among the most able to write a constitution in the context of the junta's uncertain attitude toward such a document. The assembly membership also included a core of experienced Saigon politicians who generally agreed on the basic principles that should be retained. What finally emerged was less a product of partisanship than of consensus already existing among well-known political figures.

Of the total number of voters, 65 percent cast their ballots against the Thieu-Ky ticket, far from the majorities that elected Diem. The large number of candidates put forward, however—ten tickets in all—divided the votes against the Thieu-Ky ticket into proportions, the largest not exceeding 20 percent and the average a mere 7 percent. Except for the Dzu ticket, which placed second, few actual policy differences existed among the candidates. All espoused generalized programs of social revolution. One editor noted: "The electoral campaign is already in full swing, but most electors still remain undecided because the programs of all the candidates are too good for them to reject."[36]

Those candidates who included the largest number of issues in their platforms, such as land reform, peace, continued economic development, and national independence, however, received the largest number of votes.[37] While this suggests that a candidate's treatment of issues is more rather than less relevant to the Vietnamese voter, it would be difficult to prove such a hypothesis. Most interpretations of the voting suggest the salience of peace as an issue and point to the success of the Dzu ticket in winning second place with 17 percent of the total votes cast. Peace as an issue had an appeal in those areas most affected by the war (as well as in those areas most opposed to the government for its conduct of the war). Yet it was precisely in these areas that both the Dzu ticket and the Thieu ticket did least well.[38] Indeed, if one interprets the vote for Dzu as a mandate for peace (as was the case in the United States[39]) then the magnitude of such a "mandate" was limited since 82 percent of the voters cast ballots for candidates who did not make peace more than a perfunctory campaign slogan and who expressed serious concern that a peace too hastily declared or one into which the Americans pressured the government would result in the take-over of the country by the Viet Cong.

The showing of Dzu and the other candidates must be put in the perspective of the political system then in existence. All tickets were organized with various degrees of success to respond to a limited constituency of either occupational, religious, or secular political groups. Dzu, for example, did well in the rural areas of the western Mekong Delta, reflecting the geographic composition of his People's Unified Front. The Thieu-Ky ticket, in contrast, was strongest in the eastern Mekong Delta, where there were concentrations of Catholics, in the central highlands, and in the coastal areas of III Corps. The support given other candidates was more geographically confined, but not what would have been expected on the basis of organizational ingredients. The two *Vietnam Quoc Dan Dang* slates and the one headed by the leader of the Revolutionary *Dai Viet* party, while predominantly I Corps political organizations, failed to carry their regions. They were beaten by the Thieu and Suu tickets, each of which received more than twice as many votes as the three I Corps parties. Tran van Huong, a former Prime Minister and champion of the rights of southern Buddhists, carried only Saigon and was beaten in the delta by the Thieu and Dzu tickets which received five and three times as many votes, respectively, as the Huong ticket. The remaining tickets based upon less well-known groups and personalities received scarcely any votes.

The elections demonstrated the bankruptcy of most established political parties and organizations in South Vietnam. The parties seldom were able to unite their leadership or to convert quasi-secret organizations into effective, influential organizations. Indeed, even in the areas of their greatest assumed popularity they were often unable to command enough support to carry the areas. The lessons of the presidential election were clear to one political leader: "With a few less civilian candidates and a few more votes we could have won the election. In the future we must work to reduce our differences so as to improve our ability to win votes." But this would require reorientation of most political groups and development of new bases for political mobilization.

The Upper House election demonstrated the profusion of noncommunist politics. The election reflected neither the coalescence which the drafters of the electoral law had hoped for nor the avoidance of strong particularistic tendencies that have given birth to such diversity in the first place. A total of forty-eight ten-man lists presented themselves for election, representing virtually every major and minor political party and organization as well as the principal factions within those groups.[40] Of the candidates registered, 85 percent listed Saigon as their place of residence and 90 percent of the winners concentrated most of their professional and political activities in Saigon. Groups which had the most cohesive organization and could count upon the clear support of limited constituencies were far more successful than groups which had extensive ideological appeal but less disciplined control over voters. Elections rewarded those political forces with the most limited appeal and created substantial disparities between the number of seats won and the number of votes received (see Table 3-3). By calculating a particular party's share of the total vote, the fragmented nature of the Vietnamese political system also becomes evident. Social, occupational, and religious cleavages divided both the parties and the electorate into many factions, and no party could receive a substantial vote when the probability that any two voters would choose the same slate was about one out of five.[41] In the Upper House election the fragmentation of the total vote was sufficient to reward parties polling a minority of the votes with a majority of the seats.[42] The results of the election suggested that the forced or opportunistic coalescence of political factions into lists was less essential to electoral success than the need for individual groups to maintain their control over a segment of the electorate.[43]

This fragmentation of the political system also produced electoral victories based upon small percentages of the total vote in the Lower House elections. A total of 1,172 candidates representing a mixture of local and organizational interests ran for election to the 137-member House.[44] The only attempts to centralize the selection of candidates came

Table 3-3 Electoral performance of selected Upper House slates

Slate cluster	Number of slates	Total votes received	Seats won	Share of total vote (rounded percent)
Movement for the renaissance of the South	3	1,204,497	0	5
Neo Can Lao	2	1,033,037	10	4
Tan Dai Viet	4	1,775,996	0	8
Toan Viet	4	1,966,970	0	9
Revolu- tionary Dai Viet	4	1,789,056	10	8
Vietnam Nationalist party (VNQDD)– Hoa Hao Social Democratic Party	8	3,232,019	0	15
Associated Catholic slates[a]	3	1,802,311	30	8
Nong-Cong- Binh (Farmer- Worker-Soldier Movement)	1	980,474	10	4
Other slates	19	7,878,761	0	35[b]

[a]These slates included those of the Greater Solidarity Force and two associated Catholic splinter groups of the National Social Democratic Bloc and the Social Good and Social Justice Bloc.

[b]The remaining slates polled an average 414,671 votes each, a 2 percent share of the total votes cast.

from the national Catholic organizations and I Corps regional political parties. While most of the candidates ran as independents on the basis of their reputations in their constituencies, some organizational candidates were chosen by the central executive committees. An independent's decision to run usually took into account the kind of support that could be expected from local organizations considering where the candidate was likely to be most popular, or, in the case of those receiving organizational backing, where cadre systems could be developed to practice the equivalent of door-to-door campaigning on behalf of the candidate.

In contrast to the Upper House campaign, Lower House candidates seldom appeared in joint meetings, but tended to function independently, concentrating on areas of maximum population density, often the provincial capital or districts where they felt they were most popular. In addition, the candidates tended to deemphasize their affiliations with party, religious, or regional organizations, and the campaign leaflets of the successful candidates appeared to have promised more or to have discussed local issues more fully than the losers'. In general, the more specific the appeal made by candidates on local issues the greater the probability of their election. Party candidates who advanced little more than a few slogans such as "Preserve National Sovereignty" or "Construct a Real Democracy" were not preferred to nonparty candidates who promised to work for local reforms of the government and community social welfare and public works projects. While the tone of the campaign was locally oriented and people were urged to vote for those who tended to promise the most, the electorate was not exhorted to vote for those most representative of the population but those deemed best able to represent it. One political leader observed: "Last month in voting for the Upper House we were concerned mainly with national issues and with electing those slates that consisted of people with some degree of national stature. In the Lower House election we have been concerned with electing those who best know the aspirations of the people and who will struggle for them in Saigon." Lack of emphasis on political organizations was probably also due to the parties' lack of prior concern for, or involvement in, the struggle for political rights within the provinces.

The outcome of the Lower House election reflected both the campaign strategies of the candidates and the weakness of most political organizations. Candidates generally tended to seek only the support required for a plurality, concentrating their efforts in areas where they were likely to get the most votes. As a result, most candidates won with an average of 15 to 20 percent of the total vote, and most of the voters came from a specific district, often the province capital. Few candidates won election on the basis of votes received outside the provincial capital, and only eleven deputies received a majority of the votes cast. Eight of these, however, were elected to seats reserved for ethnic minorities that were generally uncontested. The success of the three nonminority deputies who received majorities was mainly attributed to the efficacy of local nonparty support that developed for the candidate throughout the province.[45]

The appeal of political organizations in the Lower House election was directed toward a limited range of existing sympathizers within each province. Little effort was made to use the elections as an opportunity to extend the bases of organization and support. The Farmer, Worker, Soldier Movement (FWSM), for example, was organized in an effort to appeal to Vietnam's working class. Centered around some of Vietnam's elder statesmen such as former general Tan van Don, however, support for the FWSM was found primarily in the Saigon metropolitan area; it lacked appeal for farmers. Its provincial organization, as measured by electoral success, was not impressive.

In the splintered politics of the Saigon area (236 candidates for 15 seats) the FWSM received a little more than 8 percent of all votes cast, and its provincial success was largely the result of the minority candidates affiliated with it (five of eight FWSM provincial deputies were Montagnards). FWSM Vietnamese deputies from the provinces were elected by small pluralities (17 percent, 18 percent, 24 percent). Victory through plurality and reliance upon minority candidates suggests that the extent of this movement's political base throughout the country was not broad; its deputies were positioned in only five regular (that is, nonminority) provincial constituencies. A similarly broad occupational appeal was employed by the southern-oriented Movement for the Renaissance of the South (MRS) which first appeared in the 1966 elections for the Constituent Assembly. However, of the seven MRS deputies elected to the Lower House, only one was from outside the Saigon-Gia Dinh area and MRS hopefuls made a poor showing in election contests throughout the delta. In the capital area, MRS deputies were elected by less than 5 percent of the total votes cast, which compares favorably with Saigon-Gia Dinh proportions received by other groups. Despite claims to the contrary, the MRS organization did not effectively organize the delta. A third group, Vietnamese Confederation Labor (CVT), fared poorly, electing only three out of nineteen candidates.

Considered the best-organized and cohesive political entities in Vietnamese politics, national Catholic organizations elected twelve deputies to the Lower House and contributed to the election of one additional representative in Bien Hoa. Local Catholic organizations, in addition, were instrumental in electing seventeen other deputies to the Lower House. The results of the Lower House election demonstrate the ability of the Catholics to organize. In each area of their demographic concentration at least one deputy was elected. In addition, Catholics tend to be divided into northern versus southern-born groups, paralleling also their rural-urban organizational components. Of the two principal competitors, the Greater Solidarity Force (GSF) and the Catholic Citizens' Bloc (CCB), the GSF appear to be stronger in terms of Lower House representation. GSF support was responsible for the election of eleven Catholic deputies from primarily coastal II and III Corps provinces, but the major areas of plurality strengths (23 to 33 percent of the total votes cast) were in the highland province of Kontum and Vung Tau. The CCB, in contrast, elected only two deputies, both from Khanh Hoa, with a combined plurality of 42 percent of the total vote.

Seventeen out of thirty of the Lower House Catholic deputies were elected through local rather than national support. Five were elected from the Gia Dinh with a combined plurality of 20 percent of the total vote. Five additional locally supported candidates received substantial votes ranging from 24 to 73 percent of the total vote in Lam Dong, Vinh Binh, Phu Bon, and Kontum provinces. The remaining seven showed only average plurality strength and were elected from the delta area. It would appear that Catholic strength rested in stable and well-organized local communities and groups rather than in the presence of a well-supported national movement.

Demographically the largest group of Vietnamese, the Buddhists, were the least organized. Deeply split within the hierarchy of the priesthood, Buddhist lay political organizations have never been able to endure beyond the temporary coalitions required for their struggle movements. Adherence to Buddhist factions has become, therefore, primarily a matter of individual commitment, and deputies who were elected as An Quang supporters tended to rely upon the cadre systems they were individually able to mobilize for the election. A total of fifteen militant Buddhists were elected, primarily from central Vietnam. In those provinces most affected by the war, militant Buddhist deputies received above average pluralities, but there is little evidence to suggest that such support was generated by appeals to end the war. Most militant Buddhist deputies tended to deemphasize their antiwar feelings and concentrated instead upon platforms stressing social justice and public works projects. In addition to these declared militants, thirty-eight other Buddhists were elected as independents or as candidates affiliated with other political groups.

The Cao Dai and Hoa Hao religions, perhaps the strongest and best organized non-Catholic political forces in the Mekong Delta are highly factionalized, but remain essentially unchallenged in their areas of concentration. The Hoa Hao were successful in six provinces of the Delta, turning in two majorities and a number of substantial, above-average pluralities. Each Hoa Hao deputy elected, however, represented a different faction of the religion. The Cao Dai, similarly, were divided into two factions that were both successful in electing their deputies.

The election revealed the limited appeal of Vietnam's two principal secular nationalist parties, the *Vietnam Quoc Dan Dang* (VNQDD) and the *Dai Viet*. Though the VNQDD claim considerable strength through I Corps, their organization is based in the three southernmost provinces of the area. In addition, VNQDD factions served to divide their political base even further. The *Ky Bo* faction elected more than half of all VNQDD Lower House deputies (five out of nine) with above-average pluralities in Quang Nam and Quang Tin as well as with unpredicted victories in Binh Dinh and Tuyen Duc provinces in II Corps. The Vu hong Khanh faction shared VNQDD success in Quang Nam and Quang Tin garnering approximately the same proportion of votes in each province (20 percent and 40 percent, respectively). The Quang Tin proportions are among the highest of the pluralities achieved throughout the country and indicate that both factions were apparently well organized in this province. The Nguyen tuong Tam faction, similarly, is strong in Quang Ngai and elected both of its candidates with a combined majority over other candidates.

Challenging the VNQDD and the Viet Cong for political hegemony in I Corps, the factious *Dai Viets* are considered strong in the two northernmost provinces of South Vietnam (Revolutionary *Dai Viet*) and around Saigon in the III Corps area (*Tan Dai Viet*). In the Lower House election, however, *Dai Viet* strength was solid in I Corps, and their candidates garnered more than average pluralities. Seventy percent of Thua Thien province, for example, voted *Dai Viet*, and the group partially influenced the near majority of Nguyen dai Bang (a militant Buddhist) in Hue. *Tan Dai Viet* strength surfaced in Quang Ngai, a Nguyen tuong Tam VNQDD stronghold, and the *Dai Viet* candidate did as well as his VNQDD counterparts (all averaging 24 to 28 percent of the total votes cast), though he was the only successful *Tan Dai Viet* candidate out of ten hopefuls.

The inability of most groups to function outside a few limited geographical areas is clear. While data were not reported in detail to permit a comparative analysis based on the results of the Upper House election, the only major difference suspected between the two elections would be the decline in the number of seats won by Catholics which, as suggested previously, is attributable not to a decline in that religion's local organizational cohesiveness but rather to the bounds of provincial constituencies which made it impossible for Catholics to register successes outside their areas of principal concentrations. For groups like the FWSM or the CVT which attempted to construct broadly based campaigns, the elections signaled the limitations of appeals based solely upon rhetoric and centered upon a core of national figures who hoped to unify Vietnam's many splinter parties and organizations. For the parties and interest groups with an appeal limited to provincial or regional areas, the elections demonstrated not the effectiveness of their organizations within those areas but the extent to which factional strife and outdated conceptions of organization had hindered efforts both to appear cohesive and to demonstrate convincingly the popular support such movements could muster. A multiplicity of political organizations does not necessarily foster competition among them,[46] and, in the case of South Vietnam, such diversity tended to result not in efforts by all groups to expand but to consolidate their bases of support.

Representation presupposes political community. Of all the values which members of a political community might share, those which define the permissible bounds of conflict are crucial to the development of representation. Representation regulates political conflict generated by the demand of social forces for political participation. By providing an arena where peaceful competition between central authority and social forces can take place, representative government "facilitates interchanges between authority and the spontaneous groupings of society"[1] by promoting through negotiation and compromise a balance between such political forces. This process requires social forces to articulate interests and to agree that such articulation be directed at a particular institution; it also requires that the institution respond effectively to such interests.

The skill with which constituencies express their demands determines the representative's perception of his job and the talents it requires. Through organized and concerted action, constituents function to control both access to public office and the character of the office. There is considerable room for action on the representative's part, but the field within such action should take place is determined by the constituency. "The representative must act independently; his action must involve discretion and judgment; he must be the one who acts. *The represented must also be capable of independent action and judgment, not merely being taken care of.*"[2] In a praetorian polity such as South Vietnam the relationship between the constituency and its representatives, however, is just the reverse. Because the constituency is often not capable of independent action, the skill with which a representative can create both interests and demands is instrumental to the constituency. The representative determines the character of his constituency's participation in political life; he can work toward expanding the goals of the constituency because only from his position can the need for such a development be perceived. Representation, under the conditions generally associated with low levels of political community, requires the development of a shared attitude among political actors about the milieu from which they have come and, more important, the kind of milieu they would like to create by political action. Representation requires the creation of interests as well as of mechanisms to respond to such interests.

Representation and Elite Selection

The elections that established the Second Republic in South Vietnam did not select a new type of participant in politics or create a new institution whose members closely resembled the character of the total population. The concept of elite change resulting from either new political requirements after independence or the enfranchisement of hitherto nonparticipant masses (as was the case in the United States, India, the Philippines, Turkey after 1945, or Ceylon[3]) has been based largely upon the argument that such change reflects an increase in political competition and a wider sharing of skills required for mobilization.[4] In the case of South Vietnam, however, the spread of political competition has not fostered significant changes in the status or skills of those participating in politics. Rather, political competition both among and between groups and the government has underscored the stability of elite-dominated politics.

The goal of those responsible for elite selection—party members, party leadership committees, the electorate—has been and remains that of selecting elites best qualified to deal with other elites. At the local level, for example, villagers tend to select those with the most prestige attached to their respective social position in order to have the village effectively represented in encounters with government officials. In the village and hamlet council elections of 1967 almost 80 percent of those elected were either already local officials or were drawn from among the elder generation of farmers that represented the elite of the locality.[5] This pattern also held for the elections organized in 1969. Younger and presumably more progressive farmers and residents generally tended to be unsuccessful in their bid for election.[6] Similarly, political organizations and groups normally select those among their membership most closely resembling the social elite both as a reward for their participation in organizational affairs and as a means to assure the ability of the group to bargain and deal effectively with the governmental elite. The average voter also tends to choose not those representative of himself but those who are part of the social elite.[7]

Selection of elites is a form of political participation. The study of social backgrounds, consequently, is as essential to an analysis of the nature of political participation as it is to the study of elites.[8] Rather than demonstrating the extent to which segments of the population have been left out of the process of government or politics, social background analysis provides insight into the nature of political leadership. Indeed, the assumption made here is that, even given a situation where the Vietnamese voter was free from any pressure, he would essentially make an elite-determined selection rather than an issue-oriented choice between candidates. As a result, it is assumed that the elite which now participates in politics will largely retain its characteristics and its social position in the future. In this sense, Vietnam conforms to the findings of most comparative studies of legislative recruitment:

> One of the firmest generalizations which can be made about the social composition of legislatures is that they do not mirror their populations. That anyone thought they should have, or expected them to, is doubtless a result of the Nineteenth Century liberal perspective of much commentary about legislative life. Systematic and substantial biases in the recruitment process of every known system produce legislatures whose members over-represent business and professional occupations and under-represent the working class populations. Similarly, parliamentarians are highly over-representative in educational attainment.[9]

Such biases do not, however, necessarily eliminate opportunities for the masses to participate in politics. If political and social groups seek to maximize their bargaining positions vis-à-vis each other and the government, elite selection can achieve that objective.

The social backgrounds of those elected to the National Assemblies since 1956 reflect their elite nature and thereby their essential similarity. Assemblies of the Diem era contained only a narrow segment of the political elite, while the assemblies of the Second Republic include representatives from virtually every noncommunist political force. The striking feature of the comparison is that it is impossible to distinguish between the two sets of institutions on the basis of traditional criteria used to make political distinctions in Vietnam. Regionalism, religion, ethnicity, and educational and occupational distinctions are more reliable indicators of the complexity of the elite than of political differences within it. Political divisions are, consequently, of more recent vintage; they are defined by political experiences and political socialization.[10] Traditionally, religious differences coincided with political divisions in the society at large. More recently, however, religion has become less reliable as a political indicator. Buddhists have both supported and opposed the regimes in power, as have Catholic politicians. Indeed, between the assemblies of the Diem era and the establishment of the Lower House, the salience of religion as a political indicator markedly declined. Vietnam has experienced not the secularization of religious differences but the politicization of secular differences quite apart from religious concerns.

The selection of elites by the Vietnamese electorate appears independent of politics. This is clearly indicated by the similarity of social characteristics which existed between the assemblies of the First and Second Republics (see Table 4-1). In the First Republic, the selection of candidates and winners was determined by President Diem. In the Second Republic the selection of candidates and the outcome of the elections were largely free from such intervention on the part of the junta. The differences in political intervention implied in each case appear to have had little effect upon the social characteristics of those elected.[11] The elite status of the elected deputies is clearly seen from their educational and occupational experience. Virtually every study of developing societies has noted that one of the principal ingredients of the gap between the masses and the elite is education.[12] In Vietnam the distinction between the masses and the elite produced by education was less politically significant than the effect educational processes had upon the cohesion of the elite itself.[13] From the dynastic to the colonial and independence eras, discipline, not intellectual development or independent thinking, tended to be the prime goal of the Vietnamese educational system. During the decades in which most of the elected deputies came of age, the mid-1930's to the mid-1950's, the tensions between those with a purely Vietnamese education and those with a French education were great, but both kinds served to differentiate between elite and mass in Vietnam. Education remained a privilege of the few respected by the many. Because it was scarce, education was regarded as a primary means to train a governing elite and to assure its loyalty to the system.

Most deputies believed in the ability and the right of the elite to govern, and they felt that the Vietnamese voter shared these assumptions. The likelihood that farmers would not be elected to the assemblies of the Second Republic was of evident concern to deputies of the Constituent Assembly as they wrote the electoral laws. As will be suggested in Chapter 8, most deputies argued that constituencies should be based upon units no larger than a province, and they sensed that many would finally have to be based upon districts within provinces. Some deputies, moreover, viewed

Table 4-1 Profiles of South Vietnam's elected assemblies (percent)

Characteristic	Estimated total population	Constituent Assembly winners	Lower House winners	Lower House losers	Upper House winners	Upper House losers	Diem I	Diem II
Education:								
None		–	1	NA	–	NA	–	–
Primary		10	7	NA	2	NA	2	3
Secondary		38	45	NA	23	NA	41	33
College		29	39	NA	60	NA	36	38
Graduate Study		11	7	NA	15	NA	8	5
No Data		11	–	NA	–	NA	13	20
Occupation:								
Teaching	1[a]	20	19	17	18	21	19	18
Civil Service	3[b]	20	29	20	7	9	25	23
Business	11	18	15	14	12	13	16	20
Armed Forces	7	15	19	13	12	11	2	2
Law	–	8	3	2	17	8	9	8
Medicine	–	9	7	2	8	7	5	6
Journalism	–	1	4	2	5	8	5	3
Engineering	–	2	–	2	8	4	1	4
Politico	–	2	4	2	3	–	8	8
Agriculture	73	3	1	4	–	1	2	2
Property owner	–	2	–	–	3	1	5	2
Architecture	–	–	–	–	2	–	–	–
Economics	–	–	–	–	2	–	–	–

Confucian scholar	–	–	–	–	–	–	–
Retired[c]	–	–	–	–	2	–	–
Student	–	1	–	–	2	–	–
Notable	2	–	–	–	–	–	2
Local councilor[c]	–	–	–	2	–	2	2
Priest	–	–	–	–	–	1	–
Midwife	–	–	–	–	–	–	1
Employed by US	3	–	–	–	–	–	–
Domestic servant	2	–	–	–	–	–	–
No data	–	20	–	16	–	–	–

[a]Percentage is of the total labor force which in 1967 was estimated at 5,600,000 persons. Estimate for teachers includes public and private school teachers from the primary to vocational and university levels.

[b]Percentage includes all permanent and temporary employees with the exception of approximately 30,000 public school teachers in the Ministry of Culture and Education who were listed in the separate category for teachers.

[c]Occupation not further specified.

the election of farmers and their representatives as crucial in establishing the legitimacy of the National Assembly if it chose to vote no confidence in the government. They argued that, since the President of the Republic would probably be a city man, the rural population ought to be assured of a voice in the government. Those who opposed granting the power to vote no confidence in the government to the National Assembly argued that such power could not be based upon the expectation that farmers would be elected or that their direct participation in the assembly would be appropriate. As one speaker declared, "Representatives of provinces in Congress are not necessarily the farmers, but a large number are the men of the provincial capitals. This is clearly shown by the experiences in all nations so far. The city people are always better trusted because they have more experience than farmers."[14]

The closest Vietnam has come to nonelite, populist representatives was in the 1967 elections. The "politico" tended to come from the religious sects of the Mekong Delta or the established nationalist parties of the I Corps area; in most cases they tended to be older than their colleagues and to have had little more than a primary school education. This traditional politician is now a fading feature of Vietnamese political life, increasingly confronted by both challenges from within the parties and competition from without. The portrait of the local political organizer arriving each day at his party headquarters and ceremoniously attending to administrative paperwork in the morning and tea and conspiracy in the afternoon is being displaced by that of younger, better-educated leaders devoting most of their time to an outside career (usually teaching or a local civil service post) and leaving party business for late at night in kerosene-lit offices or for Sundays in their homes. In 1967 an interviewer seeking local party leaders would have been relatively successful during the working day. By 1969, not only had many of the old faces been retired, but a party headquarters was usually empty during working hours as most members of the leadership committee were at their jobs. In some instances the old faces remained, but they were unwilling to speak until a group of younger members was summoned.

The professional is replacing the politico, and in the constituency-based houses of the National Assemblies the proportion of teachers and civil servants has remained relatively constant at around 40 percent of the total membership. At the province level, the teacher is generally regarded with deference and respect provided he has been a long-term resident of the province. Most deputies elected from the teaching profession had been involved in community affairs for some time either through participation in organizations similar to the American PTA or through efforts to found local primary and secondary schools. Such candidates tend to run independent of party organizations, their campaign organization being based upon former students.[15]

Deputies elected to the Upper House reflected occupational experiences quite different from most deputies of the constituency-based group. Of the Upper House deputies 75 percent had college or graduate educations, compared to less than 50 percent of the deputies in the constituency-based assemblies. Liberal and technical professions account for approximately 40 percent of the Upper House and only 8 percent of the Lower House. The Upper House emerges as perhaps the best-qualified legislature in Vietnam's history, but it contains essentially the elite of the Saigon metropolitan area. The Lower House tends to be composed of the more parochial elite from the provincial capitals. Indeed, a frequent criticism of the Lower House has been that its deputies were poorly educated and that they lacked the necessary talent to effectively participate in the lawmaking process. Some nonparticipant observers have even attributed the poor relations between the Upper and Lower Houses to educational and occupational differences between the two bodies, underscoring the way occupation and education remain primary sources of division within the elected elite. Interviews with Upper and Lower House deputies also suggest that conflict between the two houses stems from the constituencies that each appears to serve, as well as from the relative inexperience of Lower House deputies in the process of government and from the disdain with which the latter are regarded by the more highly educated and professional members of the Upper House.

In the Second Republic the proportion of professional military officers elected to the National Assembly differed substantially from the proportion of military officers elected to the assemblies in the Diem era. This difference does not reflect an increasing tendency for the officer corps to intervene in politics since this has been a prerogative of only senior generals. The number of military officers elected to the assemblies of the Second Republic suggests both the politicization of the officer corps and the differing attitudes of those entering politics toward that development. Indeed, the military has become politicized as those making decisions on promotions and assignments of military officers have increasingly looked not to the professional credentials of officers but to their political credentials. While it is generally assumed that the military officers elected to the 1966 and 1967 assemblies were basically designates of the regime in power, a survey of the backgrounds of elected officers (see Table 4-2) coupled to interviews with them suggests that they are a considerably more diverse group. Especially in the Lower House, most army officers elected were motivated to run not because of their sympathy with the Thieu government but because of their dissatisfaction with the weakened morale of the officer corps resulting from the Thieu-Ky conflict.

Table 4-2   A profile of armed forces officers elected in 1967

Characteristic	Upper House	Lower House
Regional origin[a]		
Northern Vietnam	1	10
Central Vietnam	3	5
Southern Vietnam	2	11
Ethnic origin		
Vietnamese	7	22
Chinese	–	–
Khmer and Cham	–	3
Montagnard	–	1
Unknown	–	–
Religion		
Mahayana Buddhist	3	10
Theravada Buddhist	–	3
Catholic	2	9
Confucianist	–	1
Hoa Hao	2	1
Cao Dai	–	1
Moslem (Cham)	–	–
Protestant (Montagnard)	–	–
Ancestor Worship	–	–
Montagnard (animist)	–	1
Undeclared	–	–
Political position		
Pro-Ky	3	8
Opposition	3	6
Independent-Neutral	1	9
Ethnic minority	–	3

[a]One officer was born in France. Northern Vietnam refers to the area of present-day North Vietnam south to the 20th parallel (Thanh Hoa Province). Central Vietnam refers to the area south of Thanh Hoa to the borders between the II and III Corps military regions. Southern Vietnam includes the present-day III and IV Corps area.

No single group or religion[16] appeared dominant among the military officers elected to the National Assembly in 1967, and there were important differences between the type of officers elected to each house. In the Upper House, where the most direct appeal was made for the military vote by Tran van Don's Farmer, Worker, Soldier Movement (FWSM), four of the officers elected were generals and three of these were on Don's list, suggesting the limited appeal these figures had for the soldiers and the officer corps. In contrast, no general officer ran for election to the Lower House, and most of the military deputies were either lieutenant colonels or captains. The regional distributions in each House are proportionately equal except in the case of officers born in central Vietnam. The relatively higher proportion of Upper House officers reflects the fact that most of the generals promoted to that rank in the Diem era were central Vietnamese; thereafter this regional group declined as promotion favored a proportionate shift to southern or northern Vietnamese. Military officers of both houses tend to be ethnic Vietnamese although the four nonethnic Vietnamese officers in the Lower House reflect the gradual liberalization of commissioning policies in the early and mid-1960's, which allowed some minority soldiers to be commissioned to command specially recruited units or to work as advisers to the province government for minority affairs.

More significantly, the military officers elected were by no means predominantly supporters of either Thieu or Ky. In the Lower House the largest identifiable group of military officers have maintained their independence from either faction and, while they tend to support the government, they have also worked to draft legislation to reform the promotion and assignment system within the armed forces in conjunction with disgruntled civil servants who sought similar reforms in the civilian ministries. These deputies, labeled "Independent-Neutral," believe they represent the great majority of the officers who have been in rank for at least ten years and consider that they have suffered because of favoritism which deprived them of promotions and easy assignments. Allied with these officers in reform efforts are military officers who have openly declared their opposition to the government either by joining an opposition bloc, by consistently opposing the government's legislative program, or by their affiliation with the militant Buddhists. In the Upper House, on the other hand, opposition is centered around an effort to construct a new political movement and here lines tend to be drawn over less substantive issues than in the Lower House. The core of opposition centered around

Tran van Don until his retirement in 1970, and around other military officers elected on his list.

Military officers, like the leaders of the civil servants, do not, by themselves, constitute the core of either pro- or antigovernment movements; nor are they separate from other groups that have formed. Military officers entered alliances with other deputies based upon their experience within the profession rather than as a result of a clearly defined institutional ideology.

As a microcosm of Vietnam's social elite, National Assemblies reflect its internal differentiation. The significance of such differences lies in what it indicates about the salience of elites to government and politics in Vietnam. While level of education and occupational experience, critieria of elite status, of any given individual differs from one level of government to another, each level appears to be dominated by those with relatively similar characteristics, suggesting that Vietnamese tend to select elites to represent them based on the nature of the position. The assumption underlying this hypothesis is that the Vietnamese electorate selects elites that they consider capable of dealing with other elites. Elections represent opportunities not for direct participation of voters in decision-making processes but, rather, for the identification of those able to make decisions. The cluster pattern within the elite elected in the Second Republic—namely Upper House versus the Constituent Assembly and Lower House—suggests that such a distinction possibly was made in deciding upon candidates for the Upper House that placed them "a rung above" those elected for the Lower House. Finally, such stratification has significance not only for the ability of representatives to bargain with nonelected elites but also for their ability to work together within the legislature. Indeed, that elites are internally differentiated is less significant than the degree of correspondence that may exist between social backgrounds, dividing elites into coalitions that reflect their political interests. Social homogeneity, similarity in background and experience, greases the wheels of political cooperation at the elite level.

Political Divisions within the Elected Elite

While social structure and cultural traditions define elite status in Vietnam, divisions within the elite are functions of the level of political mobilization achieved in the polity at large. The less intense this mobilization, the less intense the conflict within the elite it produces. In

Vietnam popular political mobilization has not been extensive. The political organizations of the nationalists have traditionally been based upon identities that existed among members of a particular religion who also tended to represent distinct regional groupings.[17] At the start of the colonial war for independence there were perhaps as many as six such political organizations in the South; by the end of 1969 there were more than sixty.

This growth in the number of identifiable political organizations has not, however, been matched by an expansion of political participation. Leaders of some of the most prominent and active organizations of the 1950's have even noted that the salience of their organizations has markedly declined. Leaders of the Cao Dai, for example, claim that the religious factions account for no more than a few hundred partisans and that their political leaders have fled to Cambodia to escape government repression. Leaders of the Hoa Hao, similarly, claim that the religious base of the political organization is extremely small. As one politician has noted, "The political factions of our religion are not significant today to the religion as a whole since the most active faction members constitute only about 200 persons who have always been involved in factional disputes. To the mass of the people, Hoa Hao is today largely a religion and their concerns are with the practice of it."[18] Another leader observed that, "most of the people today follow the religion and not its factions. Thus factionalism is relatively unimportant and I myself ran for election to the House independently of any faction. A few years ago this would have been impossible because the people were much more involved. Now they have become wary of factional leaders, and they question the purposes of such groups. Politics has achieved little for them in the past and unless this changes in the future they will have little incentive to support the groups which now exist." Catholic political leaders have also noted that support for political groupings based upon religion has tended to decline. As one leader described the situation,

Catholic politicians are divided into two groups: those who support the *Nhan Xa* party and those who support the Greater Solidarity Force but the population is divided against both of these organizations because in the past they have shown little interest in helping the people. When I say the population I really mean the priests since the people follow their guidance and advice without question. When I was considering running for election, for example, I sought to win the support of the priests. They told me that if I joined one of these movements they could not ask the people to support me since neither of these organizations had done anything for the people; they only served to enrich their leaders. Many of my colleagues have told me of similar experiences, and on the whole we do not believe that the people will follow these parties and support them as they have done in the past.

Leaders of established political parties in central Vietnam also reported that both factional divisions within the parties and of the parties themselves were not significant to the population.

The people want things we have in the past not concentrated on providing, and I believe they are going to judge us in the future on our performance. Let me offer an example. In my province the Viet Cong recently distributed a leaflet which said that any person who was a member of one of the nationalist parties was their enemy, and they would be primary targets of the Communists' terrorism. In one village I spoke with a group of people who were party supporters in the past, and they said that unless the party could influence the government to protect them they had no reasons to continue to support us. To them it did not make a difference whether one figure led the party or another, only what the party would do for the people.

Buddhist political leaders as well have noted that their followers increasingly demand that any organization provide tangible benefits to the people.

These comments highlight the decline in efficacy of religious and regional politics, especially when such a decline is measured across generations. Appeals based upon religious affiliations have tended to produce less than desired results. Catholic and Buddhist parties alike have encountered increasing difficulties in gaining the support of the faithful, and leaders of such groups have acknowledged that, unless the bases of their organization changed, they could count upon only a limited amount of popular support.

Appeals for the organization of southerners and the creation of southern political organizations have been similarly ineffective. Parties once based upon a regional identity have either begun to abandon it as the focal point of the organization or have virtually atrophied as effective political forces. While the salience of regional and religious differences may reemerge in the future as the primary ingredients for constructing political organizations, such differences do not now constitute a principal obstacle to cooperation within the elected elite. In fact, religious and regional differences have never been a primary obstacle to intraelite cooperation. Instead, political socialization and the resultant generational gaps this process creates define the divisions within the political elite.

During the Diem era, the only route to national politics was through government-organized parties. In the Second Republic individuals could compete for election without support from the junta or its leaders. As Table 4-3 indicates, there is greater diversity of groups and among participants in the Second Republic's assemblies, especially the assembly elected in 1967 as a result of the relatively open nature of the contest. In the First Republic, Diem's party tended to recruit a disproportionate number of central Vietnamese, especially Catholics, who had openly declared their support of the regime. While no data on religion is available for the assemblies of the Diem era, there is little reason to doubt that they were predominantly Catholic as this was Diem's own religion, a preference exhibited in his regime's philosophy and in the recruitment of Catholics into progovernment parties. One Buddhist, who was a deputy in the assemblies of the Diem era and a member of the *Can Lao* party, claimed that there were "no more than ten" Buddhists in the assemblies but many more—"perhaps as much as 40 percent"—in the ranks of the *Can Lao*. To be sure, these Buddhists were largely those who accommodated themselves to the Diem regime.

During the Diem era the principal vehicles of political socialization for most members of the assemblies were the political movements constructed by the Ngo family. In the first assembly practically half of the deputies elected were local and national officers of the Personalist and National Revolutionary Movements. In the second assembly this portion increased to almost two-thirds as most incumbent deputies were reelected, to be joined by newly elected party officials. Municipal and provincial councillors who, by election for the assembly's second term, were not affiliated with officials in the government parties, were not renominated and were replaced by provincial-level party chairmen. The proportion of deputies with no prior political experience was small in the First Republic, the reflection of a government-sponsored organization functioning as a mechanism for the recruitment of the legislature. As suggested in Chapter 2, few differences on policy issues existed among those elected to the assemblies during the Diem era. New deputies had been socialized into politics by an agency which stressed loyalty to the President of the Republic, and they behaved accordingly.

In the Second Republic, in contrast, no single political party or

Table 4-3 Political profile of selected National Assembly deputies (percent)

Characteristic	Total population	Constituent Assembly winners	Lower House winners	Lower House losers	Upper House winners	Upper House losers	Diem I	Diem II
Regional origin								
Northern Vietnam	6[a]	27	24	33	38	41	16	10
Central Vietnam	35	30	32	31	29	18	40	37
Southern Vietnam	59	42	43	33	33	39	39	33
Unknown	–	–	–	3	–	2	5	20[b]
Ethnic origin								
Vietnamese	85	86	84	97	95	93	97	95
Chinese	8	3	4	1	2	4	–	1
Montagnard	3	3	6	–	–	2	–	1
Unknown	4	8	7	–	3	1	3	3
Religion								
Mayahana Buddhist	62	31	38	6	22	9	NA	NA
Theravada Buddhist	3	3	4	–	–	–	NA	NA
Catholic	11	29	26	4	50	8	NA	NA
Confucianist	5	8	4	–	10	1	NA	NA
Hoa Hao	9	3	3	2	3	4	NA	NA
Cao Dai	9	3	3	1	2	4	NA	NA
Moslem (Cham)	–	–	1	–	–	–	NA	NA
Protestant (Montagnard)	–	1	1	–	–	–	NA	NA
Ancestor Worshipper	–	–	–	–	2	–	NA	NA
Montagnard (animist)	–	–	–	–	1	–	NA	NA

Undeclared	–	16	13	86	10	74	NA	NA
Prior political experience								
National assemblies	NA	2	19	2	29	13	2	46
Provincial assemblies	NA	19	12	7	3	4	13	2
Appointed government posts	NA	13	3	2	15	6	13	8
Municipal and local councils	NA	7	4	1	–	1	14	8
Positions in parties and other political organizations	NA	21	39	1	8	2	48	21
Undeclared	NA	39	27	87	48	73	10	21
Prior electoral experience	NA	31	31	10	32	19	28	48

Sources: Republic of Vietnam, Office of the Prime Minister, Directorate General of Planning, *Vietnam Statistical Yearbook, 1966–67, Vol. 13* (Saigon, 1967); *Vietnam Statistical Yearbook, 1967-68, Vol. 14* (Saigon, 1968); United States Agency for International Development, *Education Division Report* (Saigon, 1968); Office of Joint Economic Affairs, *Annual Statistical Bulletin, II* (Saigon, 1968); field notes and interview data; Wesley Fishel, "Analysis of 1967 Elections," undated, unpublished mimeo, Department of Political Science, Michigan State University; Vietnam Cong Hoa [Republic of Vietnam], *Nien-Giam Thuong Nghi-Vien* [Yearbook of the Upper House] (Saigon, 1970); Vietnam Cong Hoa, *Nien-Giam Ha-Nghi-Vien* [Yearbook of the Lower House] (Saigon, 1968); Vietnam Cong Hoa, *Nien-Giam Quoc-Hoi Vietnam* [Yearbook of the Vietnam Congress] (Saigon, 1956, 1959); Allan E. Goodman, "Government and the Countryside: Political Accommodation and South Vietnam's Communal Groups," *Orbis* XIII (Summer 1969), pp. 502–525.

[a]Percents may not total 100 due to rounding error.

[b]For convenience, figure includes one deputy born in Laos.

institution served to socialize the deputies into politics; nor was the election of a candidate determined by his link with any government-sponsored group. Catholics were elected in the areas of their principal geographic concentrations, and the Buddhists in theirs, but in both cases only a small proportion of those elected had run as declared candidates of particular religious organizations. More than three-quarters of all Catholics elected ran as independents and disavowed any connections with Catholic parties. Similarly, slightly less than three-fourths of all Buddhists elected had run independently of the religion's hierarchy and its nascent and quasi-secret political organizations. In post-Diem assemblies the proportion of deputies with no prior experience markedly increased in the Constituent Assembly and in the Upper House, while only a small increase is evident in the backgrounds of those elected to the Lower House. In the case of the former two bodies, the lack of deputy involvement in politics prior to their election reflects the bias in each body toward construction of lists headed by nationally known politicians but filled by candidates with established competencies outside the field of politics. In contrast, the Lower House had the highest proportion of members with prior experience in political organizations. How did socialization into politics affect the capacity of these deputies to accommodate at the microlevel of politics to conflicts within the society at large?

Political Socialization: Bases of
Conflict and Accommodation within
the Lower House

Career Patterns

The existence of many political organizations in Vietnam has made for diversity but not divisiveness. Most political leaders will argue that these differences have largely been the result of outside influences. French colonials elevated Catholicism to a level of such political significance that conflict between Vietnamese who wished to preserve the traditional culture and those who wished to ignore it was viewed as inevitable. So also, it is argued, the war is an artificial division in Vietnam that made differences between northern, southern, and central Vietnamese more significant than they had ever been in the past. American intervention in Vietnam, finally, is held responsible for the emergence of narrowly based, repressive regimes that increasingly tend to rely upon American resources for the support which should have been sought from the population.

Whether this assessment of events is historically correct or not, to Vietnamese political leaders it underlies a view of politics that stresses not the bases of conflicts within the society but the bases of accommodation. If political conflict in the past has been the result of outside interference, then, they argue, no inherent obstacles exist to impede political cooperation between diverse social and political forces. Vietnamese and Western historians have noted that one of the primary features of rulership has been a continual search for compromises in the face of obstacles (largely externally generated) to goals such as unification and unencumbered sovereignty. So also, in more recent times it has been suggested that Vietnamese politics since the end of World War II has been characterized by cooperation and accommodation among political groups in times of turmoil and instability.[19] Common to both historical and contemporary interpretations of the process of accommodation and political compromise in Vietnam is the theme that such cooperative enterprises depend upon incentives provided. Most Vietnamese political leaders have suggested that, given the need for cooperation, even the most diverse collection of groups or individuals can work together.

The process of accommodation is inherent in Vietnamese politics, and, it has been suggested, it indicates a latent sense of political community. As one Vietnamese observed,

> The basis of politics in Vietnam is our sense of communal responsibility, and we use the term *Cong-Dong Trach-Nhiem* to denote it. *Cong-Dong* is the word we used to describe a community; it means a collectivity, a cumulation and adding together of people on the basis of what they have in common. *Trach-Nhiem* means responsibility. As you know both communities and responsibilities can increase or decrease, and we think that an increase in community is followed by an increase in responsibility. In the past the size of our communities were small, their responsibilities limited, and, because of these two features, their power was also small. Today, we tend to employ a larger conception of the term. If our community identity increases, so, too, will our power provided we are responsible to the larger interests this usage of the term implies.

Implied in this statement is the belief that, until recently, there has been neither common ground nor incentive to find common ground on which a communal identity might be developed. This lack of common interest stems partly from accommodations political groups have been able to reach with the government, thus making the search for intergroup accommodation less pressing,[20] as is indicated by this examination of the relationship between the political complexity of the Lower House and prospects for political cooperation and accommodation among its members. In a political milieu that values accommodation, participation in the Lower House has tended to emphasize not only the fragmentation of that milieu but also its integration. The House, by providing an arena in which diverse interests could be reconciled, has served as an arena of group-to-group accommodation.

Indeed, South Vietnam's Lower House deputies reflect the skills that survival in such a milieu requires. Almost three-quarters (72 percent) of the deputies entered political life as young professionals (that is, in their twenties). Only a small portion entered politics while still high school or college students (see Table 4-4). Owing to the highly politicized nature of the major service occupations—military, civil service, and teaching—an early awareness of politics or, in some cases, an early commitment to one political movement or figure was necessary. In working one's way up the career ladder, it was not unusual for civil and military officers to change their religion to assure their chances of promotion. Leaders of the 1963 coup were scheduled to be converted to Catholicism before the end of the year in return for promotion. In other cases, a deputy's career might involve a process of accommodation most often described in the following way. After the development of political consciousness, a deputy could confront an issue or personality that would lead him to withdraw from effective political activities. Because most deputies had become involved in politics early in their careers, however, involvement tended to continue. Almost all deputies interviewed reported reaching some point at which they clashed with the prevailing authorities. During withdrawal the future deputy would often change his career, job assignment, or place of residence. Usually he returned to politics about the time of the Constituent Assembly election, but he preferred low visibility until the status of elected government and the tenure of its members were more certain. Such accommodations are viewed as rules of the game when occupations are based upon politics rather than professionalism.

The Lower House deputies shared common historical experiences. Since the generation gap between the deputies is relatively small (59 percent of all deputies were between thirty and forty-four years old at the time of their election), they were exposed to a common range of experiences: the last year of the Indo-China war; the Geneva settlement; transformation of the nationalist movement into a communist one; division of their country;

Table 4-4   Career[a] patterns of Lower House deputies

Career variable	Number	Percent
Age at entry into politics		
Student	12	8
Junior professional or official	88	64
Midcareer professional or official	39	28
Agent of initial political socialization		
None	19	14
Religious sect or organization	52	36
Student organization	5	4
Political party or other organization	47	34
Military academy	16	12
Career changes before election		
None	99	71
One change	30	22
Two or more changes	10	7
Political experience[b]		
None	37	27
Campaigning	18	13
Elected local office	19	13
Political party or other organization	64	46
National Assembly, First Republic	5	4
Constituent Assembly	14	10
Viet Minh (pre-1954)	8	6
Community action project	6	4

[a]Biographical information is available for a total of 139 deputies although there have been 140 deputies since 1967. In 1967, 137 deputies were elected: one resigned his seat to accept an appointment in the Inspectorate Branch of the government; four died while in office (two of natural causes and two as a result of Viet Cong terrorism); one was captured and is currently being held prisoner by the Viet Cong. So far three vacancies have been filled through by-elections.

[b]Numbers and percents will not total due to the possibility of multiple observations.

the exodus of approximately one million persons from the north; the rise, repressions, and fall of five regimes; the establishment of two constitutional republics.[21] In addition, most deputies also had some direct organizational experience prior to their election. Almost half of the deputies (46 percent) held office in either a political party, organization, or interest group while another quarter of the deputies (26 percent) actually had participated in an election campaign prior to 1967 or had held a locally elected office. Socialized into politics by political organizations far more stable than the governments of the period, the deputies, 70 percent of which had first participated in politics under the aegis of a political organization, valued the need for accommodation in the interests of both professional and political survival. Similar patterns of socialization and the sharing of common experiences produced a tolerance for political diversity: "we deputies think that the legislature can be regarded as a hand. The hand has fingers all of different sizes and yet it is a very versatile organ of the body. A legislature also has many members, and we are searching now to find out how with this diversity it can function as an effective organ of government. We are looking for ways to live with our differences."

Role Characterizations

While a variety of role conceptions emerged in interviews with the deputies, all stressed the tentative nature of their characterizations: "Our own self-characterizations may be important to a scholar but he must not also forget that we exist in a relationship with other deputies who have different ideas of their jobs. The important thing is not that we are different but that we realize we must work with others." Differences in role-types do not rule out possibilities for either change or accommodation. Instead, a diversity of roles is regarded as essential to the effective functioning of the legislature, provided, of course, that a basis of accommodation can be developed to integrate the functions that each represents.

Two elements were central to the roles created by deputies. First, a deputy's role was intimately tied to a perception of himself as elite.[22] All deputies tended to describe their relationship to the population hierarchically in the same way that the Confucian value system prescribed the relationship between a father and his children or the emperor and his subjects. The deputy believes the population shares this orientation: "The people elected me because they felt I had the qualifications to compete with the province chief in a way that none of them could." Or, as another put it, "I was elected because I was a doctor and the people respected me for my work." Such comments reflect an acute consciousness of their status vis-à-vis the population. Few deputies ascribed their election to effective political organization or effective campaigning. Essentially, the role of the deputy is to act as a leader of the population, and the population is expected to support those leaders who merit respect: "A deputy's relationship with his constituency depends upon and is built up by the sentiment of trust. Deputies are elected for their past work. They need prestige, and this is gained by having both a prestigious occupation like that of medicine and by gaining the trust of the people. Once elected, deputies must try to build this trust, and they will be reelected because they have maintained the trust of the people rather than because they have attempted to modernize them through public works and welfare projects. It is the fate of the elite to be those who are trusted and the fate of the masses to do the trusting."

The second major determinant of a deputy's role appeared to be motivation for seeking election to the Lower House. Although most recognized the uncertainties inherent in their position within such a new institution and politics, the reason most frequently cited for running for office was a personal desire to gain leverage with which to work for a specific reform or project. Deputies had generally experienced injustices themselves, and their reforms were directed at the educational system, the civil service, or the military profession. To many, the impetus for reform also came from a highly developed sense of a religious or professional ethic of social service. One deputy, for example, stated that he viewed politics as the extension of social service work:

> I was a doctor working in an overcrowded district of Saigon that you would call a slum. One day a woman brought her child to me for treatment of a serious skin disease. I treated the child as I could and then gave the mother medicine and instructions on how to bathe the child. The next day I saw the mother washing the child in the local canal. Its polluted waters were the very source of the infection, but she had no other source of water. Then I realized that medicine would not help people unless there was also political action to make the government improve their living conditions.

Another deputy noted that his participation in the House was a principal means of working for peace: "My religion preaches that all men should live together peacefully. The only way to do this is for all men to work for that goal. There are many in Vietnam who do not believe in this and would like to destroy those of us who seek peace. In the Lower House I am free to speak up for peace and I am trying to make laws so that those who are against peace will not destroy those of us who are for it." And, finally, it is felt by some that the House provided a means to reconcile differences among the religious groups that exist in Vietnam. "My religion has taught me that all religions should work together. In the House I am learning to work with the leaders of other groups. When we learn to work with each other and trust each other, then religions will not try to destroy other religions, and they will not divide our society so sharply." Those deputies who identified most closely with their religion in an ethical and political way tended to define their role in the most accommodative terms.

A third reason frequently mentioned as instrumental in a deputy's decision to run for the Lower House concerned their own personal careers. Thirty-nine deputies (28 percent of the total) entered politics at the midcareer point and, of these deputies, all but seven entered politics specifically to run for the Lower House. Another 16 percent had changed their careers at least once before their election to the House. For these deputies, the decision to run for the House was due in large part to a desire for more gratifying work experiences than they had previously found. Some ran simply to effect a change in their career in the civil or military services. One deputy, for example, stated: "After ten years in the provincial administration I realized that I had gone as far as I could, and the work had become routine. The one job I really wanted was impossible to get since you have to be a military man to be a province chief." Another deputy ran as the only alternative to avoiding a dull career in the civil service. He had become politically involved on the "wrong side": "After the 1963 Revolution I supported the Buddhists though I am not Buddhist. My superior, however, was a Catholic and resented my position. I was assigned as a result to a faraway province that had no need for my skill. If I remained in the civil service I felt I would never receive any promotions and never have an interesting job." A similar dissatisfaction with the lack of promotions and challenging assignments was expressed by those deputies who were military officers: "I was promoted to Major within one year after my graduation from military academy. But then my general fell from power, and I have not been promoted in eleven years no matter how well I did my job. I felt there was no future for me in the military, and running for the Lower House was the only way I could be discharged from the service. Also, in the House I would be able to work for legislation that would change the procedures by which officers are promoted." Another deputy declared that election to the Lower House was the only way in which he could move from one profession to another: "I have been in the military for fifteen years, and during the past few years I took a course in law. I felt that fifteen years was enough time to give to the military service, but I could not be admitted to the bar since the military would not assign me as a law officer. I ran for the Constituent Assembly in 1966, but lost. I found that I enjoyed politics and felt that I could work well with others. I sought an assignment as the community relations officer for our military base and used that position to prepare for the elections in 1967."

The fourth reason cited by deputies as instrumental in their seeking election was the desire to use the House as a base to build new political organizations. These Lower House deputies tended to be young (25 to 35 years old) and were concerned about mobilizing other young people into politics who were dissatisfied with politics in the past. Most were drawn into such work by national movements or figures, but then found that they had to sustain the mobilization effort on their own: "I became interested in the role of young people in politics through the National Revolutionary Youth Movement of Ngo dinh Nhu but left the movement as soon as I learned more about what Nhu was doing. Ever since then I have worked with young people to develop our own political movement." Citing the encouragement he received from General Duong van Minh, a leader of the 1963 coup against Diem, another deputy observed: "General Minh called me back from the army, gave me a high position in the Youth Ministry and told me to work to get young people into the government. When Minh was ousted, the regime no longer seemed interested in doing this, and so I tried to do it myself. Soon I met others who were also interested, and, after leaving the government, we tried to do this at the local level. Now we are all in the Lower House."[23]

The more concrete a deputy's statement of what motivated him to run for election, the more concrete his description of his role as a legislator. The deputies who sought election primarily to build new political organizations, for example, have viewed their role as just that. The "mobilizer" aims at building new political organizations or revamping older ones, providing ways for the population to organize themselves.[24] The mobilizer does not necessarily seek to gain entrance into the power structure but to compete with it and change the nature of the government. Central to the operational premises of a mobilizer is a belief in the efficacy of community action and a belief that community action can only be as effective as those who seek to stimulate and lead it. One mobilizer who successfully organized a community development project observed that leadership was the key to successful political action but that leadership depended both upon the ability to organize and the ability to inspire popular confidence. "If we could get the people to trust the leaders of the project initially and if the leaders could plan effective self-help projects, the people would begin to gain confidence in themselves and trust the project." Mobilizers came to the Lower House with a record of intimate constituency involvement. The population tended to view them as persons dedicated to serving and intervening with the authorities for their interests. The demands of political mobilization, insofar as the deputy's attention to them are greater than his constituency's, have, however, tended to reduce the mobilizer's visibility in his constituency.[25]

Deputies who ran for the Lower House to combat injustice and promote institutional reforms tended to see their role as that of lawmaker. As one such deputy observed, "The function of the Lower House deputy is to make laws and work for the interests of the province at the central level." Initially seeking a position for whatever leverage it might afford to promote a specific reform or project, the lawmakers generally were successful in achieving their limited objectives. In one case success was limited only to changing the personnel practices of the Lower House's civil service staff, but the lawmakers felt it would provide an example for the rest of the government. Typically the lawmaker felt that the changes needed in the GVN could only be accomplished through the gradual development of laws and the rule of law.

Initially, the lawmaker did not see the necessity of a new political organization to support his objectives, feeling, rather, that good laws must precede political mobilization. He believed that gradually, as the constitutional system became established, comprehensive laws would provide the framework for changing the character of the government as higher levels of mobilization were achieved. As a result, these deputies did not consider constituency service part of their job. One deputy, who admitted he had practically no casework, suggested: "The function of the Lower House deputy is to make laws—and they should be left alone to do it." But another lawmaker who successfully pressured the central government into providing a new central market system for his province found that he began to receive requests for assistance from his constituents. The deputy reported trying to resolve a few of these problems with hardly any success at all. "The Congress is not the place to work for the people's problems but to make laws for them. While my position has been unquestionably helpful in knocking on doors and seeing ministers to get my market plan approved, the frustration in trying to solve the population's problems has been great. I felt more effective when I was a local official, and right now I feel like simply returning to my province and being on the province council where I can accomplish more for the people." Indeed, lawmakers whose initial objectives were fulfilled and who had become increasingly occupied with constituency problems also noted their increasing frustration in the position. One of the most prolific law drafters observed: "Constituency-deputy relations are disappointing to both parties. To the deputy because he feels his role should be one of legislating in Saigon instead of building projects and intervening for the people in the provinces; for the constituents because the deputy's power to intervene is very limited."

Lawmakers who experienced this frustration expressed a preference to run for an office other than that of legislator, an office that would put them in closer relationship with the people. "I would rather be a province chief than a deputy. The reason for this preference is that as a deputy I am not able to manage the projects I would like. It gives me hardly any chance to develop my creativity, and it is difficult to let the people know what you are doing. At least at the province level you can map out a project to help the people, carry it through, and see the results. The people know it is your work." Another deputy remarked: "At least as mayor[26] one has directly within his powers the ability to satisfy immediately the needs and problems of the people." In terms of future aspirations it would appear that the lawmakers are divided into two types. Those who have been successful in attaining their reform objectives and have also developed relations with their constituents tend to seek positions of more immediate power outside the legislature. Those who achieved their reform objectives but have not developed a close relationship with their constituents seek either to maintain their position within the legislature or to advance to higher ranks in the government.

The agents are those deputies who were nominated by and, in their view, owe their election to particular groups. An agent, consequently, believes that his primary duty is to defend the interests of that particular group. "I ran for the Lower House to continue at the national level the struggle for . . . [my group's] political and civil rights." The group may be the people of a particular district, the members of a particular political party, a faction of a particular religion, or the members of a particular occupation. The agent believes that by acting in the interest of his group he is acting in the national interest as well. Often the relationship between the elected agent and his constituency is predetermined. In return for the legislator's attention to the interests of the group at the national level, the party or group will preserve his electoral base in the province.

A final role type to which most of the very active deputies subscribe was that of educator. Most teachers, professional men, and higher-ranking civil

servants considered themselves in this category. The educator believes that
the population must be made aware of its needs and its rights but that at
present this cannot be accomplished through efforts to develop new, or
reconstitute old, political organizations. "We cannot build effective political organizations because the population will not trust them. The population won't trust politics until they can have some trust and confidence in
themselves." The educator maintains that the population also has little
confidence in the present governmental system. As one deputy observed:
"The Lower House deputy's primary role is one of explanation to the
people since they do not have confidence in local and provincial councils
in the face of the province chief and administration." Thereby the
educator seeks to fill a void which has been characteristic of provincial
government. But at the heart of the educator's conception of his role is the
conviction that the population must be made aware of its own rights. "In
addition to intervening on behalf of those citizens unjustly detained in the
province's Phoenix program,[27] a principal function of the deptuy is to
educate the population about their rights under the constitution." Once
the population knows of its rights, the educator maintains, they can be
stimulated to protect and advance them; at that point, the educator
believes that political mobilization will become important.

Frequently the educator uses the device of school construction to raise
the level of popular awareness. Assuming that education is a right
guaranteed to all by the constitution and a value highly held in the rural
environment, he attempts to stimulate the demand for more schools
through meeting with local leaders and officials. But basic to his approach
is the belief that the people must be personally involved in such a project.
"The only way to involve the people in their own self-development is to
offer to match only their own efforts."[28] Through involvement in the
self-development process, the educator maintains that the nature of the
demands and expectations of the population can be changed: "The real
needs of the population are not the ones they always talk about [such as
protection from arrest, compensation for war damage, and others]. People
only bring up aspirations when their property is damaged or they are
personally affected. The Lower House deputy, however, must bring out
their real needs, stimulate their thoughts to have them discover the real
needs of their community. The population must be educated and drawn
out to a point where they can talk about their real interests." To the
educator the job of the Lower House deputy is not only to serve as a
medium for the expression of popular aspirations, but also to create such
aspirations.

The educators are divided, however, on the question of how to create interests. One group maintains that interests can only be created through developing a close relationship with the population by serving their interests. Only then can he educate the people about their rights. "If people know they have certain rights, then they will also realize they have certain interests." The chief problem encountered by this group of educators is the reluctance of the population to stand up for its rights.

One deputy related an incident he regarded as typical of this problem. He had observed a constituent paying a bribe to an airline ticket agent and a policeman in order to secure passage to Saigon. The deputy introduced himself to the constituent and explained that a bribe was not necessary to purchase transportation tickets and that the corrupt officials should and could be punished. The constituent, however, refused to press the case, fearing that he would suffer reprisals from the police for doing so.

> If we could get enough people to fight against this sort of corrupt behavior we could shake up the whole system under which it [corruption] flourishes. The people must be made to realize, however, that they have a right to live without corruption. This is a very difficult job.

Indeed, an educator's intervention for the population is intended to be not a special favor to the persons involved (that is, a bribery without the bribe) but part of his job to protect their rights.

The second type of educator believes that the people must be made aware of their rights, but he is temperamentally not inclined toward constituent service work. This educator is usually part of the intellectual elite, and his work is limited largely to writing for popular newspapers, conducting seminars with concerned groups of young students, and drafting laws. Basically, the intellectual in the Lower House feels that the population must be educated about the meaning of the war. He believes that, when enough people are so informed, something can be done to stop the war. The intellectual spends most of his time trying to gain influence among the leadership of political and religious groups with a view toward displacing the older leadership, directing the group into new but unspecified forms of political activity. They disclaim any political ambition themselves and register their dislike for acting like politicians. As one such deputy observed: "My only duty is to work for the good of the nation, and that good is peace. While it may be true that other activities [like intervening for the population] are important to get reelected, I believe that this is only a hypothesis which I will test if I run again." Campaigning is regarded as trivial activity. Such deputies intervene for the population when the case is serious enough to merit individual attention rather than as a matter of course. The intellectual feels that he makes a contribution to politics not by what he does but by what he has the courage to stand for.

In the foregoing discussion of deputies' roles and motivations, little attention has been paid to the divisions of party and organization that exist between them. This has been done not to suggest that, with the exception of the agent, few differences exist but because no deputy regarded them as particularly significant to their role. Even the agents interviewed suggested that their role was not identified with a particular party but with an identity of interests they shared with the constituency they represented. To defend the interests of a particular group was not viewed as preventing cooperation with other deputies as long as the welfare of the agent's constituency could be advanced. By and large the differences in deputies' roles resulted from the diversity of political objectives which existed within the House and the different approaches to such objectives. Representation thus appears as political attitude rather than political difference; both are a function of experience.

Characteristic of each of the role types identified was the desire for influence over the process of government; different conceptions of role consequently reflected diversity of opinion about how influence could be developed. Political influence in Vietnam, however, required political power. The need for political power also implied the necessity of political cooperation. As the deputies interacted, they noted that such interaction tended to produce the common ground upon which political differences and their roles could be accommodated in an emerging consensus of national interests.[29] Each type of deputy came to realize that the political system and those who controlled it were unable and unwilling to provide what they demanded.

Chapter 5
Government under the Second Republic: Consolidation versus the Creation of Political Power

For the noncommunist government to compete with the Viet Cong required the participation of Vietnam's diverse sociopolitical forces. Yet little political change of this sort has been fostered by those in power in Saigon.[1] Successive governments have, instead, sought to consolidate rather than expand their narrow base of control. Western observers of Vietnamese politics have customarily viewed the executive, whether in the form of military juntas or as constitutional regimes, as the principal agent of political change. Since 1967 the American diplomatic community, in particular, has consistently looked to the executive branch not only to foster economic development in the countryside but also to serve as the prime sponsor of political reform as well. Most statements emerging from the American Mission in Saigon express either pleasure or frustration over the rate at which the executive has done either. Since Thieu's election in 1967, for example, almost all American officials have noted his efforts to circulate in the countryside and increase his stature as a national leader, to effect material improvements in rural life, and to sponsor rural mobilization. To Vietnamese, however, Thieu and his predecessors have been viewed as the principal obstacle to the very political reforms that would permit the development of an independent, noncommunist government militarily and politically able to compete with the Viet Cong.

In South Vietnam the political functions of the executive overshadow its leadership and administrative functions. Instead of fostering accommodation within diverse sociopolitical forces, the elite is often preoccupied with politics at the national level and within the military officer corps. Once in power, the ruling elite becomes increasingly isolated from the political dynamics of the society.

As one looks back on our past experience with democracy, we can see that our central problem has been one of our own making: our governments have lacked confidence in themselves. As a result, once they gain power their main efforts are focused on maintaining themselves in office rather than leading the people forward out of their troubles. Consequently, instead of broadening their base, instead of encouraging all factions, no matter how diverse their views, to join together and contribute in their own ways toward a realization of the people's dream, they have squandered most of their talent and energy in neutralizing any individual or group that is not prepared to subjugate itself completely to their direction. Caught up thus in a defensive, introverted frame of mind, past governments have usually begun by narrowing their base. In so doing they have shut out many who might be prepared to work in their own way for the national cause. Once this process sets in, personalities become involved, rumors gain credence, suspicions absorb the creative energy of the leaders. Instead of searching for ways to move forward together, schemes are devised to eliminate those who differ even slightly on how to proceed. Those who have been excluded stand aside and criticize or plot.[2]

Rather than create more power, successive juntas and regimes have sought to limit the little that existed. By relying upon the military officer corps as the base of its support and power and by clearly favoring only Catholic organizations, the Saigon government has been unable to mobilize non-communist political forces and develop the level of political community essential to compete with the Viet Cong.

Since the fall of Diem in November 1963, every junta in South Vietnam has pledged itself to "broadening the base" of government, often citing this goal as the primary reason behind each coup or cabinet change. From the November 1963 revolution through the end of 1969 there have been eleven cabinet changes, but, as one scholar observed, "insofar as top civilian office-holders are representative of that elite, it has not substantially changed its character,"[3] despite the changing character of the war and of the political and diplomatic pressures placed on the Saigon government. As Wurfel notes, "The predominance of French education and civil service experience are noticable. Separation from rural life is a consequence of most career patterns."[4] Such separation, of course, contributes to the isolation that the cabinets and the ruling elite they served came to develop during their tenure. The effects of isolation from the society, however, were not responsible for the demise of any cabinet; nor were the exigencies brought about by changes in the nature of the war or political competition within South Vietnam responsible for the changes that did occur. Such changes have only served to drain off impending political conflicts that would challenge the basis of elite rule by co-opting potentially troublesome opportunists or by purging ministerial and provincial posts of officials loyal to those who have lost in intraelite struggles.

The Executive and the Military:
The Thieu-Ky Conflict

As President since 1967, Thieu has not supported political change to strengthen the basis of his noncommunist government, but has carefully controlled the growth of political power to preserve his preeminent position within the military. The source of power for Thieu has been the support he has been able to maintain within the army and, to a more limited extent, his control over a clique of former Diemists who have gradually reappeared as influential members of the government. Thieu's primary source of strength, the army officer corps, is also a continuing source of anxiety for his rule. To lose the support of the generals or his control over some of them would remove the only base of power that Thieu has developed within noncommunist politics. It could be argued that Thieu's own self-interest would dictate that he search for an alternative base of power to insulate himself from the pressures of the generals. This would reduce his vulnerability to a coup and at the same time take advantage of American anticoup pressures and the American desire to substitute professionalism for politics in the armed forces promotion system. Thieu's political behavior since taking office has, however, made the adoption of such a strategy a moot question.

Thieu's behavior has its roots in the conflicts he witnessed after the fall of Diem. Since 1963 military interventions in politics reflected a continuing power struggle within the officer corps for control of the army rather than the government. As Milton Sacks has perceptively observed:

> there was an inherent instability in the coalition of officers of the Republic's Armed Forces which overthrew the Ngo dinh Diem regime . . . and in the ranks of the civilian leaders who, reflecting widespread public discontent [with the Diem government], supported them. There were deep-seated divisions among the military leaders, and the politicians were equally split. Moreover, the rivalry between those two forces was sufficiently great so as to preclude the creation and maintenance of a stable coalition. Even the threat of collective defeat at the hands of the South Vietnam National Liberation Front was not sufficient to restrain the various claimants for power from promoting coups and creating governmental instability in the years since the fall of President Diem.[5]

The continued presence of the military in government after the fall of Diem was a consequence of those power struggles and not the desire of generals to govern. The prevalence of revolving-door military juntas is indicative of the unsettled nature of politics within the military in that only by controlling the government could various factions within the officer corps be assured of their control over the military. As an institution, the officer corps reflected the social and political tensions within the society at large. In a society characterized by highly politicized social forces, the officer corps was no less so. The factions within the military, however, were constructed largely apart from those characterizing the conflicts between and within civilian political organizations. The changes of government that occurred in the wake of the 1963 coup, thus, reflected power struggles taking place within the officer corps and not the political system. From late 1965 to the end of 1968, however, the basic conflicts within the officer corps were subsumed under the struggle that emerged between Generals Thieu and Ky for control of the military and, thereby, the government.

Conflict within a politicized institution in a praetorian polity can be sustained rather indefinitely as long as the conflict does not weaken the particular institution vis-à-vis the other institutions and organizations with which it must contend. In the case of South Vietnam the competition between Thieu and Ky for political control of the army that began with the emergence of Ky as Premier in 1965 divided the military, but did not threaten to erode its ability to restrict civilian political organizations or the influence that the military could exert over government. The prospect of the 1967 elections, however, posed a serious challenge to the military; a military ticket had to ensure continued control over political power. To some extent, the desire for a military president may have reflected the belief some generals later expressed in interviews that, once established, the constitutional system would grow independently of the military's assent to or participation in it. Under this assumption, then, the military, like other civilian political organizations, was motivated by a desire not to be left out if this happened. Some generals also expressed the opinion that while in the past American threats to withdraw from Vietnam if the generals launched a coup had never been believed, a coup that dissolved a constitutional system in which the Americans placed much hope would surely precipitate withdrawal. Finally, the military's interest in the election probably also stemmed from their belief that ruling under a constitutional system would facilitate continued international diplomatic support. It was essential, therefore, that the elections not divide the military to the benefit of any other group in the polity.

In the spring of 1967 the personal rivalry between Thieu and Ky became a public conflict when it was apparent that both generals had decided to run for the presidency. Thieu had said that he would run, and Ky, while remaining unusually quiet, declared his intentions with the appearance of signs throughout the country declaring "The government of Nguyen cao Ky is the government of the poor people." In addition to reducing the chances of a military ticket winning, an election in which two generals ran could seriously divide the military and expose its factions to attack from several of the larger civilian parties whose allegiance both generals would need. The conflict between Thieu and Ky over the election issue was resolved during the course of a three-day meeting of all generals on active duty in the Armed Forces Council. The meeting produced a single military ticket headed by Nguyen van Thieu. This decision, perhaps more than any other single event, was an indication of the fact that Thieu had the control or support of the senior RVNAF generals. By August 1967 the Thieu supporters included three corps commanders and five division commanders, plus the commanders of the airborne, ranger, and artillery units. Ky, in contrast, had the support of only one corps commander, in addition to the Secretary General of the junta's National Leadership Committee, the director of the police, and three cabinet ministers. Thus, Thieu and Ky each had essentially different rather than competing bases of support: one based on officers of the line; the other based on cabinet and staff officers.

Ky had been faced with the problem of running the government for almost eighteen months, requiring the support of his most powerful and loyal supporters in the ministries and administrative posts. His academy classmate, General Loan, used the powers of the police to keep dissident line generals effectively in check. Needless to say, the cabinet had no regiments of its own, and Ky depended upon generals who did. The Thieu candidacy provided the generals with an alternative to continued support of the Ky government. Thus far, it appears that, whenever the generals are offered a genuine alternative to the one among them then in power, they opt for change.

The decision of the Armed Forces Council and Thieu's subsequent election in September signaled that he had the nominal support of the senior generals. Thieu now needed to consolidate his position within the army by removing Ky's men from their commands. It has been said that for approximately six months after his election Thieu feared the possibility of a coup to return Ky to power. Thieu's fears were so strong that he thought the first shots fired when the Viet Cong launched the Tet offensive of 1968 were from soldiers loyal to Ky marching on the presidential palace. Pressured by the American ambassador not to do so, Ky probably lost the power necessary to launch a coup and saw all of his major supporters removed from power, either by accident or design. General Loan, the commander of the police, was wounded during Tet; Chief of the Joint General Staff Cao van Vien resigned without explanation in April; General Le nguyen Khang and his anticoup marine division stationed around Saigon were soon replaced by ranger battalions commanded by officers committed to Thieu; in June an American helicopter misfired a rocket that landed in the midst of a meeting of six of Ky's most important field grade supporters. With Ky's base of political support within the military virtually decimated, Thieu was able to proceed with his consolidations under the guise of the four changes in cabinet made from 1967 through 1969.

Since 1967 the principal concern of President Thieu has not been to lead the struggle against the Viet Cong but rather to consolidate the base of his support within the military officer corps. All of Thieu's campaign pledges, most notably that of land reform, have been considered or implemented more slowly than their utility in the struggle against the Viet Cong would suggest. The nature of Thieu's efforts to consolidate his support can clearly be seen when put in the context of the cabinet changes he engineered to remove Ky from power. By superimposing the formal cabinet and presidential structure of the government on the Thieu-Ky conflict, two developments are apparent. First, Vice President Ky had been eclipsed by President Thieu by the end of 1968. To some observers of the presidency, Thieu's consolidations were not considered complete until the middle of March 1969, when the formation of the second Huong cabinet resulted in the ouster of the Minister of Land Reform and Agriculture, the last Ky man in any position of prominence. The irreversibility of Ky's eclipse became clear as early as mid-June 1968, however, with Ky's resignation from the chairmanship of the People's Self Defense Force (PSDF) committee. Constitutional limitations on the powers of the Vice President permitted Ky to chair three powerless advisory committees and specifically proscribed him from holding any other position in the government.

The PSDF, created in May 1968, was a semitrained and equipped civilian militia nominally controlled by village leaders but highly dependent upon district military officers for support. It showed signs of becoming a national organization, but it lacked a leader. For Ky, such a power vacuum could have become an important element in a bid for the presidency in 1971. It would certainly have done more to replenish the supporters he had lost than the positions offered in the advisory councils set up by the constitution. And Ky's appeal as a leader of these forces, enhanced by his impassioned speeches to publicize the PSDF, was great enough to cause Thieu concern. In less than a month, however, it became clear to Ky that remaining in the post would diminish the power of the PSDF as both a political and a military organization, for he would be permitted none of the power necessary to establish the PSDF as an effective militia force. In explaining the reasons for his resignation to a journalist of the *Xay Dung* [Reconstruction] daily, a northern Catholic newspaper, Ky observed, "I have said that the organization of the People's Self Defense must be considered a national policy. It is natural that the person responsible for the carrying out of that work must have full power in his hands from the point of view of personnel as well as means. . . . If I am in charge of that organization, I shall have to call in the Ministers to meet with me now and then in order to give them orders. I resigned because I found it logical to do so. That is all."[6] Examining the resignation in political terms, it was concluded: "The dispute between President Nguyen van Thieu and his Vice President had finally come into the open. But, since national unity is the inescapable price [for victory] . . . when our national leaders prove themselves at loggerheads, how can they be united on the great ends for which our people are fighting?"[7] The establishment of the PSDF as an effective organization, in Ky's view, would require powers beyond those which his struggle with the President would permit.

The second development involved Thieu's efforts to consolidate his own position. Changing or reshuffling cabinets was an important political device to diminish Ky's power in the army. The first cabinet under the new constitution was announced on 9 November 1967 and formed under the leadership of Prime Minister Nguyen van Loc. Loc, a lawyer, poet, and novelist from the Mekong Delta, was a close friend of Ky and had planned to run for the vice presidency on his ticket. Loc chose his ministers from a list of prospective candidates submitted by both Thieu and Ky. The composition of the cabinet included only one figure both close to Thieu and having national stature. While on the surface the composition of the cabinet appeared to be a conciliatory gesture on the part of Thieu, most observers felt "that the cabinet will be the scapegoat if the new government runs into early problems. They argue that it has been formed without prominent figures so that it can be reshuffled without arousing public opposition."[8] The cabinet represented a facade behind which the conflict between Thieu and Ky could take place, and so serious were the effects of the conflict that, by the end of the year, it was clear that the government had "been frozen into immobility, in the opinion of qualified observers, by the increased tension between President Nguyen van Thieu and Vice President Nguyen cao Ky."[9] The tenure of the Loc cabinet depended upon the outcome of the Thieu-Ky conflict, and, by May 1968, Thieu had emerged as victor. The stage was set for Thieu to begin removing army officers loyal to Ky from positions of power.

At that time the cabinet of former Prime Minister Tran van Huong succeeded the Loc cabinet under the twin banners of national unity (a variant of the broaden-the-base-of-the-government theme) and anticorruption. The new cabinet included figures of national prominence that the Loc cabinet had lacked, but these figures were by and large closely allied with President Thieu. In particular, the appointment of General Tran thien Khiem to the powerful position of Minister of Interior had the effect of returning Khiem—a classmate of Thieu's in the military academy and a close friend ever since—from exile as ambassador in Taiwan to a position of considerable power and influence on the basis of his loyalty to Thieu. In addition, Huong's own genuine desire to stamp out corruption in the military and administrative services played an important role in diluting the power base of military officers loyal to Ky. Half of the country's forty-four province chiefs were replaced as a result of this anticorruption campaign and the support it received from the Minister of Interior. Indeed, most of the officials removed during this period were military and civilian officials loyal to Vice President Ky, and they were replaced by Thieu supporters. It is significant to note Huong's various public statements about the progress of the anticorruption campaign; no high-ranking officials were mentioned. In a statement summarizing the effect of the campaign in late August 1968, Huong, for example, cited the action taken against one major, four lieutenants, one service chief, four service cadres, and two minor police officials. Of this group, four were dismissed for the abduction and rape of a minor.[10] In Huong's view, misconduct by officials in these ranks greatly damaged the ability of government programs to win the support of the rural population. Nevertheless, Huong also knew that such minor-level officials were not the primary source of corruption. In numerous speeches Huong referred to the need to attack the roots of corruption at the level of the province chief and higher, rather than simply at the branch level. This, however, would constitute an attack upon the system of rewards that loyal officers could expect when they were appointed province chief. The thrust of Huong's anticorruption campaign was blunted by the political purposes for which Thieu permitted it to be launched, namely, to replace officers loyal to Ky. On March 12 the Huong cabinet was reshuffled to include five new ministers loyal to Thieu and to oust those few figures left in public office who were not aligned with him.

The Khiem cabinet, formally presented on 2 September 1969, represented the final act in the eclipse of Ky and his supporters.[11] Contrary to the demands of the press and the publicly articulated goal of "broadening the base of the government" cited by Thieu in announcing the formation of a new cabinet, the Khiem cabinet narrowed the base of the government:

> An "expansion of the political base" of the government can only be reached through a cabinet comprising either representatives of powerful political parties and groups, or prominent political figures supported by the people although being independent.
>
> However, the majority of the new cabinet members are strangers having no political background. Therefore, it will be quite difficult for the new cabinet to attract the people's attention, let alone move them psychologically in order to broaden the political base of the government. The natural reaction of the people in the face of strangers is indifference.[12]

The view of political leaders and organizations was that at this particular juncture Vietnam needed an institution to foster cooperation between and unity within noncommunist political parties and organizations. Only a government whose base was broad enough to include the nationalists' diversity of political interests could compete effectively with the Viet Cong.

The appointment, consequently, of prominent Diemists who had been instrumental in the organization of the *Nhan Xa* not only foreshadowed the favor of the government which the *Nhan Xa* apparently had gained, but it also cast serious doubt on the sincerity of government efforts to reconcile Catholics and Buddhists. One Catholic leader, a promoter during 1969 of Buddhist-Catholic cooperation, observed, "I do not think that the *Nhan Xa* is exactly the same as the old *Can Lao* party of President Diem. They have been moderate so far in their actions and do not merit the same kind of reputation that the *Can Lao* had. But for the government to favor them so clearly without also favoring any balancing Buddhist political organization will make the people suspicious."[13] Shortly after this interview, the *Nhan Xa* organized, with the sponsorship of the Ministry of Information, a nationwide commemorative service on the anniversary of Diem's death that paralleled the celebration of Vietnamese National Day, the yearly celebration of the 1963 coup d'etat against Diem. The Catholic leader then wrote in a personal note that "the recent ceremony on the anniversary of Diem's death has increased the suspicion of the Buddhists about the government's motives. The prospects for greater Buddhist-Catholic cooperation under government sponsorship which I had been urging the President to facilitate are now very bleak. Many of my people, too, fear the *Nhan Xa* now because of this ceremony."

Apart from its politics, the Khiem cabinet appeared to be one of the most competent and professional that had governed South Vietnam. Indeed, the greater number of cabinet ministers have impressive professional credentials in law, economics, and the technical occupations. Most Vietnamese felt, however, that such a cabinet was required in 1967 in order to facilitate the design and implementation of national policies and development programs. By the end of 1969, however, the fundamental need of the government was not professional competence as much as political skill in developing support for the government from alienated political organizations. Inflation and agricultural backwardness were no longer the real enemies; the real enemy was the Viet Cong. The primary need was national unity. In a pessimistic mood, one political leader asked me: "Why do you want us to have a competent government? So they can better spend the money your government is giving our government and so your Congress will not complain about our corruption? Vietnam does not need money or American programs now; we need to be politically united against the communists. Look at the Viet Cong. They are very strong and also very poor, but they will win here if we cannot match their political strength. If Saigon loses the war, the present government will go to Paris or the Bahamas and count its money; I will have to stay here and live with the Viet Cong."

In its development over the past two years, the cabinet has not been a source of major political change in Vietnam of the type needed to compete with the Viet Cong. Thieu, motivated by his interest in stability, has functioned to consolidate political power rather than to create it. The overshadowing of Vice President Ky was part of a strategy that Thieu had to adopt as a means of controlling the military, as long as the officer corps remains the principal center of power in the polity. Controlling the aspirations of the army officer corps has required careful distribution of rewards via the promotion and assignment system to maintain the position of those generals and their retinue who are loyal to Thieu. Some had hoped that US pressure under the Vietnamization program and the increasing need for a professional, effectively led army would induce Thieu to remove political considerations from military assignments. But Thieu may well prove unable to sponsor such a transition, as consolidation of support for Thieu within the military is not likely to be a passing requirement but a continuing concern. As suggested in Chapter 4, factions within the officer corps have not disappeared with the demise of Ky. As long as Thieu turns to the army for support without developing nonmilitary bases of power, he will remain vulnerable to the same pressures that led to the downfall of Ky. To destroy the bases upon which Vietnam's political generals command their officer's loyalties, in Thieu's estimation, would probably result in a coup.

In addition, most Vietnamese feel that Thieu has increasingly isolated himself from civilian politics by reliance upon an exclusive group of political advisers. In estimating Thieu's relation to civilian political organizations and the population, one Lower House deputy drew a series of concentric circles to illustrate Thieu's isolation. "At the center, of course, is Thieu; surrounding Thieu are perhaps four to six advisers. Next come the generals and the army officers and then come our many political parties and religious groups. Finally, the outer ring of the circles represents the population." But survival for Thieu depends upon his ability to control the military rather than to displace it as a political force in South Vietnam.

The Impact of Consolidation upon the
Process of Government

Just as President Thieu appears to have become increasingly isolated from civilian politics, so also does it appear that government bureaucracy has developed an institutional immunity to conflicts within the governing elite, and it is not likely to support political change or reform. Vietnamese feel that it has become increasingly isolated from the needs of the population and the demands of the war. Indeed, neither the war nor the constant succession of cabinets appears to have particularly impaired the growth or recruitment of governmental institutions. The civil service, for example, has grown steadily in size from about 50,000 in 1956 to about 175,000 in 1969, and the number of civil service departments has increased from less than ten to nineteen as the development programs of the government proliferated at a rapid rate with the support of American technical assistance and economic aid. Even when the 1963 coup d'etat overthrew Diem, the civil service changed little save for a few vulnerable and outspoken pawns.

The apparent constancy in the civil service, however, has not meant that government programs have been effectively administered. Particularly since 1963, the institutional reaction to coups and cabinet changes has generally assumed the following pattern: the rumor of an impending change spreads and is evaluated; based upon the evaluation, the work of the institution slows to a snail's pace, and programs in the countryside are virtually held at a standstill awaiting the outcome of the expected province chief and corps commanders purges. The level of institutional activity tapers off and is held constant until well after the formal changes are made (usually from two to six months after the cabinet has been reshuffled). Activity eventually picks up and gradually returns to the normal pace of work before the change, but not to the pace required in light of either the backlog of work or any changes associated with a shift in the intensity of the war. "As long as changes are postponed the country is damaged. Since the date of the cabinet change announcement all of the cabinet personnel have an attitude of waiting, unenthusiasm, inactivity, no creative opinions, no efforts..."[14] And one American provincial adviser who served two nonconsecutive tours of twelve months each in two different provinces observed: "So far I have come here about one or two months before a cabinet crisis. Saigon would never believe the slowdown in activity that greets me, and I leave only one or two months after a change has been fully absorbed. As a result I figure that the government and I have done in all about four months of work in twenty-four." While the constitution may have provided the government with immunity to organized violence from the right, it has not protected the polity from the war or the threat posed by the Viet Cong. Political change in South Vietnam over the past decade has been costly, not to the stability of governmental institutions but to the progress they were able to make in the effort to defeat the Viet Cong.

The Thieu government's preoccupation with consolidating its bases of power, coupled with the isolation it has fostered within the bureaucracy have also, moreover, blunted the thrust of the reforms endorsed and financed by American assistance.[15] American efforts have not fostered the political reforms required to absorb the assistance that could strengthen the government vis-à-vis the Viet Cong. The goal of an independent, noncommunist government in the South required that the Saigon government concentrate on the political mobilization of the rural population. Development assistance, rather than facilitating such mobilization, however, made it unnecessary. This failure is related to the fact that American financial and military assistance supplanted the need for the GVN to mobilize the population in support of the war and governmental development programs. Also, the United States' consistent pursuit of stability for the Vietnamese government blunted the development of a stable political system based upon a broad base of support among the population. One prominent Vietnamese official has summarized the relationship between American assistance and its impact on government and politics: "The more aid Vietnam gets, the faster and deeper the process of social differentiation, blocked vertical mobility, and alienation of town and country will become, widening the gap between people and the government and making the struggle against communist subversion and the establishment of a balanced and viable [government for] Vietnam more difficult."[16]

Instead of supplementing the resources of indigenous Vietnamese development programs, the United States virtually became the prime mover of such efforts.[17] One long-time observer of politics in Vietnam characterized the situation by remarking that "we continue with the naïve notion that nation building is saturating the country with American advisers."[18] Rather than fostering the reform of the government, the US succeeded only in restructuring the way in which it operated. Rather than changing the behavior of its officials, development programs accomplished the reverse by hardening Vietnamese attitudes against changes the US believed essential. Rather than supplementing government efforts with US monetary and staff assistance, the development of such functions was preempted. The providing of an American combat army to fight the Viet Cong, for example, forestalled the need for the government to mobilize its own population and to gain the legitimacy and support necessary to do so. Financial aid to the government made unnecessary the collection of taxes and the revamping of an outdated taxation system. Tax collections almost ceased during 1967-68. As one scholar recently observed:

> We had committed ourselves to helping the South Vietnamese build a nation, but we had failed to see the essential revolutionary prerequisites for doing so .... We also attributed legitimacy and capacities to the government of South Vietnam which it did not have. We supplied it with virtually unlimited money and material to do what it could not possibly do .... Although we used the word "revolution," we meant rather material inundation: the spewing forth into an unready countryside of

vast quantities of matter, from tin roofs and pigs to schoolhouses and community centers. The fact eluded us that these things had little to do with the structural changes which were so necessary for the achievement of our objectives.[19]

The material inundation of the countryside, however, was a tactical error. The fundamental mistake of American policies was that they failed to realize the political ramifications of our assistance. Winning the country-side was a political task requiring political mobilization to counter similar efforts by the Viet Cong; committing the GVN to such a goal constituted a political as well as an administrative challenge.

Imported into such a milieu, American development assistance did not supplement an established governmental commitment to ameliorate the grievances of the rural population; instead, it preempted the need for such a commitment to develop. The more we pursued development programs and the harder we pushed the government to accept them, the more the Vietnamese considered the programs American inventions and, thereby, American responsibilities. By concentrating our developmental and politi-cal reform pressures within the government bureaucracy, we chose the path least likely to bring results since the *sine qua non* of our presence was based upon unfaltering support to the generals who controlled power. And since US military support was a primary means by which the generals stayed in power, continued support became the primary political imper-ative of the government's leadership.

What Vietnam required by the inauguration of the Second Republic was not only an alternative to the Viet Cong but also an alternative to the tendency of those in power to limit the amount of power in the system in order to strengthen their position. A new basis of politics had to be created, and this required the development of an arena independent of the military and its politics. Surveying the political institutions that existed at the time, it was clear that only the newly created legislature possessed such potential. Unlike the cabinet or the presidency itself, the Lower House was directly linked to the population and contained within its membership representatives of virtually all the noncommunist political forces in the society. Most of these political forces had little or no influence within the government, and subsequent developments tended to make clear the need for the expansion of political power within the political system as the legislature began to challenge the executive. The creation of a new basis of politics for Vietnam required the creation of new sources of political power for its participants.

Chapter 6

The Executive versus the Legislature: Political
Competition and Institutional Imperatives

The development of a governmental role for the Lower House required
the creation of a political role as well; essential to both was the need to
develop bases of cooperation between deputies. Unlike the public bureaucracy, which managed over time to insulate itself from politics, and
unlike the executive, which never substantially reflected the country's
political diversity, the Lower House was neither insulated from politics nor
homogeneous in political composition. The political demands that
emerged within the Lower House thus reflected the introduction of a new
element into Vietnamese politics at the level of the national institutions:
efforts to regulate and subordinate particularistic interests to those
considered institutional and thereby public interests.[1]

The Role of the Lower House

The Lower House shares with the Upper House the power to vote
legislation, ratify treaties, approve declarations of war and its termination,
pass on declarations of a state of war involving the abridgment of civil
liberties or requests by the executive for grants of emergency powers to
deal with war-related crises, and generally control the government in the
conduct of national policy by interpellating government officials or by
voting no confidence in all or part of the cabinet. In contrast to the
Constitution of 1956, Vietnamese legal scholars regard the Constitution of
1967 as containing a rather liberal grant of legislative authority.

> The Assembly's legislative power covers all aspects of national life. No
> single regulation of life is beyond the power of the legislators: from the
> exercise, restriction, or deprivation of citizen's rights, the problems of
> ownership, interests, contracts between private individuals and associ-
> ations, etc. ... to the organization and functioning of public agencies,
> the problems of public order such as penal laws, procedural law, budget,
> taxation, military service, nationalist, personal status, civil status, mar-
> riage, family, succession, labor, industry, social security etc. ... Our
> Constitution merely states briefly about the Assembly's lawmaking
> power, or more correctly, does not specify the scope of that power.[2]

Legislative authority, however, was viewed as distinct from a grant of power. Indeed, framers of the constitution sought to describe only the most general principles of legislative authority so as not to restrict the growth and development of the institution, a common practice in drafting most constitutional prescriptions of legislative powers.[3] Implementing the principles of the Constitution would depend upon the means devised by the legislators. Thereby, the authority of the legislature as a governing institution was linked to its functioning as a political institution.

The only compelling reason for a dominant executive to accept the decisions of the legislature had to emerge on the basis of what the legislature actually represented. Consequently, the ability of the legislature to effectively innovate policy (that is, to have policy proposals adopted) would depend upon its ability to create the political power necessary to influence the executive; the legislature had to represent a political force and thereby a voice that the executive could not afford to ignore. Legislative efforts at policy innovation were also viewed as a form of political competition between the executive and the political forces it represented. Such competition did not necessarily have to threaten the tenure or security of the executive. Rather, political competition between the two branches had to be defined within a framework that would render the competition acceptable to the executive (thus guarding against the assembly's dissolution) and at the same time provide a basis for cooperation among political forces. At the microlevel, deputies had to create the political community that was lacking in the polity at large.

Composed of diverse groups, the legislature faced the initial task of regulating its partisanship and rationalizing interaction between political forces that would facilitate the development of policies and their translation into specific legislative priorities. The problem was particularly acute in the Lower House, where a diverse membership made prospects for achieving consensus on any particular issue extremely bleak. Most deputies, however, realized the necessity to achieve cooperation and consensus relatively early, a process hastened by the executive's constant threat to legislative autonomy. The realization of a need for cooperative efforts precipitated the search for sets of issues where such cooperation was practicable.

By the end of 1969 two bases for cooperation emerged within the House. The deputies agreed that preservation of legislative autonomy was essential to the proper functioning and future of the constitutional system, and they viewed their principal objective as "helping to improve the lives of the people." This provided a basis for cooperative efforts among deputies of diverse political affiliations since the action it could engender was based not upon these affiliations or hence upon their ability to resolve all outstanding political issues but, instead, upon the recognition that the legislature per se was important and that its independence ought to be preserved.[4] The second basis grew from the political doctrines of the political groups with which deputies were associated. All expressed in their ideology notions of "social justice" and "the people's welfare," and all believed that in their own way they had thus far struggled for such goals. Their association in the Lower House provided an opportunity for combined efforts; the maxim that what would benefit one group would tend to benefit all groups came to replace a prior notion that what benefited one group represented a loss to others. Legislative goals functioned to deploy political interests around bases of cooperation and accommodation rather than conflict.

Initially, however, a concern for legislative autonomy was not widely shared among the deputies. Progovernment deputies tended to expect that they would develop a working relationship with the President based upon his need for a majority bloc to facilitate the passage of legislation. Opposition deputies, similarly, believed that executive domination of the legislature was inevitable and couched their objectives in rather conservative terms, resigning themselves to existence as a permanent critical minority with little hope of influencing government policy. Between these two groups, however, were deputies drawn from both sides who were concerned that executive dominance would inhibit the development of the House and other newly created institutions. Quite to their surprise, they found themselves thrust into positions of leadership within the House and aided in their work by the failure of the government to develop a working relationship with its supporters. As one of these deputies remarked, "Thieu could have had this Assembly in his pocket with very little effort. At the time of our inauguration a majority of the deputies were known supporters of the government, and all that Thieu had to do was take them into his confidence and recognize their existence as a majority bloc that would be quite responsive to his wishes. Thieu's failure to do this resulted in great disappointment within the ranks of the progovernment deputies, and many of them began to see their role as requiring more independence from the executive than they had originally anticipated." These deputies sensed a disaffection of government supporters with efforts to achieve unity, with their failure to dominate the House elections, and with their agreement with opposition deputies to deny the executive his request for emergency powers to deal with the Tet offensive of 1968. At some point between January and April 1968 the deputies initially concerned about legislative autonomy decided to constitute themselves as an informal leadership group and work behind the scenes to seek bases for cooperation on the issue of legislative autonomy.

The House leadership group functioned to promote accommodation between diverse political interests and groups and balance the growth of the House as a political institution. This leadership included not only those deputies who held elected positions within the permanent secretariat, committees, and legislative blocs but also a core of deputies who, over time, emerged as leaders in House affairs. These deputies tended to organize debates, prepare legislation, and handle the rather tenuous and acrimonious relations between both Houses and the executive. The deputies sought to commit the majority of the membership to legislative autonomy and policy innovation, and they arranged a framework within which diverse groups could cooperate.[5]

In interviews deputies expressed considerable reluctance to describe in any detail how the process of commitment had worked. They stressed that the work of this group took place behind the scenes, and to reveal details might jeopardize the group. Some public information subsequently appeared in a Saigon paper which, while not bringing to light specifics about the core of influential deputies, did present a description of one prominent deputy, perhaps a member of the core group. "The remarkable role that this deputy plays in the House, as recognized by practically all deputies and officers of the House, is to bring out plans [and give] direction in many of the Lower House's activities silently [that is, subtly]." (*Tin Dien* [12 November 1969], p. 1.) But the absence of a cordial and effective relationship between the executive and the legislature, reflecting not only the President's disdain for the Lower House but also the House's capacity and inclination to challenge the President, was essential to making such cooperation significant. Conflict among institutions of varying complexity is essential to the development of the capacity for fostering cooperation and accommodation to balance the weaker and the more complex. The role of the Lower House as a political and a governing institution developed in response to the conflict between it and the executive.

Executive-Legislative Relations:
The Significance of Conflict

Executive-legislative relations are seldom smooth, for what is at stake is political power. Constitutional prescriptions that allow both branches to share power usually function to legitimate this conflict rather than to resolve it. Cooperation between the two branches may signal either that one is dominated by the other or that each for the moment is content with the existing distribution of power. Conflict between the two is almost certainly a sign of the one attempting to displace the other. The establishment of the Second Republic introduced such conflict to the process of government in Vietnam. The April Constitution required that the virtual monopoly of the executive in making laws be shared with a National Assembly. During the colonial and the Diem eras the relationship between the executive and the legislature was straightforward and unambiguous: the legislature was subservient to and dominated by the executive. The cooperation of legislative institutions in implementing executive policies did not, as a result, reflect the sharing of common interests between the two branches of government but rather the degree of control the one was able to wield over the other. Legislative interests did not simply coincide with those of the executive; they were created by it. Linked to politics by parties and groups directly controlled by the executive, moreover, those issues on which legislators initially differed with executive views were resolved largely outside the framework of the assemblies.

The publicly articulated conflict which emerged almost from the inauguration of the Thieu government represented a considerable departure from past experience. Early manifestations of institutional differences were viewed by staunch government supporters largely as the inevitable result of including in the National Assembly members of the opposition; the deepening of this conflict and the sharpening of the issues around which it centered, however, indicated that the concerns of the opposition were more widely shared than had been anticipated and that the assembly had begun to discover that, like the executive, it, too, had a distinct political identity. Indeed, in this case, the conflict between the executive and the legislature suggests not deterioration of governmental processes but political progress.

Most Constituent Assembly deputies, in fact, had in mind a process that initially involved conflicts between the government and a National Assembly that would result in no suitable means of establishing working relations between the two branches. It was felt that this conflict would be centered upon claims made by both President Thieu and the Lower House to be the sole representative and guardian of the people's interests. Thieu would, and indeed subsequently did, argue that due to his preeminent position as leader of the government he alone could see the "big picture" and, thereby, rationally determine national needs and priorities. The Lower House, similarly, would, and did, maintain that, because it was elected by the people and was in constant touch with their needs, that it alone could determine priorities. The claim forced both parties to transform the basis upon which they were elected.[6] From the purview of the executive, the conflict would represent a fundamental challenge to political order, and the relationship between the two branches would depend upon how it was resolved.[7] Provided that, during this phase, the Assembly was not dissolved by the President or subverted by attempts to attain support by bribery, the second stage would witness the gradual reduction of outright conflict and the establishment of working relations on issues where common interests could be developed. This phase would begin on the eve of the election of a new Lower House. If the elections reflected the success of those deputies seeking to create political organizations independent of those supported by the executive, the process of accommodation between the two branches would continue, and coordination and harmony would be achieved. If, however, the elections of 1970 and 1971, as was the case in 1967, should prove only the weakness of political organizations, the legislature would come increasingly to resemble the rubber stamp assemblies of the Diem era.[8]

The Lower House's relationship with the Thieu government from 1967 to the end of 1969 remained in the first phase, conflict. The primary channels of communication provided in the Constitution for executive-legislative relations were special conference and compromise committees, the blocs, sense of the assembly resolutions, interpellations, and a liaison ministry for assembly relations within cabinet and executive communications. During the life of the Constituent Assembly, executive-legislative relations were conducted primarily through the use of special committees delegated by the Assembly to resolve points of particular controversy with the National Leadership Committee.[9] The use of special committees by the Lower House, in contrast, substantially declined; today they are rarely used. Two special committees set up in the early days of the House have been dissolved. House conflicts with the executive have been channeled through the workings of regularly established committees and, until recently, the use of interpellations of government ministers in plenary sessions. By the end of 1969, it appeared that the executive was no longer willing to participate in the interpellation process in the Lower House. The Prime Minister refused to appear, noting that "there was nothing left to say."[10] While he did not entirely rule out future executive participation in interpellations, he did suggest that the preferred site of future encounters would be in the Upper rather than the Lower House. For a time, the Lower House also used the device of sending to the executive minutes of various meetings that touched upon or reflected policy differences between the two branches. The drafting of petitions and, later, the passing of formal resolutions declaring the sense of the House came to replace the practice of transmitting meeting minutes as a means of making clear House positions. By the end of 1969, however, no satisfactory mode of executive-legislative communication had developed, reflecting the continuing conflict between both branches.

Upon reflection, deputies tended to view the deterioration of even the potential for a working relationship between the House and the executive as the result of a vicious circle. When it became clear that the President was not going to trust the House or even its supporters in the legislative process, these supporters asserted their independence by opposing government policies. Such opposition served only to reinforce Thieu's belief that cooperation with the legislature was impossible. One deputy summarized the situation as: "Executive-legislative relations have been poor owing to the fact that legislators have continually criticized the executive, and the executive has been unwilling to trust the deputies."

Lacking a basis for mutual trust, executive-legislative relations consisted of form rather than substance. Cabinet ministers would appear for interpellations and present their position, would listen to the criticisms of government policy made by the deputies, then restate their position and take their leave. In interviews with both deputies and cabinet ministers it was clear that each side felt little was gained in these exchanges, and both sides felt the other was wrong. Similarly, committees working on bills submitted by the President would request a meeting with him to discuss controversial provisions and suggest a means to avoid a clash. Deputies reported that the President usually agreed to these requests and met with committee representatives, but, again, the exchange accomplished little. One deputy who had had many meetings with the President felt that he "has never taken us into his confidence." Other committee officials reported similar reactions to meetings with the President and also noted that the attitude of the President tended to set an example for the rest of the executive departments.

Committee members seeking additional information and clarification on particular bills reported that their requests were viewed with disdain by the entire executive branch. One deputy noted: "The President has no respect for the National Assembly as an institution, and this attitude is also manifested in the lower echelons. I suppose these lesser officials reason that, if the President has no respect for the assembly, then they are not required to have it either. As a result we get very little cooperation in our deliberations, and the President gets a poor bill from the committee, which the assembly will not pass." While most deputies viewed the essence of executive-legislative relations as that of compromise and negotiation, the executive did not. Two reasons were advanced to explain the executive's attitude. A minority of the deputies who commented upon the state of executive-legislative relations felt: "The primary reason for such poor executive-legislative relations is that the executive is filled with military men who are too accustomed to the chain of command, who expect their orders to be carried out without question, and who are unskilled at the negotiation necessary to working with legislatures. This problem pervades all of the government both in Saigon and in the provinces." Most deputies found ways of working with the military in the provinces, however. Although Thieu and Ky might take this view, most of the officials in the executive were civilians with whom communication was possible.

Most deputies suggested, however, that the legislature was viewed by Thieu as lacking popular support. Deputies who subscribed to this view regarded Thieu as a cautious politician who would only recognize the significance of an institution if it materially improved or threatened the tenure of his regime. Believing that the House was of little consequence, the President felt no need to take it seriously. The responsibility for working with it could be delegated to others, and any expedient means of controlling it was acceptable. To these deputies poor executive-legislative relations underscored the need for effective political organization both within the House and within the polity at large.

Most deputies believed that the principal site for working out executive-legislative relations should be the committees, where requests for executive clarification of particular issues could be directly linked to efforts to achieve compromises between contending sides. The real ability of the House to influence government lay in its ability to affect the budgetary process, according to this view. The power of the purse, it was argued, gave the House considerable control over the execution of national policy. This potential was largely undeveloped. As one progovernment deputy who was on the Budget Committee candidly observed:

One of the problems with the growth of the power of the legislature has been that it lacks the facility for negotiation with the executive that a strong and neutral Budget Committee could provide. The committee in the past has tended to be largely proexecutive and not an effective spokesman for the legislature.[11] We have our difficulties though in preparing even our report due to the lack of cooperation from the executive. By the time we have all the required documentation the deadline is at hand, and we have all we can do to just submit the budget in a form that the deputies can debate. Thus when it reaches the floor it is violently attacked but inefficiently debated. The real place for opposition to occur is within the committee itself so that we can work out the major problems with the executive before the budget reaches the floor. Right now, we simply lack the ultimate lever that a Budget Committee should provide in its dealings with the executive.

To activate such a lever would require the effective organization of the blocs, a process only recently begun.

The failure to develop coordination and harmony between the executive and the legislature was thus related to the absence of vehicles for cooperation and the executive's preference to subvert decisional processes whenever possible. The potential of the two institutions to foster greater cooperation and, thereby, increase support for each remained undeveloped. Formal assembly blocs could have provided a means to handle differences between the branches in private, as in the case of the Constituent Assembly. In particular, it was expected by progovernment bloc leaders that the executive would develop special relationships with their organizations and come to value their support. The shifting nature of the bloc membership and its instability until recently has been a major factor in the executive's reluctance to establish any formal relationship. When the executive has met with the blocs or with their executive committees the interaction has not been significant. The executive committee of the *Dan Tien* bloc characterized one meeting with the President, for example, as "mundane." The President made a statement stressing the need for a strong government in the face of communist threat and of false peace hopes generated by the Paris Talks, Viet Cong propaganda, and American diplomacy. The President also affirmed the need for a close working relationship between the executive and the legislature. Amenities were exchanged but participants in the meeting felt that it lacked significance. "We just could not get down to speaking about the problems that really faced the nation and the ill will that has grown between the legislature and the executive," one member suggested. Cabinet ministers have upon occasion appeared to address weekly bloc meetings on national problems and policy, but deputies viewed their remarks as too general and the exchange too superficial to improve executive-legislative relations. Deputies who participated in such meetings, of course, recognized the need for communications to be opened and realized that it would take time before communication could be improved. Still, in their view, the contacts were too few to achieve that goal.

In addition, the impetus for coordination and harmony that should have come from the Thieu government did not materialize. In particular, the ministerial office in charge of liaison established with the Loc cabinet in 1967 failed to develop an organizational framework for cooperation between the executive and the legislature. The first appointee had a record of long experience in government administration and prior to his appointment was the Director of the Special Commissariat for Administration, the agency that organized the 1967 elections. The purpose of the office was to provide a formal point of contact where members and officers of the legislature could refer both constituency problems and requests for the interpellation of various ministers. The liaison office decided, for example, which ministry would have jurisdiction over particular problems submitted by deputies on behalf of their constituents and, in turn, the office tried to establish a uniform policy to apply to all ministries in the handling of such problems. The Minister had hoped to develop within the government procedures similar to those used in the United States, where congressional inquiries receive special attention and swift action. The ministries, however, were slow to develop offices to handle congressional requests. Most ministry-level bureaucrats believed that congressional inquiries were bothersome.

The liaison office, in addition, was given only limited staff and resources to develop contacts within the legislature. During the Loc cabinet the focus of the contacts made were within the Upper House, the Lower House being considered irresponsible. The emphasis on developing contacts within the Upper House was a strategic decision on the part of the government. The Upper House was decidedly progovernment and pro-Thieu, and it was felt that troublesome provisions of Lower House legislation could be dealt with more expediently when the particular bills reached the Upper House. As a consequence, the American Mission's views on certain legislation, presented to the Prime Minister, made their way into the legislature at this level rather than at the drafting stages in the Lower

House. While the liaison office has gone through four changes of directors since its establishment, its functions and the scope of its activities and staff have remained limited.[12] For their part, deputies have regarded the Liaison Ministry with suspicion. The sincerity of the Thieu government's desire to promote working relations with the legislature has been regarded as a rhetorical commitment only. The Liaison Minister himself has been viewed primarily as the executive's man,[13] and the consistent reliance by successive ministers upon the Upper House for legislative purposes has been resented.

Another reason why a working relationship failed to develop between the executive and the legislature was the executive's use of extralegal means to influence legislative behavior. President Thieu drew only upon a small circle of advisers in formulating policy with regard to the legislature. In the view of many deputies, the effect of relying upon advisers was to isolate the President. The focal point of criticism centered upon the activities of a wealthy Saigon pharmacist, Nguyen cao Thang, who, until his resignation on 30 June 1969, was officially a Special Counselor to the President.[14] In virtually every case where deputies have tried to approach the President to resolve differences or seek clarification on government policy they were blocked, as one deputy put it, "at the door of Mr. Thang's office." Another deputy characterized "communication" with the President in terms typical of other reports of attempts to establish a dialogue. "Every time we tried to see President Thieu we were forced to go to Mr. Thang's office, and Thang refused to arrange an appointment for us. In our last visit, for example, Thang said that any requests to see the President or any letters addressed to the President's attention would go through his office first. Mr. Thang then produced his reply to our last letter which simply said that what we wanted to see the President for was irrelevant to his recent statements on the matter and that it was, therefore, impossible to arrange an appointment. We left the Palace bewildered and frustrated."[15] In light of this and similar occurrences deputies were extremely critical of the way the Thieu government handled executive-legislative relations. Thang, a member of the National Assembly of the Diem era and one of the individuals handpicked by Diem to draft the 1956 Constitution, would have been regarded by the deputies in any event as a less than desirable candidate to deal with the legislature since he had played a role in making the legislature a rubber-stamp institution under Diem. The deputies' initial suspicion of Thang was reinforced once his approach to executive-legislative relations became clear. Thang's objective apparently was to work to create a progovernment majority bloc through which the wishes of the President could be easily made into law and through which the forces of opposition could be rendered insignificant. Had Thang been successful, little detail of his method of operation would have become publicly known. Because the method chosen by Thang created a scandal, however, many of his activities became matters of public record, precipitating a major crisis over the question of legislative autonomy.

The thrust of Thang's efforts, on the basis of the accounts appearing both in House debates and in the vernacular press, appeared to be to create a progovernment bloc of deputies through bribing those deputies most likely to be supporters of the government. The figure involved was reported to be the equivalent of about $2,500 US.[16] From interviews with Lower House deputies, Thang was reported to have had some success with the approach. More moderate supporters of the government, however, considered this tactic an outright insult to the integrity of the House and attempted to make their protests known to President Thieu. By the time this private effort was launched, moderate deputies suggested that Thieu was so isolated from the legislature that there remained no feasible way to approach the President without Thang's knowledge. Thang's efforts were, however, publicized in the Saigon press. Public criticism against the House was unrelenting. House members had been involved in corruption before,[17] and, in the view of many, Thang's efforts merely confirmed an image of the House as a rubber-stamp legislature. Thang himself was the subject of more cautious criticism. It was well known that, as a Saigon pharmacist, he was regarded as the "King of War Profiteering" and that "he had done nothing for the country but make himself rich."[18] But because of his closeness to the President, any who dared oppose Thang would be liable to severe reprisals. With the normal channels of public exposure substantially blocked, some deputies decided that they would have to rely upon parliamentary immunity to attack Thang and demonstrate to the executive that continued support of Thang would be detrimental to both the cause of improved executive-legislative relations and the reputation of the Thieu government in general. A special House committee was formed to investigate Thang's role in buying members' votes. The committee announced that it would submit its report to the Inspectorate in accordance with procedures outlined in the Constitution.

The committee, composed of four of the most respected members of the House, was overwhelmingly opposition in political orientation. Based upon interviews with its members, it was clear that one member was definitely linked to the An Quang Buddhist while the other three regarded themselves as An Quang sympathizers. Two of the members were outspoken critics of the government, one was a moderate, and one committee member, Tran ngoc Chau, was the Secretary-General of the House. He was universally respected as a fair individual and one who, during his tenure as an officer of the House, had maintained a balance between criticism and support of the government based upon his perception of the national interest. It was never certain whether the committee membership reflected simply a grouping of those who felt strongly about the issue or whether it reflected a deeper consensus on the need to counteract the activities of Mr. Thang and encourage the President to act out his rhetorical commitment to improve executive-legislative relations. Deputies who would comment at all on the purpose of the committee in interviews[19] suggested that it was formed with the latter purpose in mind and that its membership reflected those courageous enough to become publicly involved. Regardless of the intent of the committee's organizers, however, it precipitated a major crisis between the legislature and President Thieu and served to underscore the hostility between the two branches of government.

In October 1969, Deputy Chau, who had not sought reelection for a second term as Secretary-General, circulated a document suggesting that the Lower House investigate those "public criticisms" which alleged that "a number of important functions of the Lower House office and committees in the 1969-70 term were gained by those representatives who were supported by Mr. Nguyen cao Thang's powers and financial means." Chau's approach was cautious, suggesting that the matter came under the House's responsibility to discipline its members. It was also suggested that any evidence that implicated presidential adviser Thang would be forwarded to the Inspectorate or the Special Supreme Court.

In response to Chau's statement, Thang arranged an interview with Vietnam Press, the official government news agency, and countered Chau's charges by branding Chau a "left-behind communist cadre in the National Assembly." Thang alleged that the executive had evidence that Chau had worked for the communists since his appointment as chief of a province in the Mekong Delta and urged the Lower House to try Deputy Chau for high treason.[20] For the next four months, the "Chau case" became a cause célèbre of officials and politicians in Saigon and Washington who either supported Chau or denounced him as a communist. The executive succeeded in stripping Chau of his parliamentary immunity and convicting him before a military court which sentenced the Deputy first to twenty years at hard labor and then, under review, reduced the sentence to ten years. Subsequently, Chau's lawyer appealed to the Supreme Court on the grounds that the method by which Chau was stripped of his immunity was illegal,[21] and the Court ruled that his conviction was illegal, thus inviting his lawyers to process a new appeal for reconsideration of the case. While the tempest was brewing, the executive hurled a variety of charges against the House questioning its anticommunist character, threatening military intervention should Chau fail to be convicted, and setting off a series of riots and demonstrations both in Saigon and the provinces that threatened the lives of many deputies if they failed to condemn Deputy Chau. While the details of this crisis were well reported in the United States and need no repetition here,[22] the crisis was extremely significant as a lesson to the deputies concerned about the independence of the legislature.

The view of the Chau case held by most deputies was that the preservation of legislative autonomy—of which parliamentary immunity was a vital part—required that the House become a vital political force. That deputies actually did sign the petition was taken as an indicator of their profound dedication to anticommunism as much as an indicator of their corruption, and editorial and other political commentaries during the period reflected both viewpoints—usually within the same article.[23] Executive contempt for the House as a political force and its prerogatives was manifested by Thieu's insults and threats during the crisis and by the government-sponsored demonstrations. Unless the pace of political mobilization for all groups could be heightened, deputies feared, "No force on earth would prevent this country from becoming a dictatorship and Thieu its dictator."

Since Chau himself had organized no political party and remained independent throughout his tenure, it was widely believed that Thieu saw him vulnerable. Even moderate supporters of the government recognized that no deputy's position could be considered secure unless it was linked to a viable and dynamic political force that Thieu could not afford either to ignore or malign. The Chau crisis signaled an imperative to all political forces that effective coalescence was required both for the eventual introduction of the Viet Cong into the political system and for the more immediate danger of the growth of dictatorship within the government itself. To deputies in the Lower House, moreover, the crisis demonstrated that what bases of cooperation they had been able to discover among themselves had to be transplanted to the polity at large. Overarching cooperation at the elite level and even the support of other constitutional institutions such as the Supreme Court could not replace effective political organization. For the Lower House to function as a political institution, political power had to be created.

The Search for Legislative Autonomy and the Limits of Constitutionalism

The House and Law-making

Before the Chau crisis, the majority of the deputies did not view the absence of a working relationship between the legislature and the executive as being related to political causes. Most appeared to believe that there would be a gradual improvement as the House continued to assert its independence from the executive, thus requiring the President to woo and cooperate with the progovernment bloc. The dominant view was that competition between the President and the House for legislative initiative was essentially competition between two branches of the government and not between two distinct political forces. Even opposition deputies did not want to suggest that political competition was involved for fear of provoking a reaction from the right that might result in dissolution of the Assembly. All political forces in the House recognized that they were unprepared for political competition with a powerful executive. And the consensus among most deputies was expressed by one: "All political activities must be kept at a low key because no political force is yet able to challenge the President." The House came to rely upon the support of other constitutional institutions in its struggle for legislative autonomy, and it couched all major opposition to executive requests and legislation in questions of constitutionality.

What began as a search for legislative autonomy by the House gradually emerged as a search for bases of political cooperation that could link the functioning of the House to politics in society at large. The limits of the legislature's appeal to the Constitution to curb the executive made clear the need for greater involvement in political mobilization of the population. The search for legislative autonomy transformed the House from an institution of ratification to one of law-making. While the Chau case made clear the need for individual involvement in politics, it also served to establish that conflicts between the House and the Thieu government were fundamentally political in nature and required the development of a means for the House to influence the policies of government.

Since its inauguration in 1967, the Lower House has dealt with two major types of issues: those generated within the context of the 1967 Constitution and involving the organization of special councils, and those generated within the broader context of the war and Vietnamese politics. One deputy noted: "The work of the Lower House during [its] first two years has been in a sense predetermined. The Constitution required it to establish the structure of government in South Vietnam by establishing, organizing, and putting into operation a variety of councils, courts, commissions, and branches. In addition to this work, of course, the legislature has had to deal with a variety of crises and internally generated political issues." The April Constitution required that the legislature establish an independent judiciary that included a court system created by specific legislation as well as a Supreme Court and a Judicial Council.[24] The constitution also required that the legislature establish a number of "special institutions": a Special Court to be composed of an equal number of senators and Lower House deputies with competence to decide the impeachment of high officials; an Inspectorate to conduct investigations of public officials and private citizens and recommend appropriate punishments to the courts; an Armed Forces Council to advise the President on military affairs; and a Cultural and Educational Council, an Economic and Social Council, and an Ethnic Minorities Council—all designed to advise the government on relevant matters. Except for the Ethnic Minorities Council, these special institutions generated little controversy in the Lower House, and their establishment was straightforward.[25] Differences of opinion did emerge during the course of debate on these councils in the Lower House. But such differences were largely over the details of their organization rather than either their role in the GVN system or the powers ascribed to them.

The legislature was also given five explicit tasks. The Constitution required that laws be drafted which would establish a system of due process for all citizens, govern and guarantee freedom of the press, provide regulations governing political parties guaranteeing the freedom of the political opposition, establish a just system of labor regulation, and provide for the reorganization and regulation of local government and administration. While these tasks were prescribed for both branches of the legislature, the Lower House took a lion's share of the initiative.[26]

Following its inauguration, the Lower House met almost continually. From October 1967 until January 1970 the Lower House was in session 589 days with five regular and nine special sessions. Table 6-1 provides a picture of the sequence in which the constitutional and other legislative

Table 6-1 Regular and irregular sessions of the Lower House

Session	Type of session	Major agenda items
31 Oct.– 21 Dec. 1967	Regular	Inauguration; validation of member's election; drafting of House rules and organization; discussion of mobilization order; investigation of imprisonment of political opposition
5 Jan.– 14 Mar. 1968	Irregular	Completed rules drafting; recovery from Tet offensive; selection of committee members; rejection of executive's request for autonomy in economic and financial affairs for one year to cope with Tet offensive; discussion of national budget
1 Apr.– 30 June 1968	Regular	Rejection of the Upper House's Amendments to the national budget; discussion of law governing freedom of the press, general mobilization, Paris Peace Talks, political party law, Supreme Court legislation; interpellation of Foreign Minister, Prime Minister; passage of Mutual Aid surtax and war risk insurance legislation; updating legislation dealing with executive powers during a state of war
1 Aug.– 31 Aug. 1968	Irregular	Discussion of legislation establishing the Inspectorate and the Economic and Social Council
4 Sept.– 30 Sept. 1968	Irregular	Considered Upper House amendments to pending legislation and approved requests for the organization of by-elections to replace deputies who had vacated their offices
6 Oct.– 31 Dec. 1968	Regular	Election of new House officers and committee membership; discussion of Upper House amendments to State of War and Inspectorate Bills, the significance of US decision to stop bombing North Vietnam; consideration of legislation on establishment of Cultural and Educational Council, 1968 budget supplemental and 1969 budget interpellation of the Prime Minister

(continued)

Table 6-1 (continued)

Session	Type of session	Major agenda items
6 Jan.–14 Jan. 1969	Irregular	1969 budget
4 March 1969	Irregular	Consideration of request for a by-election
7 Apr.–30 June 1969	Regular	Consideration of remaining special constitutional institutions to be established; discussion of due process, executive action to increase taxes, provincial and municipal elections law bill; interpellation of Minister of Information on press policy, Minister of Interior and others on the Phoenix program; considered amendments to political party law
3 July–10 July 1969	Irregular	Submission of land reform legislation by executive; no confidence expressed in petition against Huong government; continued consideration of press statute
23 July 1969	Irregular	Consideration of an executive request
18 Aug.–5 Sept. 1969	Irregular	Consideration of national budget, land reform bill, and tariff modifications
6 Sept.–10 Sept. 1969	Irregular	Consideration of special court legislation, Economic and Social Council
6 Oct. 1969–31 Jan. 1970	Regular	Taxation, national budget, Chau case

tasks were taken up and the rapidity with which they were handled. The Lower House was not particularly rapid in processing legislation; in almost every case considered by the both Houses, the Upper House acted in approximately half the time. Senators maintain that such swift action demonstrated their concern for the importance of the issue at hand and, hence, their greater sense of responsibility compared to the behavior of the

Lower House. The Upper House, however, has less than half as many members as the Lower House; on any given issue it also has roughly half the number of speakers. Debates in both Houses are characterized by their repetitive nature. Unlike two-party legislatures, for example, where each party may designate one or a limited number of speakers to argue their position, the fluid bloc structure in Vietnam almost precluded the designation of spokesmen. As such, the debates are useful codifications of the dominant positions maintained by particular blocs and coalitions of deputies, but they reveal very little of the work that has gone on behind the scenes in preparing legislation. A more significant indicator of legislative initiative lies in the work that took place apart from the formal floor debates.

By the middle of 1969, a hundred pieces of legislation had been considered by the Lower House. A little less than half of this legislation was submitted by the executive, but in declining proportion as Table 6-2 suggests. Over time the four major sources of legislation also tended to specialize their interests. The executive, for example, submitted a large proportion of the draft bills providing for establishment of special institutions required by the Constitution, as well as six international treaties for ratification, five bills providing the organization of by-elections to fill vacancies caused by the death or resignation of deputies, and five bills seeking authorization for administrative changes within executive departments, in addition to submitting six bills dealing with the national budget and supplemental appropriations. These bills accounted for almost three-quarters of the total legislation submitted by the executive to the Lower House. From 1967 until mid-1968 the Lower and Upper Houses submitted their own versions of bills establishing the special institutions, as well as their own versions of the laws governing the freedom of the press and the establishment of political parties. By the fall of 1968, however,

Table 6-2 Bills submitted to the legislature by branch of origin

Year	Executive	Lower House	Lower House-Upper House	Upper House	Total
1967	0	1	1	1	3
1968	30	15	5	7	57
1969 (midyear)	14	16	4	6	40
Total	44	32	10	14	100

the nature of draft bill submissions from all three sources had changed. The executive tended to submit bills relating largely to matters of administration within its own departments, which were treated in a straightforward manner. The major exceptions were the bills dealing with land reform and taxation. The bills submitted under the joint authorship of senators and deputies tended to parallel those submitted by the executive such as land reform; before mid-1968 each body tended to draft and submit its own version. Upper House bills after mid-1968 tended to deal largely with issues relating to the conduct of business.

In contrast, the Lower House, after this date, tended to broaden its horizons as the other sources of legislation tended to narrow their focus. In 1967, the bills originating in the Lower House were drafted in response to pending legislation submitted by the executive and dealing with general mobilization and with the regulation of political parties. By mid-1968, however, the Lower House committees and blocs began drafting legislation dealing with the organization of local government, the legal authority of the executive to act independently of the legislature in time of war, the punishment of political prisoners, and the establishment and guarantee of due process for all citizens. In 1969, the concern over due process expanded as was demonstrated in the attention paid to the reorganization of local government and administration. This effort accounted for more than one-third of the new bills drafted in the Lower House.

In contrast, the Upper House tended to follow the executive's lead in its legislation drafting and reflected, no doubt, the closer relationship between these two agencies than that between the executive and the Lower House. The growing legislative initiative of the House was directly related to the development of working groups that included deputies active in constituency service work,[27] both in the drafting of legislation and the functioning of House committees. The twin concerns of the necessity to establish due process and the need to revitalize local government and administration grew out of the shared perception that taking the initiative on such issues was vital to demonstrating to the executive that the legislature must not be ignored in domestic policy making.

The scope of an institution's activities is determined by the role its members ascribe to it. In the case of the Lower House the growth of its activities and involvement in national government and politics was gradual, reflecting the cautiousness of individual commitment. As suggested in Chapter 4, the dominant attitude of those seeking election to the House in 1967 was one of uncertainty about the legislature's relationship to

Vietnamese politics. For those individuals who took the chance to enter politics in 1967, few had any faith that the principles of the constitution would govern the presidency of Nguyen van Thieu.

For purposes of analysis, three phases of growth in the scope of the Lower House's activities can be identified, although the boundaries of each phase are not precise. Each is approximately defined by the type of legislation drafted. In the initial phase, beginning with the inauguration in 1967 and lasting roughly until the Tet offensive of 1968, the scope of the Lower House's activities remained limited to the work delegated to it by the constitution. During this phase, the work of the House was routine, its legislative output low, and its debates desultory.

In the second phase, lasting roughly until the end of 1968, the House was increasingly preoccupied with defining its role and position in the government. Its members were active in constituency service, and the House itself encountered increasingly stiff resistance from the executive and the Upper House to any of its policy suggestions. Debate was strident, the structure of the blocs fluid, but its legislative output, while well below that of the executive, increased. From a concern with the establishment of constitutional organs during the first phase, House bills came to reflect a growing concern over the prerogatives of the executive and aimed at correcting the legal loopholes that, as a result of numerous decrees promulgated by successive ruling juntas, gave the executive wide latitude for arbitrarily abridging civil rights.

In the third phase, beginning in 1969 and continuing to the end of the first term, the House attempted to innovate policy. The legislative output of the House substantially increased, and a growing consensus about its role emerged among the deputies. The nature of political alignments, as reflected in the bloc structure, tended also to crystallize. Three major concerns were reflected in the legislation drafted: the need to curb executive prerogatives, the need to increase governmental responsiveness at the provincial and local level, and the need to establish the due process prescribed in the constitution. Translated into political terms, these priorities reflected what, in the view of most deputies, were essential prerequisites for the creation of political power. To avoid being regarded as a mere decoration of the executive, the legislature had to indicate early its intent to accept fully the role created for it in the Constitution. But it was increasingly apparent that an appeal to constitutionalism would not suffice to assure autonomy or influence.

Rather, the fate of the legislature would depend on its political organization: internally, the bloc structure had to be regularized and bases of cooperation among the blocs had to be developed. Not the construction of political organizations, but the development of a system upon which they could be based was imperative: political organization had to be protected from reprisals by local police, and linkages between the groups and the government had to be developed. The establishment of a system of due process was viewed as a step toward securing the right of political organization, while restructuring the process by which local and provincial governments were established was viewed as a way to create a new system of politics.

The propensity of the House to innovate policy was related to three elements: the prevailing attitudes about the role and position of the legislature vis-à-vis the executive, the scope of individual deputy activities, and the political structure of the House. Challenged by the specter of a strong and dominating executive, the House had to create rather than acquire an identity. As the clarity of the role and position of the House increased, deputies began to link individual activities in their constituencies with political organizations to the functioning of the House as an institution. The House was used as a formal processing agency for constituency complaints, and as a forum for various groups to articulate positions on major political issues. Internally and informally, however, the leadership and management of the House came to be shared among and determined by the coalitions of interest that had developed between deputies inclined to constituency service and political mobilization. To the mobilizers, the House provided an arena to advance the cause of their particular group and explore means of combining with like-minded organizations; to those deputies less inclined toward political organization, the significance of the House lay in what such activities demonstrated to the executive.

The political mobilization and constituency-oriented activities of the deputies tended to get the House involved in the process of creating new policies to reform government and expand participation, the House leadership tended to mediate between opposing interests in the drafting of legislation, and the activities of deputies and their involvements determined the specifics of the innovations that were ultimately embodied in legislation.

At the time of its inauguration three general attitudes characterized deputies' beliefs regarding the position of the House in the government system. One attitude maintained that the House must become a source of political mobilization for or against the Thieu government, a base from which opposition and progovernment movements could "take off" in their efforts to organize the population. Another attitude maintained that the House, given its limited real power, could at best function as a strong supporter of the executive and at worst would become its instrument. Associated with this view would be the majority of the progovernment deputies, deputies of the Diem era assemblies, and a number of deputies elected from the 1966-67 Constituent Assembly. These deputies did not view their own positions within the government or access to the ruling elite as contingent upon the development of the House, but rather upon the clarity with which they could make their progovernment positions known to whomever would prove to be the victor in the struggle between Thieu and Ky for ultimate power and authority. A third attitude ascribed no significance at all to the functioning or the decisions of the House, and rather than decry its existence as a facade merely viewed membership in the House in an opportunistic way, as a means of personal advancement, aggrandizement, and income.

The membership of the House could be divided roughly into thirds on the bases of these three attitudes.[28] Little change has taken place amongst those deputies who would fall into the last category. Change in attitude has, however, occurred within the middle group. The deputy who expected that the executive would value his support based solely upon a clear declaration of support was disappointed. Even legislative blocs that have been consistently pro-Thieu have been frustrated by the lack of attention and reward for such efforts that have been forthcoming from the executive, as noted in Chapter 7. Rather, Thieu has sought to narrow his power base to only the most essential elements. His support and resources have been devoted to political activities within the officer corps and to a lesser extent within Catholic political organizations. Thus while deputies in the middle group have probably not changed their desire to support the executive, the latter's rebuff has encouraged greater interest in their establishing the position of the House as an independent branch of government. To the deputies who have sought to foster political organizations and who initially did so as an activity distinct from their membership in the House, the House came to supply local groups with the national orientation they lacked in the past. The House became an arena for political participation as well as political competition for these groups. For the first time, such groups had, within the context of national goals and interests, traded support for each other on identifiable issues.

The trading of such support and the development of common interests is more significant than any efficacy these activities may have had. The construction of more permanent and more powerful bridges between Vietnam's multiplicity of groups might eventually lead to more broadly based political organizations within the polity. The fact that the Lower House could not successfully prevent the passage of executive legislation was perhaps less significant than the cooperation exhibited by the diverse groups represented in the Lower House in constructing a united front. Constituency service, to be discussed in Chapter 8, is also significant as a political phenomena, not only because it aims at fostering mass political mobilization but also because it affords a link between the population and the national governmental system that has been missing. The changing political orientations of the deputies and the discovery of bases for cooperation set the stage for the introduction of legislation viewed as essential to restructuring politics in Vietnam.

Presidential Prerogatives and Legislative Autonomy

The search for legislative autonomy was a strategy adopted by the House to secure both its role as outlined in the Constitution and to provide grounds to further political cooperation among its members. Deputies were able to reach basic agreements on the need to preserve legislative autonomy, to vote down executive requests and legislation that contravened this principle, and to involve the Supreme Court in constitutional controversies that led to decisions increasingly supportive of the legislature. But the sum total of these efforts and of such an approach revealed that appeals to constitutionalism, unless bolstered by effective political organization within the polity at large, are only marginally effective.

The first major encounter between the executive and the legislature over the question of autonomy occurred with the request submitted by President Thieu at the end of February 1968 for the authority to regulate the economic recovery of the country in the wake of the Tet offensive. The President sought emergency power for a ninety-day period and pledged to consult appropriate members of the legislature before any laws were decreed. Contained in the President's message to the legislature were details of how the Tet offensive had affected the economy and a general summary of the problems to be faced in the coming period. The report stressed the need for the application of "a number of strong, rapid, and secret measures" to prevent hoarding and speculation, developments that would increase the suffering of the people and make recovery impossible. While deputies considered the problems of recovery grave and recognized the need for timely action, the thrust of the debate suggested that the deputies also believed the relinquishing of their constitutional duties equally problematic. As one speaker suggested: "If we do not base [our actions] on the Constitution which separates clearly [each branch's] powers, we can fall easily into the confusion our country has been in since 1963 with the constant coup d'etats and cabinet reorganizations."[29] The deputy also suggested, however, that since the constitution provided for emergency procedures within each House, needed legislation could be facilitated. The deputy concluded that it would be a tragic parody of the state of Vietnamese democracy if the first act of the legislature was to pass a law abdicating its powers to the executive.

These remarks expressed the spirit of the debate. Some deputies even argued that a grant of emergency powers for a period of only one day could produce executive decisions with far-reaching consequences. In such a case, it was suggested, the people would blame the legislature for what happened and precipitate a serious crisis of confidence in the newly formed constitutional system. Even members of the progovernment bloc argued that to accede to the request would have a detrimental effect upon the growth of democracy. As one such deputy stated, "Article 3 recognizes the separation of powers. Entrusting our power to the executive would be an abdication of our responsibility. Under the First Republic the National Assembly entrusted Diem with emergency powers on several occasions, and this brought dictatorship and a family-governing regime the results of which we are still suffering from."[30] Other criticisms of the President's request stressed that it was too vague to safeguard the people's rights. Most deputies also agreed with Tran ngoc Chau who declared that the executive already had sufficient powers to cope with the economic crisis. Chau suggested that the present burden should be shared between both branches; if it were not, he argued, then the legislature would have the reputation of "only working in the easy times."

The final element of the arguments presented focused on the question of constitutionality. Deputies who spoke to this issue argued that since the Constitution made it clear that the power to make laws was given by the people to the legislature, then the legislature could only give that power back to the people. It could not, therefore, be delegated to the President. No deputy who rose to speak supported the measure. The vote was eighty-five to ten against the President's request. Subsequent meetings of the House were devoted to the establishment of regular and special Tet relief committees, and the House considered that it stood ready to act swiftly on any legislation submitted by the President for economic recovery. No legislation was submitted, however, and no comment was made by the President on the assembly's action. Nevertheless, the question of the executive's role in the drafting and promulgation of economic legislation proved to be the principal area of controversy between Thieu and the deputies.

The April Constitution allowed considerable legislative initiative to the President. Article 43 permitted the President to introduce bills into the National Assembly while Article 45 provided the following:

1. Within the period allowed for promulgation [that is, fifteen days unless otherwise specified by the Assembly], the President has a right to send a message outlining his reasons requesting the National Assembly to reconsider one or more articles of the bill.

2. In this case, the National Assembly will meet in joint plenary session to have a final vote on the bill with an absolute majority of the total number of Representatives and Senators. If the National Assembly votes to reject the amendment proposed by the President, the bill shall automatically become law and shall be transmitted to the President for promulgation.

By translating the relevant provisions of the constitution into a diagram of how a bill becomes a law in Vietnam, the significance of the second paragraph of Article 45 becomes clear. As Diagram 6-1 indicates, the President, via Article 45, actually becomes the principal controlling element in the law-making process. Regardless of the outcome of legislative votes, the President can change the resulting bills. Such changes must be specifically rejected in the Joint Session or the President's version becomes law. The process thus established meant that the President could actually make laws while the legislature had only an advisory role in their formulation. The weakest position in the entire process was that occupied by the Lower House: its decisions could be overridden by a simple majority of the Upper House (thirty votes); the decision of the Upper House could be reversed only by a two-thirds vote (ninety-two votes). Thus, bills originally passed by a majority of the Lower House on which the Upper House does not concur actually require twenty-two additional votes in favor (the difference between a simple majority and a two-thirds vote of the deputies) of the measure to have the Lower House version stand. On bills where the President has proposed changes, a simple

Diagram 6–1 How a bill becomes a law under the Second Republic

Sources (Article 43)	Legislative process	Legislative outcomes	Executive prerogatives	Promulgation
President Lower House Upper House	Lower House secretariat →	Bill passed by both houses	Legislative version accepted	Constitutionality of bill not challenged
	Lower House committee →	Bill defeated in either Upper or Lower House →		Constitutionality challenged → Supreme Court
	Lower House debate: passage requires a majority vote of the total membership →	Joint plenary session: Upper House version can be rejected only by a two-thirds vote of total members of both houses	Legislative version amended →	
	Upper House secretariat: passed or defeated bill must be transmitted within three days →		Joint plenary session: presidential amendments stand unless specifically rejected by majority vote of total membership of both Houses (Article 45)	
	Upper House committee →			
	Upper House debate: passage requires a majority vote of the total membership			

majority of each house is required to override such changes, though the leaders of both Houses consider this a virtual impossibility. As the deputies are aware, when such a confrontation develops, the President can use his vast resources and influence to prevent the required number of legislators from attending the joint session. The effect of this procedure, in the view of members of both the Upper and Lower Houses as well as Supreme Court Justices, has been to make the President the principal lawmaker. As one Justice observed,

> A common element running through several provisions of the Constitu-tion and one that is quite against its spirit is that in actuality the executive is too dominant in the making of laws. Article 45 allows the executive to make rather decisive amendments to the laws of the National Assembly which can, in effect, change their intent entirely. The requirement that the Upper House can reverse decisions of the Lower House by a simple majority which then must be counteracted by two-thirds of the House, similarly, provides the executive considerable influence since the Upper House is dominated by the President. The President's use of these provisions has been a very effective check upon the power and the ability of the Assembly to make the laws of the country.

Putting the matter more simply, one deputy summarized what appeared to be the consensus of many deputies and senators: "While the executive is not supposed to make the laws, in fact it does."

The common concern of deputies and senators over the latitude provided the executive in Article 45 led to a series of constitutional challenges of the President's authority in the legislative process. The Lower House challenged the executive by requesting the Supreme Court to interpret the constitution. All of these challenges grew from fundamental disagreements between the executive and the legislature over economic policies where Thieu attempted to circumvent the authority of the House. The legislature viewed executive decisions and action in this field as both a threat to the spirit of the constitution and hence to legislative autonomy, and as an effort by the executive to sharply reduce the ability of the legislature to influence the government's economic policies. Deputies, in particular, rallied to these challenges both because of their own growing concern with preserving their autonomy and because their constituents were highly critical of the government's economic policies. Thus, legis-lative challenges to executive power created two important bases of cooperation among the deputies: a fundamental agreement on the need to protect legislative autonomy, and a growing responsiveness of the deputies to their constituents.

The legislature, in launching its attack upon the authority of the executive in the legislative process, challenged Article 45 directly as well as indirectly. The direct challenge to Article 45 centered upon the apparent inconsistency of the constitution that on the one hand made the legislature the principal law-making institution of the Republic while on the other hand, through Article 45, tended in practice to provide only the President with this power. The argument submitted to the Court on behalf of the legislature was based on the view that the intent of Article 45 was to establish a means to review presidential amendments to assembly legislation. When the review process is completed, the deputies argued, the question to be voted on was whether or not they would accept the President's changes. The executive maintained that the wording of the constitution must be strictly interpreted and that, therefore, the question to be voted on was whether or not the assembly would reject his changes. The significance of the dispute was that under the President's interpretation the burden of reversing his changes lay upon those who opposed it while under the assembly's interpretation the President would be required to muster his supporters. Legislative leaders acknowledged the difficulties the opposition would have in mustering sufficient support to defeat presidential changes and argued that the effect of the President's interpretation would be to make the government appear as an "absentee government" since supporters of the President's views merely had to stay at home when the joint session convened.

The legislature was not successful in its efforts to counteract the influence of the executive by means of a direct challenge to Article 45. The precedents were against their argument. Examination of the debates of the Constituent Assembly revealed that the wording of the article was literally intended and based upon the rules of that body which provided that when the draft constitution was returned by the President with changes, the assembly then had to specifically reject such changes. Moreover, it was argued that when the President did, in fact, return the draft constitution with amendments the deputies had raised no questions about the procedure at that time. The Supreme Court in its decision of 19 August 1969 held that the wording of Article 45 was clear: a majority of the legislature had to reject the President's changes. While the Court's decision was expected, legislators viewed the dictum issued by the Court as at least a limited victory in the sense that it reminded the President of the constitutional limits to his authority. The Court stated: "If the President does not share the views of the National Assembly in its interpretation of an article of the Constitution, he can promulgate the bill [in question] only after the difference has been settled by the Supreme Court."[31] The significance of this dictum was that, in view of most deputies, it specifically forestalled what deputies feared most. In future disagreements between the executive and the legislature, the executive was now enjoined from promulgating unpopular and controversial legislation that he had altered, thus avoiding a situation where the challenged law would be in force while the Supreme Court considered its constitutionality.

The legislature also involved the Supreme Court in disputes over the budgetary process. Three cases were submitted challenging the President's right to amend the national budget. In each case the petition of the legislature was overruled by the Court on purely constitutional grounds. Privately, Court members reported they suggested to the deputies that the requests for constitutional interpretation thus far received had been based upon extremely weak arguments and that the submission of such cases did no service to the cause of defending legislative autonomy. Deputies, in turn, reported that the Court, contrary to their initial expectations, did not appear to be a mere puppet of the executive and viewed with sympathy the efforts by the legislators to curb the powers of the executive. As one Court member later suggested in an interview: "We are concerned with the overall operation of the constitutional system. If one branch is being subverted, all are affected." Nevertheless, it was also the opinion of the Justices that for the Court to act irresponsibly and favor the legislature without sufficient legal grounds would not further the goal of establishing a constitutional system. This early experience with the Supreme Court was significant for the dialogue it opened between the two branches of the government. Court Justices considered themselves involved with the deputies in preserving the autonomy of all branches of the government and particularly those which were weakest. Justices came to work as informal advisers to groups of deputies preparing legislation. The deputies, in turn, came to regard the Supreme Court with respect and considerably less suspicion than they had at first. In the view of most deputies, this early cooperation was instrumental to the success later achieved when a genuine constitutional issue emerged between the executive and the legislature.

Such an issue presented itself in mid-October 1969 when, in an effort to counteract what was the worst inflation in Vietnam's history, President

Thieu promulgated an executive decree imposing 1,523 austerity taxes. The result was instant outrage. The government was charged with failing to practice austerity first and passing the burden of inflation onto the shoulders of those least able to afford it, the fixed-salary civil servants and soldiers and the urban and rural poor. The taxes increased from 100-650 percent the cost of consumer goods considered "nonessential" by the government to supply additional revenue. Viewed from the legislature, however, the taxes were anathema. The major arguments advanced against the taxes concentrated on their impact on the cost of essential consumer goods. Deputies argued that, when the price of gasoline (a "nonessential" good) was doubled, the prices of all goods requiring transportation would rise.[32] Legislators in both houses recognized that, given the existing market system in Vietnam, it would be impossible for the government to effectively control pricing and prevent the taxes from causing a general rise in prices. Moreover, they reasoned that those best able to afford the taxes would bribe officials to forestall having to pay the taxes and that these bribes could not be considered sources of revenue for the government.

Appended to the evident concern of legislators over the effect of the taxes on the population was also a continuing concern that the executive was seeking to undercut the legislature's role in economic affairs. Earlier in the year the government had ordered increases in similar taxes based upon a 1964 decree that the deputies regarded as an unconstitutional act.[33] The imposition of austerity taxes was based upon a decree promulgated in 1961, a decree that expired within a year. This served as the basis for the legislature's appeal to the Supreme Court. This time, the Court viewed the legislature's petition as raising a substantive constitutional question and within little more than a month (in contrast to earlier decisions that had taken an average of six months to prepare) issued its decision. The Court held that the President's action in imposing the austerity taxes was unconstitutional since the 1961 decree had expired.[34]

While the decision of the Court was considered a victory for the legislature and demonstrated its willingness to join the legislature in the struggle for the establishment of the constitution, the actions of the executive had provoked an even greater concern that the fundamental conflict between the two branches was likely to erupt into outright political warfare. In addition to opposing the taxes, deputies viewed the controversy as a decisive and perhaps also an irreversible decline in the possibilities of a working relationship between the two branches. The inauguration of the Khiem cabinet in the spirit of a pledge by both the new Prime Minister and the President to promote greater cooperation between the two branches had been viewed by some deputies, including those in the leadership group of the House, as a sign that the executive might alter its attitude toward the legislature. Numerous deputies suggested in interviews that their own impressions of Prime Minister Khiem were generally favorable. One deputy, who spoke for what he characterized as the consensus of the House, suggested that "Khiem appears to us as sincerely interested in the improvement of executive-legislative relations. He has told many of us that this is his wish and for that reason we shall withhold our criticism of his action in appointing a poor choice for his Minister of Liaison. We are going to wait and see." Even members of the opposition appeared to welcome the Khiem appointment and had been able to meet with the new Prime Minister. "Frankly, he is a surprise to us. He wishes to be independent from Thieu, and he appears to really seek an improvement in the relations between our two branches." The President's action on the austerity taxes, however, dispelled both the desire on the part of the legislature to invoke an era of good feelings toward the new government and the hopes of some of the deputies for an improvement of executive-legislative relations.

First, deputies stressed that they were not basically opposed to the taxes but to the way they were promulgated; it was clear to many that the President would never consider the possibility of taking the legislature into his confidence. For their part, the deputies realized that there was virtually no alternative to the taxes since devaluation of the piaster was considered unthinkable. Time was required, however, before the taxes could be announced in order to assure that the government could enforce price stabilization programs, prevent hoarding, and police the black market. Deputies had urged more effective price controls for some time, and a few had circulated to the President proposals for such controls. For the executive to announce the taxes without consulting the legislature not only contravened the constitution but, of more immediate significance, these deputies argued, it made the government appear divided and forced the legislature to oppose the President when the latter could have had its support, as one deputy put it, "for the asking." Polls taken by leaders of both the progovernment and opposition forces within the House suggested that more than a majority would have supported the taxes had the President consulted the legislature. More significant, one member of the opposition reported that the Prime Minister had been working closely with House leaders on the issue and had circulated a draft of the President's proposal to progovernment and opposition leaders to work out in advance the problem areas, thus assuring that the measure would be swiftly approved by the legislature. The deputy reported that Khiem had made a strong plea to the President to submit the measure to the legislature. The President, however, turned to his adviser Nguyen cao Thang and asked if he should do what the Prime Minister suggested. Thang's response was that the legislature would not pass the measure and that his efforts to "gain supporters" had been unsuccessful. The President then said that he would make a decision and let the cabinet know the following day; whether or not a subsequent meeting with the cabinet was held is not known. On the following day the President promulgated the austerity taxes by executive decree.

While the account of Prime Minister Khiem's efforts to cooperate with the legislature was not widely known in Saigon political circles, to the Lower House deputies he consulted the President's action made clear the fact that Nguyen cao Thang both held the President's confidence and was the principal obstacle to the President's relationship with the legislature. Shortly thereafter the campaign against Thang was launched as described above. That it turned into a "naked contest of power," as one deputy characterized it, made clear to all deputies that no possibility of a working relationship between the two branches existed. As one deputy who had worked tirelessly for a rapprochement between the two branches until that time observed: "The House has now reached a turning point in its dealings with the executive. We will not now or in the future ask for any more interpellations of government officials since past experience has proved that the sessions have come to nought. There is nothing left to say." More important, to many deputies the President's action on the taxation issues and his subsequent attack on Tran ngoc Chau signalled the clear and present need for the deputies to compete politically with the President.

The summary of one deputy who had entered the legislature as an independent, then moved to a position of support for the government "in these difficult times," and then aligned himself with the moderate opposition was typical.

If President Thieu had consulted the National Assembly before announcing the taxes, they would have been endorsed by the legislature. That the President did not do this reflects the fact that Vietnam does not have a responsible government; for a very long time Thieu, Huong, and now Khiem have been used to choosing the easy way to force their will—that is by executive decree—upon the people and their representatives who have come to expect a more democratic and popular government.

Part of the reason that the assembly has failed to have the power to control the President and therefore participate meaningfully in the shaping of government policies is that we are not yet representatives of a political constituency, that is, a group of people or political forces that are cohesive and resemble modern political parties. For a long time the executive branch of the government and the mass of the population have been separated by a wide gap; the Lower House could serve as an important link but the relationship must be based on the political organization of the people. We must work to transform the relationship between the government and the people from one of the latter's dependence upon the former to one in which the government responds to the people because they represent political forces that cannot be ignored.

Currently, the nationalists are like crabs all put in one box. They have no way out and they have begun to pinch each other. This is because on the one hand the nationalist parties have not concentrated on creating bases of support among the people and on the other because the government has not recognized the need to make a real effort to mobilize the people to support it. So far we have been playing at politics in a vacuum. The government feels no need to organize the population because it is so dependent upon the American army, and the nationalist parties have failed because they tend to rest upon their reputations. While we do not know what the American government will do in the future, it is now clear to us that our parties must actively organize the population. We must create power if we are to compete with the Viet Cong eventually, but this is also necessary if we are to make the government and particularly the President more responsive to the people.

The conflict between the executive and the legislature thus suggested the need for a new politics in Vietnam, one based not upon traditional political divisions or factions but upon the ability of political groups and institutions to mobilize the population. Representatives of all political groups, by the end of 1969, acknowledged that this was the task before them, made all the more pressing in light of the increasing isolation of the President and the prospect of returning to the kind of government—narrowly based, cabalistic, and repressive—that resembled the family dictatorship of Ngo dinh Diem. This specter, it was argued, had meaning for all political forces. The bases of cooperation emerging in the legislature had to be transferred to politics in general; a common national interest had to be created. Political action within the legislature must be linked to political organization of the polity, and the political power of the one would depend upon the political mobilization of the other.

Legislative Blocs as Political Participation:
Doctrines of Political Organization
and Competition in Transition

Legislative blocs organize political participation based upon shared perceptions of interests, identity, and goals. They are designed to increase the ability of their members to influence governmental decisions. They are also designed to make a spirit of partisanship in the legislative process compatible with the need for a legislature to handle effectively the volume of its work.[1] Whether legislative blocs facilitate or impede the deliberative process, however, depends upon the challenges to a legislature posed by outside forces such as the executive and the existence of a shared feeling among all blocs for the importance of the legislature itself. Where the volume of legislative work is minimal, for example, the blocs gain little experience working together and do not develop mechanisms for the self-regulation of partisanship. Similarly, when the volume of legislative work is originated primarily outside the body itself or when the decisions of the legislature are almost certain to be overridden by another branch of government, the blocs are likely to practice partisanship but not concentrate on regulating it.

The bloc structure of a legislature also tends to be based upon the political structure of the society. Where strong cleavages based upon distrust and suspicion exist between social forces, the regulation of partisanship may be difficult to achieve unless members, in the interest of promoting legislative efficiency, can suppress what appear to be natural inclinations toward noncooperation with other groups. Finally, blocs tend to vary in cohesiveness. Their ability to bind members to either bloc decisions or procedures for interbloc cooperation may be limited. The function of legislative blocs thus depends on the cohesion of individual blocs as well as the ability of bloc leaders to link their organization to politics both in the legislature and society at large.

In South Vietnam the legislative blocs of the Second Republic faced all of the problems described above. The formation of legislative blocs, like the preparation for the elections, was a new feature of politics in Vietnam. The blocs organized within the assemblies of the Diem era, for example, were primarily a device for the executive to provide the assemblies with the appearance of a modern legislature, but not the latitude characteristic of modern legislative organizations.[2] The members of the 1967 National Assembly did not initially share a common perception of the significance and importance of the legislature which might provide a basis for interbloc cooperation. In the first year of the assembly's term, moreover, the volume of legislative work handled was small. Procedurally, the legislative process left the legislature little initiative. Lacking an institutionally generated raison d'être, the blocs initially established were derived from the complexity of the polity at large. As such, however, the blocs themselves did not represent natural or party-dictated alignments, but, rather, shifting coalitions of individuals evincing a variety of vague objectives. And in some cases the bloc themselves were not organized to facilitate the functioning of the legislature, but to serve as support for the cliques of national political figures. The stability that such organizations were likely to foster was not great. "In case the election is freely held, a Lower House that is elected will be one of dispersion. Because a majority of deputies will be independent ones, their bloc, if they form one at all, will not be a very stable majority bloc."[3] Such blocs represented not the formal institutions associated with modern parliaments, but rather, experimental caucusing groups with varying degrees of formal organization.

The blocs were something more than cliques and something less than political parties.[4] Based upon interviews with a cross section of deputies and senators from all blocs, there appeared to exist a rather striking consensus that the blocs should serve to link the government to the organizations of the polity at large. The remarks of one senator serve to summarize the comments of many in both houses: "The essence of bloc politics—and its fundamental utility as a means of political organization—is the relationship it fosters between the executive, the legislature, and the various political forces which make up the political system." The blocs were meant to be part of a process of government rather than an alternative to it. In practice, however, neither a tradition of government nor of politics existed to support the pursuit of linkage functions alone. Indeed, in Vietnam politics as practiced by cliques, parties, or legislative blocs have not been noted for their efficacy or stability. By the end of 1969, however, rather sharp differences existed in the nature of the organizations that emerged within the framework of each house. The blocs of the Upper House, originally organized as cliques, tended to remain so despite considerable shifts in the membership and leadership of each clique. Lower House blocs, in contrast, tended to emerge as preparty organizations despite their origins, in the words of one deputy, as "friendship associations."[5] Whether as cliques or preparty organizations, the legislative blocs also represented important experiments in the organization of political participation.

Legislative blocs afforded the first opportunity for Vietnam's diverse political forces and groups to link their activities to a national decision-making process. Indeed, in retrospect, the political significance of the legislature, in terms of the mobilization of the population it could foster, appeared to depend upon the bases of cooperation that were established among its members and the transfer of such cooperation, once achieved, to the polity at large. The fact that a working relationship between the executive and the legislature failed to emerge, while a threat to legislative autonomy did emerge, was related to the changing nature of the bloc structure of the Lower House. Legislative blocs have come to be regarded as a means of organizing each house of the assembly and nationalist political forces as well. The blocs represented a form of political participation both within the elected elite and between it and the population. A survey of these blocs,[6] consequently, provides insight into how the elections in 1967 and subsequent developments within the legislature affected conceptions of political organization in Vietnam.

The Constituent Assembly as a Prelude

The legislative blocs of the Second Republic's National Assembly initially mirrored the religious and political cleavages within the polity at large. These divisions set the basis for the emergence of bloc organizations in 1967 as they did for the Constituent Assembly in 1966. In that body, newly created blocs, elected without the partisanship that characterized the competition of the 1967 National Assembly, were viewed primarily as devices to facilitate the work of the assembly in drafting the constitution. In addition, the southern deputies in particular had hoped that the creation of blocs would support their effort to organize a political party of national prominence and align it with other groups in the assembly demonstrating similar political and ideological objectives. As one deputy observed, "We had thought that by working together with other groups' leaders at the national level we would be able to discover some basis for cooperation among our groups at the local level." The blocs of the Constituent Assembly thus represented an initial attempt to group deputies according to their political leanings, to facilitate the development of positions on particular issues of the constitutional debate, and to give the assembly something more than the character of a loose collection of personalities.

During the Constitutent Assembly's year tenure, five blocs emerged and the background characteristics of each are presented in Table 7-1. By far the largest bloc, the Greater Peoples' Bloc (*Khoi Dai Chung*), included central Vietnamese Buddhists, northern-born Catholics, and a number of Chinese, Khmer, and Montagnard minority deputies, representing the civilian and military service professions. As the largest bloc, the Greater Peoples' included most progovernment deputies but had the least potential for unity. Splits occurred within the bloc, largely between those deputies loyal to Ky or Thieu, while relatively few issues divided the bloc along religious or ethnic lines. On the one hand, most of the Buddhists included in the bloc were not associated with the militant An Quang faction, but were generally those who had cooperated with both the Diem regime and its successors. On the other hand, the ethnic minority deputies in the bloc reflected the progovernment position that minority groups have generally preferred to maintain in Vietnamese politics.[7] As such, the bloc presaged the kind of progovernment support that would appear in future assemblies: a large coalition of deputies held together by individual perceptions of the benefits of maintaining a progovernment posture rather than by any incentives emanating from the government itself. In contrast, the remaining four blocs were less diverse in membership and ranged from mild support of the government to mild opposition to it.[8]

The blocs did not figure prominently in the work of the assembly. They neither averted conflicts with the executive on the drafting of the constitution and electoral laws or established a process for conflicting resolution. Rather, assembly work was dominated by those deputies of national stature who remained aloof from bloc politics. Similarly, little progress was made through the blocs towards fostering political alignments that some had hoped might develop out of the experience of drafting the constitution. Some groups declared that they would refuse to seek alignments with other groups for the purpose of forming a political party. Political leaders suggested that the central executive committees of these groups disagreed with the philosophies of those most interested in forming an alliance. Others believed that Vietnam had too many parties as it was and hoped that future elections would reduce the number of parties that could demonstrate a national following. These deputies seemed to suggest that by freezing the political party structure at the present level, more broadly based parties would develop.

With the promulgation of the April Constitution the nature of the work of the Constituent Assembly changed, and the limited formal functioning of the blocs declined. From the middle of April until the fall election, it was transformed into an election law drafting commission, and the bulk of the work on these laws was done by those who had led the drafting of the constitution. Assembly attendance sharply declined, and only a few meetings involved controversial issues. Deputies also tended to focus upon their own future plans as more than half prepared to run for election either to the presidency or to one of the new National Assembly houses. Since activists met with little initial success in seeking to develop intergroup alignments, almost no efforts were made after April.

Some felt that the experiment with legislative blocs in the Constituent Assembly had failed for the very reason they were initially organized. Blocs constructed to facilitate the work of the assembly, they argued, could not do so without coming to grips with politics. The grouping of deputies on the basis of only tenuous political sympathies did not foster the cohesion required for effective functioning or stability. Nor did the relatively short tenure of the Constituent Assembly provide much chance for the blocs to go through a period of consolidation. The management of the drafting process and the resolution of conflicts with the executive were conducted largely outside the framework of the bloc organizations. This removed one possible role the bloc could play. Finally, the Constituent Assembly lacked the challenges faced by its successor in 1968-69 in dealing with the executive, challenges that fostered crystallization of a bloc structure in the Lower House.

The Upper House: The Clique as Participation

In contrast to the Constituent Assembly, the organization of legislative blocs in the Upper House reflected the partisan nature of the elections. As such, the organization of the blocs was not characterized by an effort to form broadly based coalitions to preserve an appeal to the mass of the voters, but concentrated instead upon preserving the electoral lists as entities in national politics. Initially, the most promising list that converted into a legislative bloc was the one headed by former General Tran van Don, which received the largest plurality in terms of its votes. Known as the *Nong Cong Binh*, the bloc was constructed to have broad appeal in rural as well as urban areas and for all occupations. Its core membership, the ten deputies elected on the Don list, was evenly divided between

Table 7-1 Composition of bloc alignments in the Constituent Assembly

Background characteristic	Peoples'	Alliance	Democrats	Renaissance	Independents
I. Constituency					
Capital	6	1	5	4	10
I Corps	7	8	–	1	2
II Corps	21	2	5	–	–
III Corps	5	1	5	1	3
IV Corps	4	13	1	6	6
II. Age groups					
25–34	20	1	1	8	5
35–44	16	11	4	–	5
45–54	4	10	5	–	7
55–64	3	3	2	4	4
III. Regional origin					
North Vietnam	14	1	10	1	4
North Central Vietnam	–	1	1	–	3
South Central Vietnam	10	8	2	1	2
South Vietnam	7	14	3	9	10
IV. Ethnic group					
Chinese	2	–	–	–	1
Montagnard	8	1	–	–	–
Khmer	2	–	–	1	1
V. Religion					
Buddhist	19	6	1	6	7

Confucianist	1	3	1	–	3
Hoa Hao	–	10	–	–	–
Cao Dai	1	3	–	2	1
Catholic	11	1	12	1	8
Protestant	–	–	–	3	–
Unavailable	11	1	2	–	2
VI. Occupation					
Agriculture	–	6	1	–	1
Civil servant	9	6	2	1	3
Professions					
Education	7	4	2	6	2
Law	3	1	2	–	3
Medicine	2	–	1	–	1
Journalism	1	1	–	1	–
Business	3	4	4	1	4
Notables	1	2	1	3	2
ARVN	13	1	2	–	4
Other	4	–	1	–	–

northern and southern Vietnamese, included deputies from most religious and occupational groups, and drew support in urban and rural areas—a feature that all other lists did not share. The purpose of this bloc was to create a political organization based upon an ability to balance and coordinate the interests of the diverse groups it claimed to represent. One member of the bloc described its goals in the following way: "Simply to speak of building 'a broader-based government,' without first creating a real political program is meaningless, and will lead only to more intrigue. The Viet Cong have that kind of program, but the Americans have always confused administration with political power. The people who have so far been elected to the hamlet and village councils are only links to the district, provincial, and central governments. They are not representatives of traditionally autonomous local units. There is a lot we could learn from the Viet Cong slogan 'Let us set up the people's authority of the village.' "[9]

In its early days the *Nong Cong Binh* stressed the development of a political identity for all Vietnamese, particularly those who lived in rural areas or had resettled from a rural environment and who not only supported the central government but provided it with a political organization capable of competing with the Viet Cong at the local level. To this end, the bloc aimed at the construction of a new political party built upon the base established for its election in 1967. As one keen observer of Vietnamese politics reported shortly after the election,

> The only slate that shows any promise of developing into a serious party is General Don's. . . . Although [the bloc] has declared itself independent, it will support the government if it feels that the Thieu-Ky regime and a Premier selected after proper consultation with the senators can draw up a workable program and carry it out efficiently. Though Don, who is widely known and liked, headed the slate, its guiding genius is Dr. Dan van Sung, a veteran nationalist and onetime Dai Viet leader who publishes *Chinh-Luan*, perhaps the best Vietnamese-language daily paper in Saigon. Sung is one of the few men in Vietnam who have sought, since Diem's overthrow, to create some kind of new and workable alignment here. One of Sung's closest allies is Tran quoc Buu, the head of the Vietnamese Confederation of Labor. Buu initially had a slate of his own running for the Senate, but it was disqualified on a technicality. The *Nong Cong Binh* ticket finally included one of Buu's labor representatives, and was largely elected through the support of Buu's federation. [The *Nong Cong Binh*'s] aim is to create as wide a base as possible for the [bloc], penetrating deeply into the villages and

embracing all the divided and scattered elements of Vietnamese society....[10]

The formidable task of preserving even the balance of forces with which it was elected, however, was beyond the capabilities of the movement. By the summer of 1969, the membership of the initial slate itself had split into factions, and Dr. Sung had parted with General Don and organized his own legislative bloc. The CVT (the commonly used abbreviation for the Confederation of Labor taken from its French name) had announced the formation of a new political party designed to provide its membership with the political influence it felt was lacking in the Upper and Lower Houses. For his part, General Don launched a new coalition of forces, the National Salvation Front in order to support his expected candidacy for the presidency in 1971.

The fate of the *Nong Cong Binh* movement illustrates the difficulties that most Upper House slates had in converting their electoral coalitions into more enduring political organizations. Only the Catholic slates that did not seek to either develop a broad coalition of interest or appeal (see Table 7-2) remained relatively cohesive during the first two years of the Second Republic. The slates which tried to preserve or expand the basis of their support as essentially new and nationally oriented entities were

Table 7-2 Upper House blocs and their constituencies

Bloc	Average size[a]	Leader	Constituency
Republic Bloc (formerly the Farmers, Workers, Soldiers bloc and later the Revolutionary Farmers and Workers bloc)	20	Tran van Don	Labor, Dai Viet, retired generals, sect and minorities
Social Democratic bloc (established January 1969)	20	Dang van Sung Tran van Lam[b] Nguyen gia Hien	Catholic and Can Lao civil servants
Independents	20		

[a]Size of the blocs has varied on an average of two to three members per month and figures represent an assessment of the bloc's average size over the period of its existence. As of the end of 1969, the blocs appeared to have settled down to the proportions given above.
[b]Succeeded by Huynh van Cao upon appointment as Minister of Foreign Affairs.

unable to do so. Primarily, the failure of new parties to emerge was related to the newness of the "practice" of political mobilization as opposed to political consolidation. While the rhetorical commitment to such a practice had become characteristic of most political organizations in Vietnam, the institutional capacity for its realization remained limited. Popular distrust of all political organizations, including those of the Catholics, and personal disputes within their leadership made the achievement of even a unified superstructure impossible. Most deputies and senators interviewed, for example, attributed the failure of the Don movement to the personal political ambitions of its leader. One senator remarked: "We are tired of seeing many groups all designed to further the interests of one or a few men. When our political groups can demonstrate to the population that they are organized to serve their interests, then the people will be less reluctant to support such organizations." As the nature and structure of the *Nong Cong Binh* bloc crystallized, it became apparent that, rather than functioning as a party in embryo, Don's personalistic direction had reduced the scope of its activities to little more than that of a clique. Indeed, owing to the changes in composition that had taken place by the end of 1969, the bloc came to resemble a parliamentary rather than an electoral organization. "Typically they [parliamentary organizations] are formed within the legislature by successful candidates after they are elected rather than in the constituency by aspiring candidates in order to get elected. Candidates are elected as individuals on the basis of their social or economic status and appeal. The legislative faction or clique then becomes a means of linking them to other political activists, not a means of linking political activists to the masses."[11] The *Nong Cong Binh* became a vehicle for the political interaction of a portion of the elected elite rather than for the political mobilization of the population. In a certain sense, General Don had achieved, within the framework of the Senate, the organization of the clique that had eluded him in the wake of the 1963 coup against Diem.

Those local and regional political leaders who had initially derived much hope from the *Nong Cong Binh* movement, by the end of 1969, felt that the effort to form a national political party had once again fallen victim to the personal ambitions inherent in clique politics. Even those who had joined with Don in the initial effort to form the multiorganization National Salvation Front were increasingly critical of Don's effort to turn the movement into a campaign organization for the 1971 presidential election. One central Vietnamese leader of the movement observed: "Our program is gradually being subverted by General Don. He will only support those aspects of it that will help him get elected. Our programs of social service have not received his support nor have the programs of any of the other components of the Front. As for our part, I do not think that we can continue to appear to the people only as an organization interested in furthering the ambitions of politicians."[12] His comment suggests that political organizations in Vietnam must be linked to the population by more than personalized cadre systems. What is required is the development of interest-serving functions as part of political organizations before support for political goals can be achieved. In the case of both the Constituent Assembly and the Upper House, the legislative blocs failed to develop such a function as an explicit ingredient of their organization.

While the legislative blocs in the Upper House failed to support broadly based national parties, so also little progress was made in the direction of forming an interhouse coalition of deputies, a movement originated in the Senate. Don's movement had initially sought to include those deputies elected to the Lower House with *Nong Cong Binh* support as part of the national organization of the movement. The deputies, however, responded to Don's overtures coolly, and by 1969 most had severed their ties with Don, seeking instead to develop an independent source of support within their provinces. A few had affiliated themselves with Don's National Salvation Front, but privately expressed their dissatisfaction with the use of the organization as a front for Don's presidential ambitions. A second attempt at the formation of an interhouse coalition was launched shortly after Dr. Dang van Sung broke with General Don and organized his own bloc in the Upper House. Despite the initial expectation that Sung's appeal among the Catholic members of the Lower House would be great, no interbloc existed by the end of 1969. A Republican Bloc leader summarized the situation: "The establishment of a National Assembly interbloc has not been realized so far due to different advocations of various blocs as well as to the absence of a number of senators and representatives from the capital."[13] Upper House deputies suggested in interviews that Sung had had a difficult time convincing his colleagues of the merits of the interbloc, partly because of the lack of attendance at bloc meetings and partly because of the disdain with which the senators regarded the irascible and unpredictable Lower House. Catholic deputies, in contrast, perceived clearly the need for such a joint organization, but suggested that they preferred independence from any formal Catholic organization. Of the total number of Catholics elected, almost three-quarters attributed their election to local rather than national Catholic support. One deputy spoke critically: "Neither the leaders of our Catholic parties nor the parties themselves have demonstrated that they are concerned with anything but their own advancement. They have failed to demonstrate their sincerity to the people and the people are more and more reluctant to support them." In addition, almost all deputies interviewed felt that there were more than enough blocs organized that lacked substance. The creation of a superbloc, they felt, would be fruitless under such circumstances. On the whole, individual senators appeared to derive little political benefit from participating in a bloc organization. One senator stated, albeit enigmatically, "The blocs organize the Upper House but not its politics." Indeed, Senators appeared to be more responsive to those political movements which supported their election rather than to the potential that any one bloc possessed to serve as a national political organization.[14]

Legislative Blocs in the Lower House

The organization of legislative blocs in the Lower House reflected the diversity of the political affiliations and objectives of its members. As in the case of the Upper House, a two-bloc system was supported: "The smaller interest groups will have to either unite with each other or align themselves with larger groups in order to have some influence upon the decisions of the House. As this process takes place, we expect to see the development of two blocs, one which can defend the interest of the government and one which will criticize its policies." In the first full term of the House, a multibloc system was anticipated as members shifted from bloc to bloc until each bloc was able to establish its identity and link legislative performance to political posture.

The legislative blocs of the Lower House mirrored the complexity but not the imputed rigidity of the political system. Relatively few of those elected interpreted their election as a mandate limiting their activities or political affiliations to what had been promised during the campaign. Those deputies elected as designated representatives of particular political groups did initially appear bound by certain principles and goals of political action espoused by their sponsoring organizations, but, during the following two years, they seemed to experiment considerably with modes of political organization and actions within the framework of legislative blocs. Indeed, the deputies interviewed cited this aspect of the bloc organizations as the most compelling reason for their participation in them; the blocs helped to organize both the Lower House and its politics.

From the inauguration of the Lower House to the end of 1969, seven blocs were organized. Diagram 7-1 depicts the changes in the bloc structure of the Lower House. Of the four blocs initially organized, only one had a relatively stable membership during the entire period. During their tenure, all of the blocs appeared to function as formal legislative organizations in the sense that they met on a regular basis (biweekly in most cases), organized seminars to provide information for their members on national policies, debated in Lower House sessions, prepared positions on national issues for distribution to the press, and sought to engage members of the executive in a dialogue to clarify both contemporary and long range GVN policies. There was no roll call voting, however, and even the most stable bloc was unable to bind its members to vote a particular way on the floor of the Lower House. Deputies suggested that a bloc's ability to influence a member's vote varied more directly with its size and membership policy. The smaller the bloc, the more intimately the members knew each other and could exert pressure on the members to vote the bloc line. By controlling the size of the bloc, its leadership could expel those who deviated too often from the bloc position and admit only those deputies most likely to act in concert with the bloc. During the two-year period under study, the most disciplined blocs were the smallest ones. Blocs in moderate opposition to the government or in moderate support of it appeared to have the least success in preserving bloc discipline, and, ultimately, of remaining a bloc. Almost all deputies, at one point, were members of a bloc, and more than half of the Lower House had participated in at least two blocs during the period. The initial bloc structure of the House emerged in early 1968 and consisted of four basic groupings that, although under different names in subsequent bloc re-organizations, reflected permanent points around which the deputies clustered.

The Doc Lap Bloc: The Limits of
Catholicism

The *Doc Lap* or Independence Bloc was the most conservative and the most stable one. It consisted mainly of northern Catholic professionals associated with either the Greater Solidarity Force, the Catholic Citizens Bloc, or the Revolutionary *Dai Viet* party. At its apex in April 1968 the bloc had twenty-one members, including a number of Catholics elected without the support of the two Catholic parties who had reported that they were uncertain about making a commitment to any organizations. These deputies also differed with the *Doc Lap*'s hard-line position on

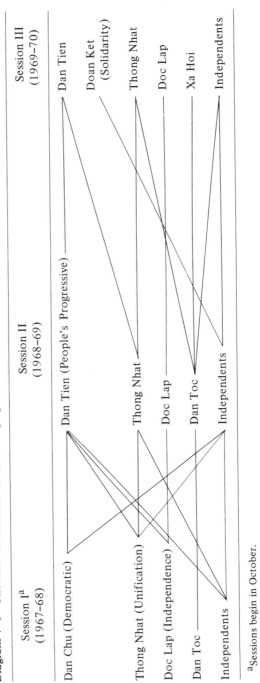

Diagram 7-1 The flow of members in the changing bloc structure of the Lower House

Session I[a] (1967–68)	Session II (1968–69)	Session III (1969–70)
Dan Chu (Democratic)	Dan Tien (People's Progressive)	Dan Tien
Thong Nhat (Unification)	Thong Nhat	Doan Ket (Solidarity)
Doc Lap (Independence)	Doc Lap	Thong Nhat
Dan Toc	Dan Toc	Doc Lap
Independents	Independents	Xa Hoi
		Independents

[a]Sessions begin in October.

negotiations with the Viet Cong and with its opposition to a rapprochement with the Buddhists. By 1969 the membership of the bloc had leveled off at seventeen and by the beginning of the third term, included only those Catholics linked to the parties and willing to support the bloc's position on the negotiation and the rapprochement issues. In addition, four new members had joined the bloc. One was a recent convert to Catholicism and a leader of the newly created *Nhan Xa* party. The three others were members of the VNQDD that had, in the early 1960's, struggled against the Diem regime and were imprisoned for it. Subsequently they adopted a hard line against those advocating negotiation with the Viet Cong. Rather than appeal to all Catholic deputies, the bloc limited its membership based on adherence to bloc positions. Voting against the line was tolerated only on issues such as land reform and taxation and never on issues relating to peace or to cooperation with the Buddhists.

The purpose of the *Doc Lap* bloc, as outlined in its literature, was to bring together "all representatives having an independent spirit and putting the national interests above those of the individual or party . . . to struggle for Freedom, Democracy and Social Justice."[15] The "national interests" referred to here apparently are those involving the broader questions of peace and the place of the Viet Cong in Vietnamese political life. One bloc member observed: "While I claim that our bloc is more disciplined than all the others, fundamentally, the most important elements determining each member's behavior are the interests and opinions of his constituency. And I have opposed the bloc position on several occasions to reflect the interests of my constituents." In terms of the bloc's principles, that such deviation may take place is recognized by adherence to the principle of "Collective Leadership, Individual Execution," in which the "seminar is the usual means of promoting understanding and finding out common policies."[16] The bloc seminar meets once each week and is designed to balance member's responses to their constituent's interests with the bloc's position on national issues. One bloc member described the process: "We meet once a week on Tuesday's in regular session, and we have occasional special meetings to deal with crises as they arise. The bloc's position is determined by the vote of the majority, but individual positions are sometimes dictated by other criteria. Thus, the bloc tends to vote for a position as a group in the House only on those issues on which we agree to accept the outcome of the voting in the bloc meetings."

This development of positions, however, was not viewed by some early

Doc Lap members as sufficient evidence of the bloc's intentions to formulate a specific legislative program. Another deputy, who later left the bloc, summarized its direction: "I helped to organize the bloc but then decided to leave it due to its lack of discipline, the lack of desire on the part of the members to formulate a long-term program of goals, and its lack of close contacts with the people. Many of the bloc members were attracted to it not because of their desire to formulate such a program but because of their involvement with the old political parties and groups which I believe lack any genuine basis of popular support. It became clear to me that the bloc was going to preserve the image of older parties rather than try to work to change them." This view of the Catholic parties tends to corroborate similar views expressed by Catholic leaders. *Doc Lap* members, in contrast, dispute this view and suggest that the principal reason for the bloc's apparent lack of discipline is that members respond first to the needs of their constituencies, and then differ considerably from issue to issue. The bloc's consensus, in the view of these members, is that deviations based upon constituent interests must be tolerated. Nevertheless, the *Doc Lap* bloc did not develop a definite legislative program beyond the level of the generalities contained in its statement of principles. Thus, the bloc acted in concert only on issues with considerable consensus, such as the Paris Talks. On others, it permitted considerable latitude, especially where constituent interests were strong. The shared identity of the bloc's members thus worked both to facilitate the development of bloc positions as well as to recognize the need to accommodate deviation where warranted.

The Dan Chu Bloc: The Limits of Progovernmentalism

To the left of the *Doc Lap* bloc, but still right of center, is the *Dan Chu* or Democratic Bloc. This bloc considered itself the government's majority, and until its demise included forty to fifty deputies. At its peak of fifty-two members in January 1968 the bloc included deputies from the ethnic minorities, religious sects of the Mekong Delta, and southern and central Vietnamese civil servants. At its demise, the membership declined by more than twenty deputies, reflecting the disaffection of some of the minority deputies and most of the southern civil servants.

As the largest bloc, the *Dan Chu* was also the least disciplined. It was able to issue fewer declarations on national issues than any other bloc, and, while it met on a regular basis, it was never able to achieve the consensus that characterized the *Doc Lap* bloc. The basic division of the

Dan Chu bloc was over support for the various personalities in the executive. Thus it became a fairly common practice to "raid" the membership of the *Dan Chu* bloc for support in Lower House elections and for votes on controversial issues. Bloc leaders also suggested that, while they had worked to create a progovernment majority, their efforts were hampered by not only the divided loyalties of its members but also by a lack of interest on the part of the executive. This problem became particularly acute with the demise of Vice President Ky at the same time that President Thieu expressed little interest in the *Dan Chu* bloc by refusing to help it or any bloc in the development of a legislative program. *Dan Chu* leaders, for their part, tended to refuse to cooperate with Thieu's adviser on legislative affairs, pharmacist Nguyen cao Thang, because of his disdain for the Lower House and his method of dealing with it.

The tentative commitment of the members of the *Dan Chu* bloc also contributed to its lack of discipline. Many members suggested that the reason for forming the bloc was to enable the government to demonstrate that its policies were supported by a majority of the legislature. As such, this commitment did not necessarily mean a commitment to any particular executive. This was particularly true under the increasing authoritarianism of Thieu. Rather, their commitment represented a generalized belief that the government must be supported if it were to deal effectively with Washington and Hanoi. For most bloc members this meant solidarity on questions relating to foreign affairs but not on domestic policies. Had the executive sought to court this group, its leaders believed, the cohesion of the members might have been extended to include support of government policies. Lacking such cooperation and support, however, the leaders acknowledged that the construction of such a large bloc on a permanent basis was virtually impossible.

The *Dan Chu* was succeeded by the *Dan Tien* bloc, organized to create a progovernment majority once the Thieu-Ky conflict had ended and the US had begun to pressure the government to expand the Paris Talks. Almost half (seventeen out of forty-two) of the original *Dan Chu* members were not affiliated with the *Dan Tien* bloc because of their disaffection with recent government policies and the growth of Ky supporters in other blocs. The *Dan Tien* bloc drew new members (seven out of seventeen) from among those who had previously remained independent, and it drew deputies who had moved away from left of center blocs to support the government against US pressures. One *Dan Tien* member explained his motivation.

I was formerly considered an independent but one with definite sympathies for some of the opposition groups in the House. But when the Midway meeting between Presidents Thieu and Johnson occurred and when shortly thereafter the Democratic presidential candidate Humphrey made his "risks for peace" speech, I became convinced that it was most important for Thieu, as President of the Republic, to demonstrate that he had the support of the country for his position on negotiations. The best way to do this was through a government—but not necessarily a pro-Thieu—bloc and that is why I joined the Dan Tien bloc. I consider my action aimed not at demonstrating support for one man but rather as support for a noncommunist government in the South.

Like most of his colleagues, this deputy also explained that he was opposed not to peace or to the achievement of peace through negotiations but to the treatment of the government that made it appear as a puppet of the United States. The deputy suggested that it was widely known that President Johnson did not consult with President Thieu in announcing the partial bombing halt in March 1968 and that "unless allies consult each other on strategic questions of great importance one ally is bound to appear to dominate the other."

All deputies, however, acknowledged that cohesion within such a large bloc was difficult to achieve and that its members still acted as individuals:

Whether or not support is forthcoming for the President depends upon the specific issue involved. Like its predecessor, this bloc still lacks cohesion and unity. On controversial matters the bloc reflects the "natural groupings" that exist within it. For example, on the issue of peace and the current [that is, July 1969] proposals offered by the President to the NLF, the bloc is divided between the northern Catholics who oppose a soft peace policy despite the fact that they usually side with the President and the southern and central Buddhists who, while they usually are opposed to the presidential point of view on most issues, tend to favor a soft peace policy. In the case of the land reform bill, the split occurred between the landowners of the bloc and those who considered themselves to be members of the proletariat.

Like that of its predecessor, moreover, the leadership of the *Dan Tien* bloc was not aided in its effort to develop bloc censensus by the attitude of the executive they sought to support. As one leader observed:

We have tried to follow the practice of reciprocity in our dealings with the President, a principle of action upon which all of our members are agreed. We must demand from Thieu a concession on his part in return for our support. If, for example, we will support him in the area of foreign policy, he must agree to take into account our viewpoints on domestic policies such as taxation. Unfortunately this has not worked. The President has not responded positively to any of our invitations for him to address the members of the bloc although he has invited the leaders to visit him at the Palace. When we did so we argued that it was not we he had to convince to support him but the rest of our colleagues. The President, however, was not in a very serious mood that day.

As a result of consistent efforts to get Thieu to recognize the importance of the bloc, the leadership was able to have one of Thieu's advisers appear at several bloc meetings. "Mr. Thang comes to the bloc meeting with President Thieu's reasons for submitting a particular bill or wanting it passed, but Thang will not negotiate on anything. He usually just states the President's reasons and then leaves with a request for our support. In certain cases, however, he has offered certain members of the bloc money in exchange for their votes. Mr. Thang is not respected by the Lower House or even among the members of the progovernment bloc." Lacking consensus and without anything but the most demeaning support from the executive, most leaders of the *Dan Tien* bloc were not sanguine about its ability to function as a meaningful progovernment force within the Lower House.

Observers of progovernment blocs in the Lower House have suggested that difficulties stem from the lack of common interests that might generate national political parties. In fact, the *Dan Tien* bloc has also been the only bloc in the Lower House to disavow the need to create a political party based upon its membership. This is partly due to the existence of the natural groupings that both reflect the class identities of its members and are reaffirmed by affiliations with established political parties and organizations. Some deputies felt that an effort to organize a party would entail reconciling too many diverse groups. At best, they suggested, the formation of a progovernment majority would become a long-term goal of the bloc. *Dan Tien* deputies also suggested that, in their view, the GVN needed stability at the top.

This need is created by the war and the demands it is making on the government to operate swiftly and effectively. We attach less of a priority to building a firm base for the government upward from the people since this would not, right now, improve the ability of the government to function. Moreover, most of the people vote for Lower House deputies based not on their cadre organizations among the population but on the deputy's ability to determine who the local influentials are and then win their support. These local influentials, in turn, ask their circle of friends to vote for the deputy. The development of a more organized party system will come in the future as we prepare to compete politically with the VC. Now we have to concentrate on making up what we have lost by having so much instability at the top levels of government since the fall of Diem.

The picture which emerges of the *Dan Tien* bloc is one of general commitment to supporting the government but with a lack of organizational discipline and incentives to do so.

The Opposition Blocs: Doctrines of Political Organization in Transition

The *Thong Nhat* or Unification Bloc is left of center and constitutes the first bloc mildly opposed to the government. This bloc underwent the greatest internal change. Originally it was a coalition of deputies of the various VNQDD, Cao Dai, and Hoa Hao factions that, in the Upper House election, had attempted to combine in an unsuccessful effort to elect a slate. From its initial membership of fifteen deputies, the *Thong Nhat* bloc had grown to a peak of twenty-nine members in October 1968, when its fortunes were linked to its support of the Huong cabinet. A year later, membership declined to fifteen members. From an initial position of moderate opposition to the executive, the *Thong Nhat* had crossed the center position to support the Huong government and then subsequently recrossed the line after the political demise of Huong. Less than half (seven out of fifteen) of its original members were left by the end of 1969. Six of its eight new members reported ties with the militant Buddhists. This change eliminated members of one VNQDD faction and one faction of the Hoa Hao and pared down the remaining faction members of both organizations. Their replacement, however, by deputies in sympathy with the militant Buddhists did not necessarily indicate that the *Thong Nhat* bloc had become pro-An Quang; bloc members explicitly suggested that they were not trying to make the bloc into an An Quang party or affiliate. Other deputies, as well as An Quang leaders, also indicated that the bloc was not officially sanctioned or its formation solicited by the An Quang hierarchy.[17] Moreover, not all An Quang deputies in the house had joined the bloc as a number preferred to disassociate themselves with any bloc.

The impact of the *Thong Nhat* bloc's transformation, was, by the end of 1969, unclear, as were its intentions to use the bloc to introduce a formal, secular An Quang interest group into national politics.

The *Dan Toc* or People's Bloc dissolved in the fall of 1969 was also left of center. Organized with the inauguration of the Lower House, the *Dan Toc* bloc contained most of the Lower House's militant Buddhists and remained relatively stable in its membership. The group also included a number of deputies aligned with the Movement for the Renaissance of the South, which later formed the core of a separate bloc. While this bloc was generally in opposition to government policies, its membership did not include those most outspoken on the floor of the House. Rather, it tended to work more to aid the Buddhists who, by the middle of 1968, had shifted from attempting to bring about the fall of governments to seeking more effective participation in the decision-making processes of the government. This shift in Buddhist attitudes toward the government was attributed by all deputies interviewed to the realization that, as a result of the Viet Cong occupation of Hue during the Tet offensive of 1968, the future of Buddhism in the south depended upon the future viability of the government. In addition, deputies noted that by working through the legislature they were able to do more toward ending government repression of Buddhist leaders than they could by remaining outside its framework.

The outspoken criticism of the government that most expected the Buddhists to articulate was replaced by a behind-the-scenes effort to bring pressure to bear on the government to cease arresting Buddhist leaders and to release those it had imprisoned. Of all the blocs, the *Dan Toc* focused least upon contemporary and controversial issues in its biweekly meetings and instead discussed future government policies toward economic development and social welfare. This emphasis reflected the intellectual character of some of the bloc's members who maintained that their principal service lay in their ability to assess future needs rather than to engage in floor fights. Behind such concerns also lay a certain essential caution that most bloc members had in regard to their public activities. "If we always challenge the government then we would face the risk of being ignored when we requested that the constitutional rights of the Buddhists not be violated by false arrest or detention without trial or, what would have been worse, the government would have redoubled its efforts to repress other Buddhists in order to silence us." The *Dan Toc* bloc thus recognized the dangers inherent in proclaiming itself the focus of the opposition in the House, particularly when there were other deputies and other blocs that could act as the voice of opposition with much less risk than could Buddhists.

The dissolution of the *Dan Toc* bloc in the fall of 1969 was ascribed to three causes. Most deputies in the Lower House believed that its dissolution was to disassociate it from the behavior of one founding member, Pham the Truc, a young, former Buddhist struggler from Binh Thuan province. Regarded as one of the "most liked deputies" by his colleagues in the House,[18] Truc "defected" during the course of a visit to Japan. There, in June 1969, Truc declared in a press conference convened by antiwar and leftist groups that he was in favor of an immediate end to the war, the immediate withdrawal of all American and allied military forces, the overthrow of the Thieu government, and the opening of the government to full Buddhist participation. For these remarks Truc was later accused of being a communist by Thieu and subsequently tried and sentenced to death *in absentia* by a military court. Members of the *Dan Toc* bloc did not approve of what Truc did or of the things he advocated. At a special session of the bloc it was decided to dissolve the bloc to demonstrate that as a group they did not condone Truc.

A smaller circle of deputies maintained in interviews that the *Dan Toc* bloc was dissolved as a result of pressure from the executive which viewed Truc's behavior as symbolic of the opposition to the regime harbored by most militant Buddhists. According to these deputies, Nguyen cao Thang bribed a number of *Dan Toc* members so that under the rules of the House the bloc fell below the number of members required for formal status. In light of the general feeling of all *Dan Toc* members toward the activities of Mr. Thang, it was highly unlikely that they would have been susceptible to such a bribe. Still it is possible that Thang threatened a number of members with arrest and imprisonment on the grounds that they were Communist sympathizers should they fail to get reelected (and thereby lose their parliamentary immunity), a development which Thang certainly could have engineered.

A third explanation for the dissolution of the bloc lies in the changing nature of Buddhist opposition within the House. While many deputies expected the *Dan Toc* members to work closely together after the dissolution of the bloc, this was not what actually happened. Some *Dan Toc* members aligned themselves with those seeking to form a new bloc to represent the interests of the southern Buddhists which later emerged as the *Xa Hoi* bloc; other *Dan Toc* deputies entered the more ideologically moderate *Thong Nhat* bloc, while still others chose not to affiliate with any and declared themselves independent. Surely these divisions of *Dan Toc* members after the bloc's dissolution existed while the bloc was still operative. As early as the summer of 1968 bloc members indicated that they had thought about leaving the *Dan Toc*. This explanation suggests that the incentives and commitments which initially brought the *Dan Toc* bloc into existence had changed over time. The Truc incident provided, in this view, the occasion for its formal dissolution but not the reason for it. Rather, the opposition deputies in the Lower House, by the beginning of the third session, had come to differ over the means of effective opposition to government policies. Some of these deputies, those most active and most involved with constituency problems in central Vietnam, tended to feel that individual action was the most efficacious and aligned themselves with no group. Those most active in constituency work in the southern area tended to seek an alignment with other activist southerners both in an effort to improve their constituency service and to organize a southern Buddhist party. Finally, those deputies most involved in Saigon politicking and in the affairs of the House tended to seek alignment with like-minded deputies remaining in the *Thong Nhat* bloc.

Two new blocs organized in the early part of the Lower House's third session also reflected the diversity of the opposition. Both blocs were essentially southern-oriented, and their leaders have suggested that, while distinct as organizational entities, they have worked closely in the past and expect to do so in the future. The first of these new organizations, the *Doan Ket* or Solidarity Bloc, is composed of deputies who had previously remained independent (six out of its total membership of twenty) and of the deputies elected to ethnic minority seats who had previously belonged to the *Dan Chu* bloc. The bulk of the minority deputies were of Khmer origin from the delta (eight out of the eleven minority deputies), one was the Assembly's only Cham deputy, and two were from the montagnard provinces in the central highlands. In addition to these officially recognized minorities, two ethnic Vietnamese deputies in the bloc developed strong ties with the Chinese community in Saigon. The grouping of all Khmer deputies in one bloc for the first time reflected the united front developed as a result of the presidential decision to revoke the status of the Khmers as an officially protected minority (carrying with it certain educational, electoral and occupational benefits). Their claim to work closely with the other newly created bloc, the *Khoi Xa Hoi*, is probably also based upon the fact that *Xa Hoi* deputies' newspapers and weekly political journals had consistently supported the Khmer claim to be a minority in opposition to the presidential point of view. Moreover, prior to the presidential decision, Khmer deputies tended to support the government as they traditionally had done. Their participation in the *Doan Ket* bloc, coupled to their newly developed tie with the southern Buddhist opposition, thus suggests a basic shift of the Khmer and minority position in general. Other minorities tended to view the presidential decision on the Khmers as an indication of the future direction of government policy toward all minorities and made similar shifts.

The occupational composition of the bloc suggests the thrust of its opposition and the nature of the changes the bloc sought to make. The *Doan Ket* bloc members were civil servants who attained relatively high-level positions in administration of their provinces or region. In most cases the government officials had risen rather rapidly in rank under the early Ky government, and by 1965 most reported that they realized they had advanced about as far as possible based on promotions and moderate to enthusiastic support for the then Premier Nguyen cao Ky. Generally disgruntled by changing political fortunes, which froze them into position while they were still relatively young, most reported that they ran for election to leave government service. Participation in the Lower House appeared to channel their personal frustration into a common desire to work for changes in the assignment and promotion systems in the civil service. It was likely that much of the bloc's activities would be directed toward the drafting of new legislation to foster such administrative reforms.[19] In contrast to the apparent mellowing of civilian officials, the one military officer that joined the bloc actually campaigned on a platform of reforms for the civil and military services including demands for a settlement of the war, a review of the promotion and assignment system in the military, improvements in living standards and allowances for military personnel, the establishment of cooperatives and commissaries for laborers and civil servants, and the use of Lower House budgetary powers as the mechanism to implement such reforms. Needless to say, none of these reforms have thus far been realized.

Until recently bloc organizations have been too unstable to develop specific legislative programs or too preoccupied with crises and controversies involving the future role of the Lower House. By 1969, signs of a change were, however, apparent to some deputies, in particular those of the *Doan Ket* and the *Xa Hoi* blocs. Most, for example, believe that, while it is by no means secure, the legislature has demonstrated that it has a role in the formulation of national policy. More significant, deputies feel that the blocs have begun to organize more than parochial interests as deputies have developed specific interests in and programs for governmental and political reforms. Most deputies believe that, in the future, the construction of legislative programs will provide the framework within which the difficulties of organizing legislative blocs and political parties can be overcome.

The newest bloc in the Lower House, the *Xa Hoi*, like the *Doan Ket*, shares a common conception of social reform and political action. The *Xa Hoi* or Society Bloc was formally established in late November 1969 although it had existed in de facto form since the inauguration of the Lower House. The core of *Xa Hoi* leadership came from those deputies who had been associated with an informal New Society group in 1967 and with several earlier movements such as the Movement for the Renaissance of the South in the 1966 Constitutent Assembly and other groups with appeal to the southern Buddhist teachers and civil servants like the *Tan Dai Viet*. The New Society group did not emerge as a bloc in 1967 because it lacked the requisite minimum number of members under the rules of the Lower House. Bloc leaders described their informal organization in 1967 as one based largely upon the affiliation of a number of deputies who were friends or who had come together during the course of their careers. One of its leaders suggested that, in 1967, "we were a natural grouping based upon friendship and mutual respect that had grown out of our work in the past." During the course of the next two years the New Society group sought to operationalize two elements that would transform the group into a legislative bloc and possibly a national political organization.

First, the founders of the New Society group felt it important to establish a working relationship with other deputies in the House and the political interests those deputies represented. As a group of southern Buddhist intellectuals, however, their appeal to non-Buddhist organizations was limited despite substantial individual experience in working closely with Catholic political organizations and local Catholic leaders. A similar lack of success greeted their efforts to establish a link with central Vietnamese Buddhists who either were in sympathy with An Quang or members of the nationalist parties. An Quang's reluctance stemmed from the unsettled nature of the religion's political policy which, while it did not preclude ties with other groups, discouraged the development of any specific working relationship from 1967-68. In addition, An Quang deputies appeared less certain of the legitimacy of the legislature since it was formally a part of the government. Consequently, they were largely undecided about the proper extent of their participation in legislative activities beyond those that contributed directly to their goal of the release of Buddhist leaders imprisoned by the government. The central Vietnamese nationalist parties, in contrast, appeared to have no qualms about participating in the newly created constitutional system, but their leaders were not committed to linking their groups with any others in the legislature or the larger political system.[20]

In response to the coolness with which the concept of joint efforts was met, the New Society group left the issue open in its negotiations with other groups. New Society deputies sought to project a basic posture of support to those groups they felt shared common interests and goals. They thereby attempted to establish a record of sympathy and support to be used to reopen the coalescence issue. By supporting other groups' candidates for election to House offices and by lending their moral support both on the house floor and in the newspapers owned by members of the group, New Society deputies sought to strengthen intergroup cooperation on specific issues. The New Society group thus attempted to demonstrate that diverse groups which were not traditionally aligned could develop meaningful bases of cooperation to serve diverse interests without adversely affecting any particular group's autonomy or independence of action.

The New Society approach constituted also a novel aspect of political organizing in Vietnam. The deputies, while aware of the present and continuing importance of traditional identities, sought to go beyond such parochial interests. New Society deputies reasoned that regional suspicions were probably based upon traditional enmities and misinformation. Once it could be demonstrated that such suspicions were groundless, through cooperation on particular issues, a principal obstacle to greater collaboration in the political arena would be removed. This perspective on political organizing and the value of regionalism was directly related to the experience that a number of the New Society deputies had with community action projects and reflected an effort to transform the concept into a political doctrine, the second feature of the group's activities from 1967-1969.

The concept of community action employed by the New Society group emphasized the ability of diverse groups and of even traditionally hostile groups to work together for a set of common goals of graduated significance. Short-term goals designed to bring short-term results were designed to give participants and leaders a sense of efficacy and confidence that then encouraged the development of longer-term plans. Ultimately the responsibility for the creation of goals and programs was directly passed on to the actual participants. Translated into political terms, this doctrine of community political action suggested that, by a series of effective demonstrations of how diverse groups can work together to achieve political ends, common ground could be found for groups to undertake a task as complex as that of organizing a national party composed of diverse elements. The core of the leadership of the New Society group originated with their association in a community action project during Saigon's greatest growth when the city's slum population doubled in less than a year with the influx of war refugees.

The four key members of the New Society group in the Lower House were among the legislature's youngest members, and all were drawn into a more active role in government at the request of General Duong van Minh, the leader of the first government that emerged in the wake of the 1963 coup against Diem. All of the deputies except one who was engaged in a medical practice were either in the army or in one of the district administrations at the time they were called to Saigon by General Minh. Some of the deputies had known Minh personally or had grown up with him in the same Mekong Delta town. Minh asked each of the deputies to work to infuse a spirit of youthfulness and dynamism in their particular ministries, and the fall from power of General Minh did not mean the removal of these deputies from their assignments. Through their association in the ministries, they decided to form a group devoted to developing the morale of the people in the countryside. In 1964, however, this goal changed when they realized the impossibility of providing adequate security for the cadre of the "development groups" they proposed to send to the rural areas to teach the population techniques of self-help and community action. Instead of focusing upon the rural areas, the group decided to concentrate upon the cities since the war promised to force large numbers of rural inhabitants from their lands into the cities. The area they selected for a community action program was in one of Saigon's outlying districts where rural migrants congregated.

The district they chose was marked by chronic poverty. Detached from the body of Saigon proper by a network of rivers and canals, District 8 had long been a haven for vice and crime in the capital and was one of the areas that the crime syndicate of the 1950's, the Binh Xuyen, had made their headquarters.[21] One of the deputies described the site in the early

1960's before the migrants had come. "In 1963 the district had about 49,000 persons and was the least-developed area of Saigon. Aside from the 15,000 northern Catholics who resettled there under the leadership of Father Hoang Quynh[22] and the 2,000 to 5,000 Catholics who moved to this area after the district in which they were living had become insecure due to the war in the delta, most of the population consisted of taxi girls, bandits, thieves and other unsavory characters. Housing was poor and sanitation almost nil. District 8 was also the garbage dump for all of Saigon and it was not uncommon for people to build make-shift houses in between 8-10 foot high piles of refuse."[23] In 1964-65 the population of this district alone increased to 300,000 persons. In 1962, approximately 57 percent of the city's population had been born in Saigon, but by 1968, in contrast, most sample surveys revealed that probably less than 6 percent of the population then living in Saigon had been born there.[24] The influx of so many persons to a city originally designed for no more than 500,000 persons but which now held almost six times that amount taxed the ability of the government to meet effectively the needs associated with such rapid growth.

The problems of those areas already chronically poverty-stricken were acute. An American official who organized aid once the District 8 program was established observed the conditions in 1965 when he visited the area as an International Voluntary Service volunteer.

In the crowded slums, families huddled in makeshift huts along rancid alleys and canals and on stilts over fetid marshes and pools. Public latrines were inadequate; rubbish was strewn on the streets; and drainage ditches were clogged and coated with black slime. Outbreaks of bubonic plague and cholera were common and nearly 200,000 cases of tuberculosis were known. Water had to be trucked into the outlying slum areas and was sold to the people at exhorbitant prices. There were insufficient schools, dispensaries, parks, day nurseries, and reading rooms for the multiplying population. . . . Gangs of vagrants, many of whom were in their early teens, freely vandalized stores and homes. . . . Apathy was high and morale low. No sense of community or national cohesiveness was felt; instead there was a mutual suspicion between the people and their government. Realizing this, nests of propagandists and terrorists had intensified their activities in the slums which the police could not control.[25]

Government development programs and American assistance, characteristically weak in the field of urban problems in Vietnam, barely touched the surface of the problems of Saigon or of District 8 in particular. Indeed, the only government presence in the district were the 1,000 national policemen assigned there who rarely ventured out beyond a few main streets since the area was regarded as being under almost total control of the Viet Cong.

The New Society deputies recognized that the people who had migrated to the district lacked the ability to help themselves as even the few Catholic priests, generally regarded as community leaders, reported:

> The people who flooded into District 8 were like plants violently torn up by the roots and thrown into a new setting. Like such plants many of them had a poor chance of survival; many had lost all their roots, or most had been damaged in the process of "transplanting." The population of District 8 was generally without roots in the rural communities from which they had been expelled by the war, and the cleavages between ways of life were most apparent in what emerged as a generation gap. Parents were no longer able to control their children, and since there were no high schools and few primary schools in the district the children had no formal teachers but many informal teachers in the ways of crime, vice, and so forth. Children no longer worshiped their ancestors and were cut off from that tradition since the parents no longer lived off the land. The war produced not only an urban problem but a sharp cleavage between the generations as well. And in the process, the village system which was and still is the basis of life in Vietnam was utterly destroyed. The community therefore did not function as one but was like what your philosopher Hobbes referred to when he described a life that was really a war of every individual against every other individual.

Although a sense of community was needed, the New Society realized that there could be no reliance upon a preexisting community or even the memory of community from life in the countryside. A new and common set of interests among diverse, uprooted people had to be developed. From these interests, goals would have to be developed, and, as the population worked to achieve them, it was hoped that the people would come to have confidence in their ability to improve their lives.

In the context of Vietnamese society, such a cooperative venture was a novelty, and novel means were required. Leaders of what was called the New Life Development Project realized that, if the people were going to build more permanent dwelling units, they would have to do so without any family knowing in which house they would reside. If the people knew their houses, it was argued, they would cease work on any other family's house once their own was completed. The project instituted a system whereby all houses underwent reconstruction and renovation, and a family could take possession of a house only after all houses were completed. Individual houses were chosen by lots. The project leaders similarly had to take possession of any materials provided by the government for homes that had been destroyed in the floods and by the war since, if individual families received supplies directly, they would sell them on the black market. To institute such community cooperation, the leadership of the project realized that they would have to project a particular image to the population and "blend in with the population of the district." Cadres who after the first month were still called by their formal titles such as Mr. Doctor or Mr. Engineer were considered ineffective since they were, presumably, unable to deemphasize social differences and were removed from their positions. Project cadre also had to demonstrate to the population that their energy was entirely devoted to the people. Finally, the cadre sought out those with potential to be community leaders and involved them in the planning process. Ultimately these individuals were elected to a development council and gradually took over all the major functions that were the initial responsibility of the project's founders.

The goal, as one of the project leaders described it, was "to help the people develop confidence in themselves. If we could get the people to trust us initially, then we could plan effective self-help projects. The payoff from these projects would be the development of the confidence of the people to improve their lives. The sooner they realized that by working together they could achieve many things that working alone they could not, the sooner we moved to the background. Now we primarily work only to bring funds from the outside into the area; all the planning of projects and control of their execution is done by the people themselves." While this digression is not aimed at assessing the success of the project, it is important to note that the concept of community action or community creation and then action proved to be a rather dramatic success. And the successfulness of the concept led the New Society deputies to apply it to the Vietnamese political community at large. Thus, in the Lower House these deputies sought to create a community of political interests that would demonstrate to diverse political groups the benefits of cooperative efforts. And the behavior of all the New Society deputies is strikingly similar to that adopted in the New Life Development Project. All have sought to adopt a low profile in the Lower House that permitted them to work effectively behind the scenes and most deputies interviewed suggested that this way of working had gained the New Society group much respect and cooperation from deputies and blocs.

Many members of the *Xa Hoi* bloc who were not associated with the New Life Development Project reported that they had similar experiences with community action projects in their own constituencies. Some, as former provincial officials, had made the concept the basis for their distribution of government aid and assistance to refugee groups and for public works projects in general. In describing his particular approach one deputy stated: "The government should not build schools for the people; the people should build them for themselves. In my province we resisted the temptation to promise the people new schools or other public improvements and required that the people must decide themselves what they wanted. Then they would come to us with their requests and we would give them the necessary supplies, money, or technical assistance. But even at that point we required that they must take an active part in the project by contributing their own labor. When the Viet Cong attacked these projects, the people defended them. In other provinces when the Viet Cong attack a school or a well the people do not defend them since they feel that such things belong to the government and not the people." Deputies in the bloc who had graduated from the National Institute of Administration, similarly, felt that community involvement was essential in both development projects and in efforts to politically organize the population. One deputy with links to the *Cap Tien* Movement suggested that "For a long time politics in Vietnam was based solely on individual personalities who wanted to create their own movements but who had no conception of how to develop common interests among their members. Now we realize the need to develop such common interests, and this is a principal technique of our organization." The philosophy of the *Xa Hoi* bloc seeks to translate community action into political action based upon the creation of communities of interests between political groups. Their doctrine of political organization is also and uniquely a prescription for political community.

The political activities of the bloc during 1968-1969 had a two-fold impact. First, the group sought to translate its prior involvement in particular communities into political support. From all accounts this was a slow process. The deputies of the District 8 project (two of the original four ran from this district) reported that the people generally tend to be suspicious of any political organization since, in the past, none have demonstrated that they actually work for the interests of the people.[26] In place of efforts to directly mobilize the population behind a political movement, the *Xa Hoi* deputies have tended to concentrate their activities on constituency service as a means of demonstrating that legislators can benefit the community by assisting the population in a way development councils cannot. The effort here has been to work toward developing the population's confidence in a system of government and to make clear the need for the community to be effectively represented. Increasingly, it was hoped that the community's interest in being represented would lead them to realize the need for effective political mobilization.

Similar difficulties have been reported by those deputies who ran outside District 8 and who were not involved in the New Life Development Project. And a similar approach has been employed, namely, the use of constituency service to demonstrate the values of effective representation. A greater degree of direct political mobilization, however, has been possible due to the existence of political organizations in the provinces where *Xa Hoi* deputies were elected in contrast to the lack of any such organizations in District 8. There have been regular monthly meetings in these provinces where four to eight *Xa Hoi* members attend as political advisers to the local leadership. *Xa Hoi* deputies also sought to develop working relationships with other groups within the Lower House as suggested previously. The issues they concentrated upon have been those with potentially great significance to other political organizations. One such issue, for example, involved the government's Phoenix program,[27] where people were arrested and summarily detained as Viet Cong suspects. In reality the program had been corrupted in many provinces; only a bribe wins a victim's release. Leaders of all political groups interviewed expressed their concern with the impact of this program and their inability to help the people arrested until it was made the subject of a formal investigation in the Lower House. The investigation was launched by members of the *Xa Hoi* group who, notwithstanding their concern for the injustices of the program, also realized the significance of their actions for all groups trying to work to end such injustices. The result of such activities, of course, was not calculated by the *Xa Hoi* bloc in terms of immediate gains but as part of a process designed to demonstrate the efficacy of cooperative action within the legislature.[28]

Bloc Competition and Cohesion

It is difficult to estimate the cohesion of each bloc beyond the remarks of deputies. In its three sessions to date, there has been only one (unrecorded) role call vote taken, and it was on a procedural question.[29]

The only measure of bloc cohesiveness is, consequently, crude. All blocs in the House competed to have their members elected to the secretariat and the permanent committees' leadership,[30] and it was presumed that all blocs agreed in their caucus on what committees and positions they would seek. The consensus of caucuses was that each bloc would try to gain as many offices as possible. Thus each bloc appeared to compete for the same objective, and the measure devised to indicate cohesion involved a count of the number of its members that each bloc succeeded in electing. Votes for the House officers, of course, were made by means of secret ballots which afforded members the opportunity to deviate from bloc candidates without their colleagues knowing it.

Table 7-3 presents the bloc competition of House officers for each of the three sessions. In terms of aggregate numbers the most successful group in electing deputies to House positions was in reality a "nongroup" composed of those deputies that at the beginning of each October session were listed as independent deputies and won a total of thirty-seven seats. Since, however, the independents represented those awaiting new alignments, it is possible to project deputies' subsequent alignments to provide a structure to the independents' apparent success. When these projections were made, only three deputies who at the time of their election were independents remained so throughout each subsequent session. The progovernment majority blocs, the *Dan Chu* and its successor the *Dan Tien*, appeared to do the best of any bloc in winning a total of thirty-three positions. They suffered, however, a sharp decline in success shortly after the *Dan Chu* bloc was dissolved and in the second session elected only seven of their members to positions compared with twelve in the 1967-68 and fourteen in the 1969-70 sessions. This decline was probably due to the confusion surrounding its dissolution. Of the committees which deputies regarded as most important, namely, Economics, Budget and Finance, Defense, and Interior, however, the majority bloc did less well than it had hoped and captured only five out of a total of twenty-three positions across all of the sessions. Moreover, the bloc was also unsuccessful in capturing the Secretariat, gaining only six of a possible twenty offices. The performance of the progovernment majority bloc in House elections tends to confirm the thesis advanced by both its members and its critics: that the bloc lacked cohesion and the ability to discipline its members. Its performance also tends to confirm the suggestion that other blocs were able to raid the membership of the majority bloc in House elections and presumably also in voting on substantive issues.

When the success of the majority bloc is coupled to that of the further

Table 7-3 Success of the blocs in Lower House elections

Office	Controlling bloc 1967–68	Controlling bloc 1968–69	Controlling bloc 1969–70
Secretariat			
Chairman	Dan Chu	Independent	Independent
1st Vice-Chairman	Independent[a]	Independent[a]	Independent[a]
2nd Vice-Chairman	Dan Chu	Independent[a]	Doc Lap
Secretary-General	Doc Lap	Independent	Dan Tien[b]
1st Deputy Secretary-General	Dan Toc[a]	Dan Toc[a]	Doan Ket
2nd Deputy Secretary-General	Dan Chu	Doc Lap	Dan Tien
3rd Deputy Secretary-General	—	Thong Nhat[a]	Dan Tien[a]
Permanent committees[c]			
Anticorruption	Doc Lap/Independent[a]	Independent[a]/Independent[a]	Doan Ket/Dan Tien
Agriculture	Independent/Dan Chu	Thong Nhat[a]/Dan Toc	Dan Tien/Thong Nhat[a]
Public works	Dan Chu/Dan Toc	Independent/Doc Lap	Dan Tien/Doan Ket
Economics	Doc Lap/Independent[a]	Thong Nhat/Doc Lap	Doan Ket/Doan Ket
Labor, Social Welfare, Veterans	Dan Chu/Dan Toc	Thong Nhat/Doc Lap	Dan Tien/Independent
Khmer Affairs	Dan Chu/Dan Chu	Dan Tien/Dan Tien	Doan Ket/Doan Ket
Budget and Finance	Dan Toc/Dan Chu	Doc Lap/Doc Lap	Dan Tien/Doc Lap
Foreign Affairs	Doc Lap/Independent	Independent	Doc Lap/Thong Nhat
Interior	Dan Chu/Independent[a]	Independent[d]/Independent[d]	Doan Ket/Independent[a]
Ethnic Minorities	Dan Toc/Dan Chu	Dan Tien/Dan Tien	Independent[a]/Dan Tien

Defense	Independent[d]/Doc Lap	Independent[a]/Independent	Dan Tien/Dan Tien
Information and Chieu Hoi	Doc Lap/Independent	Thong Nhat/Dan Tien	Independent[a]/Dan Tien
Judiciary	Independent[b]/Doc Lap	Independent[a]/Independent[b]	Independent[a]/Doc Lap
Culture, Education, Youth	Independent/Doc Lap	Doc Lap/Independent	Doc Lap/Dan Tien
Rural Reconstruction	Thong Nhat/Doc Lap	Independent[a]/Dan Tien	Independent[a]/Dan Tien
Public Health	Independent[a]/Doc Lap	Independent[a]	Independent[a]/Doc Lap

[a] Associated with the New Society Group which later became the *Xa Hoi* bloc.
[b] Associated with the New Society Group; later became Independent.
[c] First bloc listed is that of the Chairman; second bloc is that of the Vice-Chairman if one was elected.
[d] Associated with An Quang Buddhists.

right *Doc Lap* bloc a picture emerges of a rather balanced match between the forces of opposition and declared supporters of the government. Opposition forces won a total of sixty positions in all the elections, and progovernment forces a total of fifty-eight seats. Progovernment and opposition deputies alike have suggested that the relatively greater success of the opposition probably contributed to the feeling of the executive that the House was an unreliable medium to process controversial and important legislation. Opposition deputies, moreover, were considerably cheered by the evident decline in the right-wing character of the House and cited as evidence the decline in the number of positions that the *Doc Lap* bloc had been able to win. The *Doc Lap*'s success was greatest in the first election (the bloc won ten positions) and declined thereafter to seven and then only six seats. As one deputy observed: "At first many members of the progovernment *Dan Chu* bloc believed that the *Doc Lap* bloc had the support of the executive and that it must be supported. Experience has proven that this is not the case. In addition, many deputies in the majority bloc who probably wished to take a more tolerant stand on peace and other issues probably felt that unless the House appeared to take a hard line in support of the executive on most issues the President would dissolve the assembly. Now it is clear that this will not happen, and many members of the *Dan Tien* bloc are expressing moderate views more openly and support some of the moderate opposition deputies in House elections." Similar views were expressed by deputies of all political leanings who attributed the trend toward moderation on both sides of the specturm to the discovery of common interests between deputies and a common desire for the House to ultimately emerge as a mediating insitution in which diverse social and political forces could find common ways to work for the good of the nation.

The most successful of the opposition groups in House elections were those aligned with the New Society group. Across all elections this group, which operated as independents for much of the time, won a total of twenty-nine positions, only four less than the majority bloc. *Xa Hoi* deputies regarded this as evidence of their ability to win support from the members of other groups of all persuasions and a demonstration of the practicability of their concept of political action. These deputies also attributed the success of the new *Doan Ket* bloc in the elections to the cooperation which emerged between the groups over the issue of minority representation that emerged in the early fall of 1969. In contrast to these two groups that gained in support over time, the success of the *Thong*

Nhat bloc, the third element of the opposition, declined. Deputies attributed this to the impact of the activities and subsequent prosecution of one of its members, Tran ngoc Chau, Secretary-General for 1968-69, and to the reluctance of militant Buddhists to run for House offices and the reluctance of the House to elect them in light of the growing hostility manifested by the executive. For their part, the Buddhists seemed to prefer to remain behind the scenes as much as possible while supporting other more moderate groups who took the lead in forming the opposition. One militant Buddhist suggested: "We would not like to see the opposition in the House become as radical as the government supporters on the far right. Neither they nor we speak for the majority of our side, and it would be inappropriate for either of us to attempt to do so. The more moderate groups of opposition deputies also have a better chance of working with other groups that benefit us whereas we would have little chance of developing a common stand alone." Whether or not this view was widely shared among militant Buddhists was impossible to determine in explicit terms although other Buddhists tended to prefer a leadership of a more moderate sort that would form coalitions for House elections and on substantive issues. Indeed, the efficacy of blocs, as measured by their cohesion, appeared linked not to their rigidity but to the level of cooperation achieved among them.

Legislative Blocs and the Organization of Politics

The potential of the blocs is a matter of interpretation and projection that requires more hindsight than is available for the discussion here. Based upon interviews with the leaders of the blocs considered here, there appear to be three reasons why blocs were established: to maintain the character of the lists constructed for the election campaign at a somewhat higher level than mere temporary personal alliances between political figures seeking an expedient means of election; to facilitate the development of progovernment and opposition positions and coordinate legislation; to aid the development of new political parties throughout the country based on common interests.

In each instance, however, legislative blocs fell short of their objectives. Bloc organizers, by and large, had little success in preserving the cohesiveness of the initial lists. The defections of some of the principal leaders indicated that the election campaign had resulted in little more than a temporary papering over of fundamental personal and political differences that existed prior to the election. In the Upper House one list subsequently divided into two opposing blocs. The Lower House, which was not elected on the basis of national lists but from multimember constituencies, divided into an initial four blocs. In the Lower House subsequent changes of membership within any given bloc were so great that most deputies belonged to more than one bloc during their tenure. This is not to say that the changing composition of the blocs was inherently detrimental. In the case of the Lower House such changes were essential to improving the prospects for greater interbloc cooperation.

Blocs seldom functioned as effective instruments of legislation. In the Constituent Assembly the drafting of the constitution was mainly accomplished without declared bloc affiliation. The functioning of the Upper and Lower Houses, similarly, has depended upon a relatively small core of active deputies who fill their roles regardless of bloc or political affiliation. Nor have blocs been effective in organizing opinion in support of legislation.

The drafting of legislation did not appear to be a particularly bloc-oriented activity, either. It reflected, instead, the cooperation of deputies with similar interests, which varied from bill to bill. Bloc positions were more consistently presented in periodic declarations on such topics as the Paris Peace Talks, various social and ethnic minorities, and statements of political principles that the regime was urged to adopt or implement. The blocs were used as educational forums for their members on national economic and political matters, and periodic meetings were held at which efforts were made to have members of the government and other national figures appear to discuss the issues of the day. At these meetings, some attempt was made to develop bloc positions on specific pieces of legislation, but no member of any bloc interviewed felt obliged to abide by the positions that emerged from such discussions. The blocs also have elected internal committees to deal with the drafting of position statements, proposed legislation, and their own political program. A typical bloc meeting usually involved a working session where declarations were drafted or bloc positions were discussed, followed by a briefing and open discussion in which either a bloc member or an invited guest speaker discussed a particular topic of current interest. Between formal meetings the business of the bloc was handled by its steering committee.

The ability of blocs to foster the development of new political organizations has been limited although such attempts were being made. Most bloc leaders, except those who organized the Catholics, had hoped to use their bloc to provide a basis for national political organizations by linking regional and local organizations into a national framework. Such an effort, aimed at encouraging groups with little experience to cooperate with each other, however, apparently demanded a series of compromises that individual leaders were unwilling or unable to make, and so no single group of leaders could emerge with genuinely wide support, which had been the basic goal of consolidation. One leader observed: "We Vietnamese agree on the principles behind national parties but not on who should lead them. Whenever you have two Vietnamese you have a party with a chairman and a vice-chairman. When a third person is added, then you have two parties, one of which will have two factions." Moreover, the blocs and the organizations they represented provided little incentive for potential supporters to follow their program. When asked about their reluctance to join in a nationally oriented effort, many local political leaders expressed doubts about what positive benefits a national party would have for them since "they have never done very much for the people. To us it appeared as if we were contributing only to the personal careers of politicians who had very little interest in our aspirations. If we are to support any leaders in the future they must demonstrate what they can do for us before we will demonstrate what we can do for them."

In Vietnam, the benefits of political organizations beyond the local or provincial level have yet to be effectively demonstrated although most local leaders have come to accept the principle in theory. One deputy suggested why the blocs in the legislature did not spawn either new or reconstituted political parties: "The Lower House did not become the birthplace of popularly based political parties for several reasons. First, many deputies were not inclined toward constructing such parties by temperament and preferred to associate themselves with the older, less dynamic groups. Second, in general the Lower House deputies have suffered a considerable loss of credibility with the population of their constituencies since the expectations of the people were far greater than the ability of the deputy to fulfill [through constituency service work]. Third, the deputies simply lacked the financial means to organize political movements." While deputies would hesitate to agree entirely with this assessment, none would deny that efforts to create new political parties, though not entirely fruitless, have been frustrating. In general there has been some retrenchment in the effort to build new parties, or perhaps a readjustment in the rhetoric of those involved. As activists ran into problems, they came to realize the long-term nature of the process of building political organizations, made especially acute by the paucity of financial resources. Leaders stressed that their current activities were designed to lay the basis for future efforts. Interbloc cooperation and alliances substituted for the initial goal of interorganizational alliances in the political system at large.

The discovery of cooperation in the midst of a tradition of political division changed the nature of political competition within the Lower House and the stability of political alignments. The emerging pattern of political competition between progovernment and opposition elements suggested that both sides were fairly well matched in internal contests and that, despite its diversity, opposition elements appear to have found ways in which to cooperate with each other and with the more moderate elements of the progovernment majority. On basic and procedural issues, in addition, each side appears to have been able to achieve a greater degree of solidarity than was apparent during the first session of the Lower House. And, inasmuch as the emergence of new blocs beyond those at the end of 1969 was considered unlikely by most deputies, the bloc structure of the House itself appears to have reached a certain level of stability. It is expected that bloc members will come to reconcile their individual policy positions with the blocs and that the blocs will allow their members greater freedom on some issues while requiring allegiance and unity on others. As the blocs gradually change from organizations based solely on personal friendships to those also committed to specific legislative and political goals, the consensus which should emerge will provide the discipline and cohesion thus far lacking.

Deputies also consider the past instability of the blocs related to the instability of the government itself and expect that the blocs will learn to function in spite of it. One deputy summarized the bloc changes that occurred from 1967 to the end of 1969 as follows:

The shifting bloc composition and the apparent alliances various blocs have maintained with each other and the executive reflect the rise or demise of three central figures—Nguyen van Thieu, Nguyen cao Ky, and Tran van Huong. Initially, the blocs were organized in support of a particular figure against his opponents, and the demise of the early Lower House blocs reflects the rise to power of President Thieu and his ability to isolate Ky. With the victory of Thieu over Ky, a period of conflict ensued between the supporters of Thieu and those loyal to Prime Minister Tran van Huong. The fall of the Huong cabinet, the prolonged crisis over a successor to Huong, the apparent threats of Vietnamization, and American independence from the Thieu government in the field of peace seeking stimulated yet another series of shifts in the composition of the blocs. Finally, the establishment of the Khiem cabinet seemed to mark the end of the power struggles at the top, and the blocs also appeared to have reached at least a plateau of stability.

The decline of personal political loyalties as the basis of bloc organization within the Lower House has also changed the nature of progovernment support and its relationship to the growth of political opposition. In contrast to the problems the opposition alone faces in most parliamentary systems,[31] in South Vietnam both opposition and progovernment supporters appear concerned about the authoritarian character of the executive. As one deputy suggested in an interview: "We may be willing to accept a dictatorship that serves the people, but most certainly we would not be willing to accept one that only served the interests of its leaders." Deputies on both sides of the spectrum tend to relate the problem of legislative autonomy to the ability of the executive to dominate the constitutional system and suggest similar reforms to limit what one deputy identified as "those powers which tend to make the executive authoritarian." Moreover, the development of cooperative efforts to curb these powers through the drafting of legislation to create a system of due process is regarded by deputies as part of an overall strategy aimed at reversing a perceived trend rather than weakening the ability of the executive to be effective altogether. The thrust of such reform efforts, which will be described in detail in Chapter 9, is, indeed, to increase overall governmental effectiveness. As one deputy stated: "If the executive spent less time being involved in other branches of government and in trying to dominate them, he would have more time to attend to the needs of the population and improve his administrative apparatus. Take the Ministry of Interior, for example. Rather than spend most of its time working on developing more effective administrative procedures to govern the rural population, it spends most of its time involved in police work designed to capture Viet Cong but in reality its programs are rife with corruption.[32] This is work that can best be handled by the courts." Legislative efforts to reform the system of local government and create an adequate judicial system, similarly are aimed at increasing government effectiveness by implementing the Constitution.

Groups on both sides of the political spectrum also face the prospect that new centers of political activity will develop which regard the legislature and the dialogue between the opposition and the government as meaningless. The legislature would then reflect a succession of pro- and antigovernment groups which must constantly discover new bases of cooperation and develop new sources of influence. Presumably, however, the current groups within the legislature will seek to expand the bases of their support to include new groupings which would appear as their ambition to become the focus of a party system was realized. To date, the efforts of the forces of opposition have demonstrated more vitality in this regard although it does appear that, where the forces of one side appear to be well organized at the province level, more vigorous efforts are made by progovernment forces to compete. In the case of Buddhist-Catholic competition, for example, wherever the *Nhan Xa* party was strong so also was the Buddhist political effort. Where such outright competition does not exist, the pace of political organization has been lethargic. In such instances, however, Lower House deputies have worked to convince party leaderships that they must think of competition beyond the local or provincial levels. The nominally progovernment parties appear to have at least recognized the need to perform better in future elections and, by the end of 1969, had begun to step up party reorganization and mobilization.

In light of similarity in problems and objectives, it is unlikely that the present alignment of forces into opposition and progovernment groupings will remain as permanent features of politics in South Vietnam. They seem, rather, to reflect a pattern of incomplete political evolution. The Constitution has set up a system of government that provides only for the participation of nationalists in a polity divided between nationalists and communists. The real political issue in Vietnam is over support for the Viet Cong, not over support for the executive or the legislature. Consequently, the participation of diverse groups in organizing the legislature is significant in the sense that such an institution may provide the basis for a nationalist coalescence, an essential prerequisite to the eventual participation of the Viet Cong in the political system.[33] Viewed in such a light, the organization of a political opposition and of a progovernment grouping within the Lower House suggests an initial exploration of the possibility of coalescence among the nationalists. While the political mobilization required for tentative accommodation at the elite level is considerably less than that which would be required for a coalescence of the nationalists, the latter must come first.

Developments within the House alone will not effect such a coalescence, but such developments as representatives of diverse groups seeking bases of cooperation and discovering their practicability will not be without their effects upon the political system at large. As the groups recognize common problems and as their leaders are able to discover workable bases for cooperation, the likelihood of a nationalist coalescence emerging is increased. Should the prospect of competition with the Viet Cong become clear, an incentive for nationalist coalescence would exist, but such an incentive would likely produce chaos unless there were a basis for such coalescence. It is for this reason that the pattern of bloc organization in the Lower House is significant beyond the insight it provides about the nature of current political developments.

Bloc politics in the Lower House represents the first major experiment aimed at discovering bases of cooperation among Vietnam's political forces. This effort appeared to have caused the gradual movement of political groups closer toward the center of the political spectrum. In the early stages of bloc organization, the political spectrum within the House tended to reflect the positions of the various groups with respect to their traditional or inherited rivalries. On the left of the spectrum were located those forces of opposition that ranged from the mildly critical southern Buddhists to the radical, militant central Vietnamese Buddhists. As should be clear from the preceding discussion of the composition of the blocs, the opposition within the Lower House is but a cluster of groups highly critical of the government but differing in intensity and direction. As yet, little argument exists on the functions or place of a formally constituted approach within the legislature, and not all deputies interpret the constitutional preference for a two-party system in Vietnam as meaning a progovernment and an antigovernment party. Indeed, some suggest that Vietnam will eventually have two political poles reflecting the outcome of the current struggle between nationalists and communists. Others believe that the term opposition is actually a misnomer since the blocs differ very little on questions of policy as do the Republican and the Democratic Parties in the United States.

According to the deputies, opposition induces a temporary division between those groups which have been long-term participants in the government system, such as the Catholics, and those groups which have only recently demonstrated a desire to participate. Entering the political system in an atmosphere of distrust and alienation from the government, groups such as the militant Buddhists were expected to be critical of the government. Deputies holding this view believe that, given the opportunity, the Buddhists would behave very similarly to the Thieu government. Buddhism, in this perspective, then becomes a particularistic opposition that would disappear should the government make concessions to them by according them important ministries in the cabinet, for example. Such co-optation would not necessarily involve effective mobilization of Buddhist political forces—indeed, it is an alternative to it. Thus, struggle politics might come to represent not opposition to centralized authority but to a central authority in which the Buddhists have no share.[34] Were the Buddhists in power, the government would probably become less repressive, and it would be less criticized since most Buddhist opposition stems from the government's seeming preference to jail dissenters rather than to tolerate them. Beyond the issue of political repression, the Buddhists, as a group, have tended to be about as vague as other groups on both sides of the political spectrum in advancing a specific policy or legislative program. One would have expected, for example, substantial differences to have developed between the Buddhists and the progovernment supporters on the question of a peace settlement, and yet interviews with Buddhist leaders on these topics produced as hard a line as any that emerged in interviews with the far right. Thus, in terms of national policy it is not altogether clear that a distinction between progovernment supporters and the opposition can be made on the basis of articulated policy differences.[35]

Both sides of the political spectrum in the Lower House tended toward the dispersion rather than the consolidation of its adherents. Dispersion, however, is distinct from factionalization which, by its very nature, signals the breakdown of cooperation and suggests the impossibility of accommodation. In contrast to factionalization, dispersion tended to do more to improve prospects for cooperation and accommodation than would have been likely had the original bloc structure of the House been preserved. Groupings at both ends of the spectrum tended to move closer to the center while the larger groups tended to divide into smaller, more workable coalitions. In so doing, the range of deputies who could cooperate with other deputies increased. Expansion of the range of cooperation thus varied directly with creation of incentives for it, the existence of an arena in which it could meaningfully take place, and the dispersion of political forces into working political coalitions. Intragroup cooperation appeared to be a necessary prerequisite to intergroup cooperation.

Over time the forces of the political opposition both increased and mellowed as they came to cooperate with each other.[36] Undoubtedly this mellowing was due in part to the participation of the opposition in the leadership of the Lower House and its committees. Seemingly common ground for cooperation appeared to replace the initial perception of the opposition's role as one of constant criticism, suggesting that participation in the Lower House provided an unexpected level of individual and legislative political action and creativity. Even the most radical of the opposition deputies suggested in interviews that they had come to recognize a community of interests among themselves and even with some deputies of the center on the issue of legislative autonomy and legislative priorities that might presage greater cooperation in the future. Apparently, also, the cause of improved Buddhist-Catholic relations was aided by the realization on both sides that these forces could work together, and that, particularly for the Buddhists, not all of the Catholic political leaders were as militant as those of the far right. To be sure, such efforts at cooperation could be expected if the legislature were to be considered as part of the general phenomena of elite associations. Since most participants possessed similar social backgrounds, a basis for cooperation was at least a theoretical possibility, similar in nature to the one C. Wright Mills noted in his work on interelite relations. "Insofar as the power elite is composed of men of similar origin and education, insofar as their careers and their styles of life are similar, there are psychological and social bases for their unity, resting upon the fact that they are of similar social type and leading to the fact of their easy intermingling."[37] While differences in backgrounds exist among Lower House deputies, they do not appear to offer significant obstacles to interrelationships among deputies that might not have been possible within the framework of their political organizations.

Moreover, within the context of the political system the threat of executive dominance that served as a basis for cooperation probably would not have had the same effect since group relations with the executive in the larger polity are the concern largely, if not exclusively, of the individual groups involved. The legislature provided a common symbol to which all groups could respond since what affected the institution itself affected all members of the institution. And the point at which individual groups came to value the legislature as part of a constitutional system also coincided with the point at which group leaders initiated cooperative efforts. The implication of the experience of cooperation among the opposition and the limited accommodations between it and the progovernment majority on particular issues is that, over time, such cooperation and accommodation may extend beyond the legislature to change nationalist politics in general.

Similar cases have been noted where cooperation at the elite level may eventually lead to cooperation between the organizations of the elite. As one scholar has noted of the phenomenon in a polity that approximates the political and religious diversity that exists in Vietnam, "overarching cooperation at the elite level can be a substitute for crosscutting affiliations at the mass level."[38] Indeed, such cooperation between elites in legislative blocs may begin to approximate the functions of even political parties as described in one study of the relationship between social cleavages and political parties. Political parties "help to crystallize and make explicit the conflicting interests, the latent strains and contrasts in the existing social structure, and they force subjects and citizens to ally themselves across structural cleavage lines and to set up priorities among their commitments to established or prospective roles in the system. Parties have an *expressive* function; they develop a rhetoric for the translation of contrasts in the social and cultural structure into demands and pressures for action or inaction. But they also have *instrumental* and *representative* functions: they force the spokesmen for the many contrasting interests and outlooks to strike bargains, to stagger demands, and to aggregate pressures."[39] Where party systems are unable to operate beyond purely expressive functions, as seems to be true in Vietnam, and where it is necessary for them to acquire instrumental and representative functions, overarching cooperation among party elites may serve to inject these functions into such parties or informally substitute for these functions in a specific political arena when necessary.

Presumably, also, when such cooperation becomes important to the continued survival of political organizations, they may then be able to build upon the backlog of experience obtained in the more limited or experimental system of the legislature. Thus, in Vietnam, such cooperation may also work to influence affiliations at the mass level as legislators emerge as leaders in political organizations, organize new groups, or convince party executive committees of the possibilities of mutual gain from mutual cooperation with other groups. Cooperation to preserve the autonomy of the legislature could then become translated into the broader goal of enabling groups to compete successfully with the cohesive Viet Cong when that eventuality becomes imminent. The subversion of nationalistic politics by either the Thieu government or the Viet Cong appears equally unpalatable.

Cooperation and accommodation depend upon the incentives for them. By the end of 1969 they were only beginning to become apparent to political leaders outside the legislature in Vietnam. The political experiences of Lower House deputies and their experimentation with doctrines of political organization represent a feature of Vietnamese politics in which future observers may come to see either the epitaph of the Second Republic or its significance and contribution to a political process that facilitates an end to the war.

Internal war does not create politics or processes of government. This is likely to be the most tragic aspect of the war in Vietnam. When the guns are silent, the political analyst will find essentially the same political forces and governmental institutions intact as when the conflict began. The war has served to break down the traditional isolation of the village and countryside from the government, but it has not provided a system of politics to integrate the rural population into national politics. The war has created desires and expectations for governmental institutions to alleviate suffering, but it has not created, on either the communist or noncommunist sides, the capacity to do so. On the noncommunist side, the lack of governmental responsiveness and the absence of a role for legislators in internal politics have thrust the Lower House deputy into constituency service. The denouement of the Chau case, in particular, made it clear to most deputies that the essential conflict between the President and the legislature was political, and that, unless the legislature could develop sources of support within the population at large, it had but a weak defense against Thieu's authoritarianism. The legislature had to find legitimacy and a political role not just in the constitution but in the beliefs and expectations of the people. In reviewing the dynamics of this process, it is striking how little impact the war had upon political behavior. The basic tensions between the social and political forces of this praetorian polity, rather than the war per se, make clear that politics not only goes on during war, but often quite apart from it.

The mobilization of political support required the reorientation of political organizations. Doctrines of political action developed within the Lower House to foster cooperation among deputies had to be transferred to the polity at large, and the most feasible way of accomplishing this appeared to be through constituency service rather than exclusively through established political organizations. Constituency service could create interests and demands involving the population in a political process directly influencing governmental policies, a dimension lacking in the past. Most deputies acknowledged that the limited service provided through established political organizations had failed to gain the confidence of the population after years of unresponsiveness to the people's needs. Deputies also acknowledged that this failure was related to the absence of a voice for the population that might influence the conduct of the government at the national level. By the end of 1969 constituency service had become a part of many deputies' strategy to maintain and enhance the autonomy of the Lower House. The Lower House, they felt, had to create and serve a larger public interest.[1]

Basing the effort to make the House a viable political force on organizations the population distrusted would, in the view of most deputies, hardly be effective as a means of mobilizing popular support. Rather, the population had to be organized on the basis of interests and goals that would transform their relationship to the government and, in the process, also transform the nature and the purposes of political organizations. Constituency service was initially practiced by only a handful of deputies, and it was aimed at providing political groups with a new link to local and provincial government. An increasing number of deputies came to involve themselves with their constituencies as it became clear that the development of deputy-constituency relations had important implications for political mobilization because it provided the population with a means to demand changes in local government that could not have been articulated earlier. Such interaction between the deputy, his constituency, and the government also suggested that, if the population could become politically involved in demanding changes, they might also be able to directly influence the character of provincial government.

By focusing popular attention upon how aspirations could be achieved within the province, deputies' intervention on behalf of constituents demonstrated that diverse groups had interests in common that could be advanced by effective national political organization. For the House itself, constituency interests increasingly influenced the nature of its legislative work. This is not to say that all members had to engage in constituency service, but, rather, that a majority had to recognize its significance in the tasks of legislation, thereby providing the genesis for new types of political alignments. Representation by the end of 1969 involved the creation as well as the serving of interests.

The Political Character of
Constituencies in Vietnam

A constituency is a cluster of demands and demand-making structures. To a legislator, a constituency is a political entity that exerts pressures generated by needs to which he must respond. To representatives, the constituency is responsible for electing him. Constituencies, thus, have both a legal and political character. They can be viewed as a specific administrative unit of territory containing a prescribed number of voters or they can be viewed as aggregations of political interests and groups with whom legislators identify and to whom they respond. The formal constituencies in Vietnam were defined for the Lower House election as identical to administrative units no larger than a province, and the framers hoped that constituencies would come to represent politically significant units as well.

But provinces in South Vietnam are not natural political or social boundaries. Their current boundaries are the products of colonialism and war. Before the French conquest, what is today South Vietnam was divided into six provinces. The French reorganized these into twenty-four provinces. By the end of World War II, there were twenty-five provinces. Diem increased this number to thirty-seven in 1959. From 1963-1966, the number of provinces had increased to forty-five. In 1969 there were forty-four provinces and five autonomous cities. One scholar of Vietnamese public administration has noted that "provinces and their subdivisions, the districts, are only territorial subdivisions of the state, without any natural autonomous existence. The factor of boundaries is motivated by complex reasons—sometimes the rationalization of territorial organization, at other times certain administrative practices found in organizational matters in general."[2] Throughout most of South Vietnam, consequently, the identification of the population with the province as a political entity is weak. In most cases, the province is too politically complicated to permit identification with the geographic unit. From north to south, for example, along the coastal provinces of I, II, and III Corps there is a mixture of traditional Buddhist associations, old-line nationalist political organizations, and newer settlements and organizations of northern Catholic refugees. Roughly 20 percent of the population lives in this area. The Mekong Delta is a mosaic of concentrations of ethnic Vietnamese, religious sects, and ethnic minorities. Roughly 60 percent of the population lives in this area. Consequently, the identification of deputies with their provinces tended to center around particular population concentrations, rather than within boundaries drawn and eroded by administrative decrees over the years.

Constituency Service: A New
Orientation in Vietnamese Politics

Since most provinces in Vietnam are complex political constituencies, within each province exists a myriad of problems and needs—and capacities to articulate them. Thus it remains a matter of individual choice for each representative to respond to such entities as clusters of political demands. Indeed, constituency service did not appear to depend upon either the impact of the war or political complexity. Active deputies were rather evenly distributed over all provinces and came from those provinces that had experienced the most war and the most peace, from provinces with the largest and the smallest refugee populations, and from provinces and autonomous cities with diverse and homogeneous social forces and economic problems.[3] The only meaningful differences between service-oriented and other deputies were based on personality and prior experiences.

Of the total Lower House membership, one-third engaged in constituency service. Such deputies were not difficult to identify because they made their activities known to both the American and the Vietnamese communities and because there is a strong relationship between constituency work and visible Assembly participation. Such an orientation is seen in the maintenance of at least one actively functioning office manned by a permanent local representative within the constituency; in the fact that families remain in the province while the deputies are in Saigon during Assembly sessions, and that deputies travel to their constituencies at least once a month; in the promotion and implementation of one or more province-oriented development projects at both the local and central government levels; and in activity in private social welfare projects within the province sponsored by local religious and political leaders. These deputies maintain definite and regularly functioning channels of communication with their constituents and with the provincial government.[4]

In South Vietnam, those deputies most active within their constituencies also tend to be among the most active within the Assembly itself in committee work, legislation drafting, and floor debates. Table 8-1 locates the service-oriented deputy within the framework of both this and the

Table 8-1 Distribution of deputy activities: legislative and constituency service functions

	Constituency service work	
House activities[a]	Percent active	Percent inactive
Active	12	19
Inactive	19	50

[a]Indications of House activities included deputies' consistent participation in secretariat and committee work, bloc organizations, and the drafting and sponsoring of legislation.

institutional features of legislative activities. Exactly half of the total membership of the Lower House does not participate in any ostensible way in the affairs of either the House or their constituencies. The remaining members can be grouped into the three categories suggested in Table 8-1. For the 19 percent who are actively involved in House affairs but not that of their constituencies and for the 19 percent for whom the reverse is true, each reported in interviews that demands on their time had prevented them from taking more comprehensively active roles. In general, the time factor appeared to be a satisfactory explanation in the sense that those most active in constituency service work (as measured by their reference to excessive case loads) and those active in committees requiring frequent and time-consuming meetings tended to fall into these two groups. But the deputies active in both constituent and legislative work also tended to have similarly heavy case loads and were also involved in time-consuming committee work. The differences between patterns of deputies' activities probably reflect less the amount of work done as individual preference for and experience with one type of activity over another. This is not to say, however, that the two types of activities are considered mutually exclusive at the policy-making level. Indeed, almost all of the legislation originating in the House after the Tet offensive of 1968 has been drafted by coalitions of deputies which include those active in House affairs, those primarily engaged in constituency service work, and those who managed to do both. Committee-based investigations were similarly joint ventures. Taken as a group, however, the service-oriented deputies represent a distinctive influence in the House since they remain the vanguard of the effort to establish it as a national institution oriented toward responding to local and popular needs and problems.

Occupational experience and political socialization distinguish service-oriented deputies from the membership of the Lower House as a whole. First, on the basis of the interviews held and observations made of their activities, service-oriented deputies expressed a decided personal preference for this type of activity. They had chosen or thrived on occupations that brought them into contact with the population, and constituency service was viewed as a natural extension of their earlier activity. Especially for those who entered politics at the mid-career point, constituency work was described as the most personally rewarding aspect of their decision to seek such a change. In terms of the overall occupational structure of the Lower House, most service-oriented deputies came from civil service and teaching careers (59 percent) with the military, provincial businesses, and medicine accounting for another 35 percent. The non-service-oriented deputies' occupational structure was more varied and reflected a higher proportion of professional military officers and Saigon businessmen (38 percent). But the major occupational difference between both groups of deputies lay in the level of the position attained rather than the type of career pursued. The highest-ranking civil servants at the province level, for example, tended to be oriented toward constituent service, and their motivation for running for the Lower House appears to be a need to exceed the limits on individual initiative imposed by service in provincial government. So also, career military officers who served in administrative posts, such as province and district chiefs, tended, prior to running for election, to be among those for whom constituency service most nearly met their conception of the role of a Lower House deputy. It would appear that the more powerful the position previously held, the more a deputy tried to make his position in the Lower House just as influential and active.

In other cases, particularly those of the career military officers, the position of Lower House deputy may in some measure have been compensation for their inability to progress within the ranks to command positions. In the field-grade ranks, for example, of the twelve officers who were either pro-Thieu, pro-Ky, or neutral in military politics, nine were inactive when it came to constituency service. In comparison, of the four field-grade officers who considered themselves in opposition to the government, two were service oriented and one was reported to be in the process of gaining such an orientation. Similarly, of the seven neutral deputies of all ranks (who had not advanced in rank in ten years or more), three were service oriented, and two more were reported to be leaning in that direction. While the total number of officers is small (twenty) and the divisions within them even smaller, the relationship between a progovernment orientation, success in achieving promotions, and lack of constituency service is a strong one. Those deputies who have not been favored by rapid promotion and who consider themselves in opposition to the government have tended to be among the most active members of the Lower House. Constituency service, thus, could be motivated by strong desires to compensate for loss of power, either as a result of retirement or a change in political fortunes.

Service-oriented deputies also tended to have been socialized into politics at a different organizational level than deputies who were not active in constituency service work. In terms of general background characteristics, as Table 8-2 indicates, the cluster of active deputies tends

Table 8-2 Selected characteristics of constituency service-oriented Lower House deputies compared with other deputies

Characteristic	Service-oriented[a] (percent)	Nonservice-oriented[b] (percent)
Primary occupation		
Civil servant	34[c]	27
Military officer	14	22
Teacher	25	17
Business	12	16
Lawyer	2	3
Doctor	9	5
Sect politico	0	6
Journalist	4	3
Farmer	0	1
Imprisonment		
1945–1953	7	16
1954–1963	13	11
(Nov.) 1963–1966	4	2
Local orientation		
Born in constituency	43	23
Prior work experience in constituency	93	83
Place of birth by urban area and region		
Hanoi		3
Elsewhere in North Vietnam	14	31
Hue		

Table 8-2 (continued)

Characteristic	Service-oriented[a] (percent)	Nonservice-oriented[b] (percent)
Elsewhere in Central Vietnam (I and II Corps military region)	30	28
Saigon	2	4
Elsewhere in South Vietnam (III and IV Corps military region)	50	32
Declared Religion		
Vietnamese Buddhist	48	32
Theravada Buddhist	2	5
Catholic	14	32
Hoa Hao	7	11
Cao Dai	4	3
Confucianist	9	7
Animist	0	2
Moslem	0	2
Protestant	2	1
Ancestor worshipping Buddhist	7	3
Unknown; no religion declared	7	2
Election plurality		
Under 10 percent of votes cast	9	16
11-15	18	15
16-20	27	27
21-25	18	14
26-30	9	6
31-35	5	4
36-40	2	4
41-45	9	1
46-50	0	2
Over 50	2	11
Age at election		
20-25	4	
26-30	21	14
31-35	23	18
36-40	16	21
41-45	23	22

(continued)

Table 8-2 (continued)

Characteristic	Service-oriented[a] (percent)	Nonservice-oriented[b] (percent)
46–50	4	5
51–55	4	12
56–60	4	5
61 and over	0	3
Age of entry into politics		
Student	23	12
Junior professional or official (i.e., 25–35)	68	61
Midcareer professional or official	30	27
Primary agent of political socialization		
None	9	16
Religious sect or organization	43	35
Student organization	0	5
Political party or organization	41	31
Military academy	7	13
Primary political experience		
None	27	26
National campaign organizer or local representative	16[d]	12
Elected to local or provincial office	9	16
Officer of political party or organization	59	40
National Assembly deputy, 1955–1963	0	5
Constituent Assembly deputy, 1966–1967	9	11
Viet Minh cadre, 1945–1954	14	2
Community action project leader	9	2

[a]N = 44

[b]N = 95

[c]Number expresses percent of a particular category of the group rather than of the total House. Percents may reflect rounding error.

[d]Percentages do not total 100 owing to possibility of deputies having several types of prior political experience.

to cut across most lines of classification and includes, for example, deputies of all ages, from all religious groups, from all occupations, and from opposition as well as progovernment political groups. And while almost half of the service-oriented deputies were born in the province from which they were elected, as compared to only a quarter of the other deputies, both categories of deputies rank fairly high as to prior work experience within their constituencies (93 percent of the service-oriented deputies had prior work experience versus 83 percent of the other deputies). A greater proportion of the service-oriented deputies, however, were socialized into politics through religious and political organizations at the local level, as compared to nonservice-oriented deputies (84 percent versus 66 percent, respectively). Although this difference suggests that to some extent a service orientation is related to participation in political organizations, examining deputies' specific political affiliations makes clear that differences in orientation are also related to an individual's relative position within such organizations. Those deputies who ran for the House as leaders of particular groups were less inclined toward constituency service than those who ran for election as members of such groups but not as representatives of their central or national executive committees. Younger members of religious organizations tended to evince a service orientation and tended to run for election to the House either as undeclared members of their group or as independents without any factional affiliations. Indeed, factionalism as a determinant of political behavior in South Vietnam tended to be significant only for those deputies who represented leadership and hierarchies considered national in orientation. The nonservice-oriented deputies, in contrast, were much more closely identified with a particular group, and their election reflected the position they had attained within a leadership hierarchy rather than a particular conception of the role that they would play as a deputy. Similar differences exist between service-oriented and other deputies who entered politics initially through participation in political parties and organizations. The latter group's socialization occurred relatively earlier, and more of the deputies in this group were socialized into politics through the older nationalist political parties and the parties of the Diem era. The service-oriented deputies were initially involved in secular political organizations and movements more recently organized or factionalized into cliques of younger and older party members.

Finally, to deputies previously unaffiliated with currently functioning political organizations, the two years following their election represented a period in which to make new commitments. The proportion of deputies in both groups who campaigned independently from established political organizations was surprisingly high given the equally high level of prior political affiliations indicated. Thirty-nine percent of the service-oriented deputies and 44 percent of the other deputies campaigned as independents. Today, almost all of the deputies are committed to particular political organizations. The principal explanation for the different nature of such commitment lies in the reliance of the service-oriented deputy upon his constituency to reelect him. Those less inclined toward such activity have sought to enter the older and more established political groups and draw support from their membership.

The question of the nature of a deputy's popular support also has important implications for the balance between the opposition and the progovernment groups within the House. As Table 8-3 suggests, in terms of current political affiliations the opposition represents an almost even mixture between deputies who are service oriented and those who are not. In terms of the absolute number of deputies in each group, progovernment and opposition groups are relatively equal when it comes to the number of deputies having the skills needed to develop political organizations based on service to and mobilization of the population. And the rate at which active deputies who were initially independent have joined either progovernment or opposition groups has been exactly equal. Viewed from the perspective of the character of opposition and progovernment supporters, however, it is clear that progovernment groups in the assembly appear to lack a constituency service orientation.[5] The eighteen service-oriented deputies represent only 22 percent of the total composition of the progovernment forces, while the remaining twenty-four service-oriented

Table 8-3 Current political affiliations of deputies by service orientation

Current affiliation	Service-oriented deputies (percent)	Nonservice-oriented deputies (percent)
Progovernment group	18(41)[a]	65(68)
Opposition group	24(55)	21(22)
Undeclared	2(4)	9(10)

[a]Figures in parentheses are percents each group contributed to the total of service-and nonservice-oriented deputies.

deputies constitute 53 percent of the membership of the opposition forces. While it would thus appear that constituency service developed independently of deputies' pro- or antigovernment political preferences, such a finding may also suggest that the need for such activities was perceived differently by each group.

Opposition deputies, presumably, placed a higher premium upon developing a link to their constituents in order to bolster the political support they felt the opposition lacked. Moreover, that opposition deputies were able to develop effective and working relationships with the province government suggests what appears to be an emerging trait of the opposition in Vietnam: the ability to separate hostility toward the Thieu government from involvement in politics at the local level. Progovernment deputies tended to feel that the development of popular bases of support would not be required since the President would favor their support within the context of the House itself. As suggested in Chapters 6 and 7, this expectation was frustrated when a working relationship between the Thieu government and its supporters failed to develop. By the end of 1969, however, progovernment deputies had come to reassess their position, and a growing number appeared to recognize the need to become more active within their constituencies. Of the progovernment deputies active in constituency service work, more than half became active in 1969, in contrast to the opposition deputies who tended to involve themselves in such work in early 1968. Constituency service, thus, reflected not only differences in personality and political experience but a changing view of politics as well.

Patterns of Deputy-Constituency Relations

The nature and extent of the relationship between the Lower House deputy and his constituents depends upon channels of communication developed for the articulation of local problems. Initially, service-oriented deputies sought to establish contact with the population largely through the medium of personal appearances and visits to villages and market centers, the principal purpose being to discuss national issues and local problems with local leaders. From January to October of 1969, for example, the *Lower House Journal* reported that thirty delegations visited the provinces to distribute funds and commodities to war victims and refugees (eleven visits), to present contributions for the construction of community religious and educational centers (four visits), to discuss local needs and problems with villages and hamlet residents (twelve visits), to lecture on the observations of delegations sent abroad (one visit), and to investigate regional distribution and supply centers (two visits). Discussion of national or international issues was limited. When it took place, it was used more as a means to report to constituents rather than to engage them in discussion.[6]

To the service-oriented deputy, his most effective visitation work occurs in the district. These visits usually last a full day and are well organized in advance. The deputy's local representatives alert village elders to the visit and arrange for them to be brought to the district headquarters where local problems are discussed. Such a meeting provides a forum for the village elders to state their positions and their concerns while the deputy makes a short speech to reaffirm the sincerity of his interest in their problems. During the course of one meeting, for example, the village leaders expressed their desire to have another district high school constructed at a location that would require less travel over insecure roads for the students; to petition the Viet Cong delegation in Paris (the deputy had told of his meeting in Paris with the allied delegation) to stop all terrorist attacks within the province; to have greater coordination between the district administration and military forces in the area since recently, after the military had granted permission for farmers to return to their fields, a round of artillery was fired at them; to have more classrooms built in a particular village; to have the animal husbandry program improved since many animals treated by local veterinarians were still dying; and to have the road to the provincial capital open to civilian traffic more frequently. After the meeting the deputy lunched with the district chief where these problems were discussed, and the two men reviewed the progress made on some of their joint efforts involving various district public works projects. In the afternoon the deputy and his assistants visited about half of the villages in the district and talked with local political and religious leaders. The deputy then returned to the province capital and his residence and held a session in the evening with his assistants to assign priorities to the problems uncovered during the visit and to run over details for the visit scheduled for the following day.

The deputy observed that it had taken quite some time to develop these district visits into meaningful experiences for the villagers and their leaders. When he was first elected, he made only one visit to one district, where he was overwhelmed with the number of problems raised by the village leaders. He did not return for more than two months to the district because of the difficulty in establishing a workable system to process and resolve constituency problems. "I thought that the job of representing the people would be easy since I would be able to control the flow of the problems and define my duties as I went along. On my first visit I discovered that it was me and not the people who had no clear conception of my job. They had the problems, but I had not worked out a clear way to resolve them."

District visits and grievance meetings constituted a regular, but not the most frequent, form of contact between a deputy and his constituents. Most service-oriented deputies reported that their most frequent form of contact with constituents was more ad hoc, and developed from particular emergencies or crises that occurred within the province. The deputy might receive a letter from a constituent or a group of families complaining about a particular local official or problem. He might then return to the province to meet solely with that group of constituents. When a particular hamlet in the constituency has been the victim of a Viet Cong attack, killing many and destroying many homes, the deputy was usually informed by his local representatives about the nature and extent of the damage, and he was advised about the necessity of returning to console the victims. Local representatives also informed the deputy about particular deficiencies in the relief effort that had been organized or shortages that the attack may have caused. Before departure for the province or en route, the deputy would try to see how the relief efforts could be supplemented by working to overcome any obstacles at the central or the regional level or by using his personal funds or influence to supplement relief activities. One deputy, for example, provided at his own expense potable water supplies for one hundred families left homeless by a North Vietnamese attack on a district town until their request for adequate water made its way through the appropriate relief agency. By and large, deputies acknowledged that the relief programs for victims of such attacks were adequate in the short run. Only as the victims began to recover and applied for longer-term government assistance in reconstruction did the deputies have to jog and monitor the ponderous bureaucracy that handled such applications.

In the cases of deputies who returned to their constituencies in the wake of such attacks, the deputy's basic role involved expressing sympathy to those families who suffered losses. The deputy, and usually one of his personal friends from the particular village, performed this mission. Often the deputy made a contribution to these families that did not have adequate funds to provide coffins for the dead. Then the deputy would inquire as to what applications for relief had been made and check to see that the forms were properly filled out and administered. In some cases where families have been left completely homeless the deputy might offer them the use of his house until they could get resettled. If, from his investigation of the incident, the deputy believed that local security forces were lax, this would be discussed with local security officials and, in some cases, he would design new hamlet and village defense systems. By Vietnamese standards, the effort to console war victims is a rather dramatic gesture. Often victims of Viet Cong terrorism are not visited by any government official despite the knowledge of the incident, and they must come to the local headquarters to apply for relief and request emergency assistance. One district official observed: "When I worked in another province the district chief never went to see victims of Viet Cong attacks because he told us that, if any of us were killed by the Viet Cong, none of the people would come to console our families. Also, he believed that the Americans would always come to see the victims and that they had unlimited supplies with which to aid the victims while the district had nothing. In this district, however, the deputy district chief for administration always goes to console the victims because he said that when he was at school [in the National Institute of Administration] he was taught that this was part of his job and important to the government's cause. As for myself, I have no authority to help these people." To be sure, a number of explanations of Vietnamese behavior could be offered, but all would be difficult to document. Rather, the attitude of this Vietnamese official highlights one aspect of the difference in attitude that exists between the deputy and the local official. The service-oriented deputy, by providing a new channel for demands of the population, provides new ways to link the populace to the government.

That local demands exist in Vietnam is clear; whether they are articulated or not depends upon the development of effective agents and agencies responsive to those demands. Ironically, however, all of the service-oriented deputies interviewed suggested that in reality they did not particularly like or value doing constituent service work. Most felt that it was the job of the village and provincial councils. At present, such work had to be done by the deputies because, as one deputy explained, "the local and provincial councils are bankrupt—they have meager funds, little respect from the people, no confidence in themselves, and no power vis-à-vis the province chief." Most active deputies expressed the hope that in the future they would be able to devote more time to legislative affairs and leave constituency service either to well-established local representatives or, preferably, to members of the provincial and local councils. This view was shared by observers of the province scene as well. These observers suggested that the service-oriented deputies should be spending more time in Saigon representing the province than in the province itself intervening for popular grievances. The active deputies reported that they spent about two-thirds of their time on constituent service problems and about one-third on legislative matters.[7] Without exception, all deputies interviewed would prefer to reverse this division of their labor.

It is unlikely, however, that a deputy's interest and time in constituent service work will decline very significantly in the future. Much constituency service has involved problems related to war, but there is every reason to believe that problems related to peace and the multiplicity of programs aimed at postwar reconstruction will be equally demanding. Most deputies do not regard war as having changed the character of the bureaucracy, particularly that which exists in the provinces. Constituency service is also likely to become more politically significant for the deputies. While such activities and the activists involved were regarded initially as nonpolitical in nature, constituency service is likely in the future to be linked to deputies' reelection campaigns and their participation in the development of political organizations. Despite both expected substantial reforms in the operations and powers of local and provincial councils and possible election of province chiefs to the Lower House, the deputy has consciously sought to establish a two-way system of communication between the population and the government. The customary ineptness of provincial administrations and the customary impotence of the province council is not likely to die easily either in the minds of the population or, perhaps, in practice. Moreover, even the election of province chiefs and the revamping of the provincial councils does not necessarily mean that they will have more power at the national level. Only the Lower House deputy is able at times to exert the extralegal pressure on the central government to get things done. And to the segment of the population that benefited from such extralegal pressure, the tendency to rely on the deputy is still likely to be great.

Deputies themselves may be dissatisfied with a method of keeping in touch with and building the support of the population that relies more on favors done by the deputy than on legislative accomplishments in Saigon. Deputies may also perceive local and provincial councils as sources of possible competition for their own seats, which would require that they continue to devote a major portion of their time to constituent service. What is more likely to develop with time is that deputies will organize more effective local offices to do initial screening and handle the more routine cases under their signature. To some extent this has already happened with those deputies who handle a few hundred cases each month. Important to any analysis of deputy-constituency relations is the nature of the local office and its operations.

While the organized and the ad hoc visit serves as the principal contact between the deputy and his constituency, the local office functions as the primary channel of communication between the constituents and the deputy's representatives. All Lower House deputies maintain some form of a local office, usually a room in their homes in the provincial capital or at the residence or place of business of their local representatives. As the work load of the deputies has increased in Saigon, the tendency to rely upon organized and ad hoc visits to process local problems has declined, and the local office for those deputies active in constituent service work has grown in importance. Particularly after the Tet offensive, when the Assembly met almost continually for twelve months in regular and emergency sessions, even the most active deputies' time in the provinces was limited to one or two weekends per month.

Thus, the constituent increasingly looked to the staff of the local office to assist in the completion of a myriad of forms and applications required by the GVN for such things as war damage compensation, orphan's and widow's relief, agricultural loans, and draft exemptions. Prior to this, the peasant had virtually been forced to pay a substantial "fee," usually calculated as a proportion of the total expected relief to local officials, to assure that such applications were correctly filled out and processed. Peasants who refused to pay local officials for such assistance generally found that their applications were either not approved by the province government or they were unexplainably delayed within the bureaucracy until the deadline for submission had passed. In order to circumvent this process, the deputy's local office required at least one fulltime clerk with administrative experience to deal effectively with the local bureaucracy. Sometimes this function was filled by a local civil servant loyal to the deputy, but in most cases the deputies have found that a permanent staff member was essential.[8]

Inadequate financial allowance for local offices has resulted in considerable variation in style of operations. The largest proportion of local offices was headed by a member of the deputy's family, usually his wife or brother, who acted as his local representative and used their home as the local office. Such an office assured absolute loyalty of the staff and guaranteed them better treatment when calling on local and provincial officials. During the Tet offensive and at other times when local security was threatened, many constituents were comforted by the fact that a deputy's family shared their plight. As one suggested, "things cannot be so bad if our deputy has left his family here with us." Deputies' wives were a great asset since they tended to be highly qualified in their own right and were able to provide the constituent with a feeling that their problems would receive the personal attention of the deputy. With the advent of the army telephone service, deputies and their wives tended to be in daily contact about constituency problems. Deputies who were high-ranking provincial officials before their election also enjoyed the respect of their successors, and this respect was usually transferred to the deputy's wife in his absence. The major difference between the performance of a deputy's wife and a relative as local representative was that the latter, usually engaged in his own business or profession as well, tended to have less time available for constituency service work and generally limited his and his office's focus to a few particular types of problems.

A second type of local office found among the active deputies can be termed the patronage office. In this case, the local office or offices were staffed by volunteers, personally loyal to the deputy but not members of his family. These staff members had usually worked for the deputy during the campaign and tended to be employed in either the provincial civil service or the local school. They often received their job through the intervention of the deputy (after his election or while the deputy was a provincial official). In some cases, however, volunteers have come from the families of those whom the deputy has assisted with a particular problem such as having a son released from the army when drafted illegally. The patronage system tended to produce the greatest number of local offices outside of the provincial capital, and those deputies who employed this system of staffing generally had at least three offices. In one case a deputy used this system to develop offices in every village of his province. Such a system divided the burden of work more evenly since the multiplication of offices reduced the number of cases handled by any one office.

The third type of local office was well established before the deputy was elected and was put at his disposal after the election. The rarest of such offices were business offices, usually law offices, where the deputy had practiced before he was elected. These tended to be more administratively oriented since they were replete with experienced clerks and typists. The converted business office was generally found in major urban areas, and it handled more complicated problems that constituents had with the province or municipal government or with the courts. The case load of this office was generally the largest in terms of absolute numbers, and it is easily documented owing to the Vietnamese system of numbering all correspondence, often exceeding a thousand cases on file compared to an average of three hundred to four hundred for most other deputies' offices. Part of the case load was a natural outgrowth of the lawyer's own clients who sought to use his new position to resolve problems (without cost) not handled by an ordinary lawyer or the deputy before his election. Another portion of the case load consisted of referrals from other deputies who had no legal experience. Finally, case work was often drummed up by the deputy himself during the course of well-organized visits to the districts in his constituency. One active lawyer reported that he visited his district, especially those sections where he received his strongest support and those he felt likely to win in the next election, every two months to meet with the local leaders and constituents with problems he was working on. The staff in the field for these converted business offices was recruited by patronage either in jobs or in legal assistance, and the field representatives served as the principal channel of communication between the deputy and the population. It would indeed be difficult to visualize the average farmer appearing in elaborate city offices.

The most frequently encountered of the established offices were those maintained under the auspices of a religious sect or of the older nationalist parties in the I Corps region. Through such converted organizational offices the deputy was provided with clerical skills, limited financial resources to supplement his own allowances, and cadre and communications structures. In return, the deputy was expected to become the organization's man, but many have not felt compelled to serve the interests of the group automatically. In one case, an active deputy bolted from his party and is now attempting to take its provincial cadre structure with him, leaving the central executive committee with few followers. For those deputies who have remained within the fold of their organization, reliance upon it for support in constituency service has narrowed rather than expanded their concern for and appeal to the mass of the voters, despite party proclamations to the contrary. This is particularly true for those nominated from the nationalist parties, which includes some of the

Assembly's most active deputies. Such consolidation is not viewed by the deputies as an alternative to expanding the bases of their political support; rather, it is considered part of a sequence of activities aimed at the effective mobilization of the population. Consolidation is required, according to this view, because of the need to transform established political organizations by recommitting their supporters to a more dynamic conception of politics. As one deputy observed: "The population must be linked to our party not because of its past reputation but because of its present performance. Once we get our initial supporters reeducated, we can begin to work to gain the support of others." Recognizing the limitations of established political organizations, deputies affiliated with such groups tend to believe that their constituency service represents a prelude to activities that should be expanded to link old and new supporters alike to the organization.

The local office in whatever form serves as a clearinghouse for constituency demands and problems and reflects the degree of a particular deputy's participation and involvement in local politics. It has become the principal mechanism for supporting constituency service and may be organized by the deputy, depending upon his financial resources, around the members of his immediate family, around a core of loyal supporters to which limited patronage rewards are distributed, or around an existing office and staff maintained by the political party of a religious association that worked for the deputy's election. Thus, while the development of the deputies' case loads was initiated by rather ad hoc ceremonial visits to their constituencies, all service-oriented deputies have since established definite procedures and channels of communication for constituency service.

Constituency Service and the Demand Process

Most service-oriented deputies were surprised at how quickly they were put to work. Indeed, as one deputy observed: "Eighty to ninety percent of the population does not know that the deputies are supposed to make laws but thinks that they are supposed to intervene for the people's needs only." And, in the opinion of some observers, to the extent that deputies have reinforced this "misconception" by their activities, the Lower House has made a significant impact on government in Vietnam. One government minister, for example, noted that his "office had been working for some time at trying to assure better conditions of employment for workers. The labor unions have not been very successful at this because they have little influence and were more concerned with national issues than with the welfare of the workers. The Lower House deputy, through intervening for the rights of workers, has helped to focus attention upon how their rights should be protected. Thus, they have aided us in trying to convince the government that more regulation is necessary, and they have aided the workers by pressuring for changes at the provincial and municipal levels." The Speaker of the House suggested that the activities of the Lower House deputies have had an important impact on increasing political conscious-ness in the society: "The Lower House's contribution to political development in Vietnam has largely been through what it has begun to teach the people. This, in turn, is largely due to the activities of the Lower House deputies as they have intervened on behalf of the population." Another deputy voiced a similar sentiment shared by almost all deputies interviewed, regardless of how active they had been in their constituencies. "Constituency service work is the most important contribution the Lower House has made to South Vietnam's social and political life. Unlike the previous National Assemblies under Diem, the Lower House, due to the activity of some of its members, has actually helped the people." In the view of most deputies, regardless of their orientation, constituency service established a link between the population and the government that had been absent in the past.

Constituency service work and the service-oriented deputy are part of a recent phenomenon, rather than standard practice. One active deputy commented that the "current period is one of experimentation with constituency service," and, as a result, a variety of styles and types of intervention procedures has been developed. Since 1967, all active deputies noted that the number of cases with which they have to deal has steadily increased. As a result all active deputies had to institute a procedure to handle the case work as it developed. While each deputy's method of operation differs according to his own personal style, the process of intervention and its development has a number of common work elements. The load itself in many cases began shortly after the election results were announced, and it took the form of a letter from a constituent. Some deputies had a case load even before they were elected, having discovered problems during the campaign. All deputies recognized early the need for some regular system of handling cases. The first step in the intervention process involved a careful investigation of the problem presented by the constituent, usually in a letter. Initially, deputies tended to do this themselves, but, as the work load increased, they relied upon local representatives. All active deputies stressed that, to establish the validity of each problem presented by constituents, a judgment was required as to whether the demand was reasonable. In cases where the criteria of reasonableness was not met, the deputy would personally explain to the constituent why the request was unfair. The service-oriented deputy, of course, recognized that reasonable requests had a greater chance of being resolved, and the criteria applied form an important part of a deputy's strategy.

Throughout the process deputies stressed its educational nature.[9] They tended to view their role as not only to represent the constituent but also to explain the government to the population. One deputy observed that the people "need to have their problems solved and, just as important, to know how they were solved." And in the case of those deputies with little or no previous administrative governmental experience, they viewed the intervention process as one where they would also have to learn how things were done. The intervention process in all cases started at the local rather than the national level. The most frequently reported interventions involved the deputy taking the constituent's problem and, as one described it, "walking it through" the provincial government bureaucracy until a decision was reached. Walking a case through the bureaucracy was also viewed by the deputy as an important source of information on the provincial government.

One deputy, for example, described how a particular problem provided him with greater insight into the complex relationships affecting the livelihood of his constituents. The problem concerned a decision by the local military commander to declare a well-established fishing area closed after discovering three Viet Cong hiding a boatload of dynamite in the fleet. In order to get to the fishing grounds, the fleet had to pass under a strategic bridge. By declaring the fishing grounds off limits, the military commander reasoned that the threat to the bridge would be reduced. The fishermen then attempted to move to a new area, but were denied passage by local security forces guarding another bridge. The fleet then turned downstream to grounds used by fishermen from another port, but were soon ordered out by local officials protecting the grounds for their own men. The fishermen sent a delegation to the area military commander, requesting either permission to pass under the bridge or assistance in finding a new area. The commander replied that only the mayor of their municipality could make such a decision; their request was "forwarded."

Several days passed with no action, and the fishermen went to the Lower House deputy. The deputy went to the military commander, who reported that the mayor had been too busy to see him. So the deputy went to the mayor himself and found a quick and receptive audience. The mayor suggested that a naval launch escort the fishermen to a new area, thus allowing them to pass under the bridge. The launch arrived at the fishing fleet thirty minutes later.

In retrospect, the deputy observed that, because of the differences in rank and personality between the military commander and the mayor, the commander would not go out of his way to see the mayor and vice versa. What was required was someone to act as the go-between for the fishermen and the officials involved. "The problems in this area are generally created by the local military forces but, as far as the civilian population is concerned, only the city administration can solve them. The population, however, usually does not understand this and goes to the wrong office for relief. Once their application enters the bureaucracy it often becomes stuck at the wrong level. Because of my position I can follow the problems through and teach the population about how their government works and whom they must see. Now, when the fishermen have problems, they see me for advice about whom they should submit their grievance to, rather than asking me to solve it for them." By walking the problem through, not only was the immediate incident resolved but a channel for future action was also established; the reinforcing nature of local intervention—the more local institutions are used, the more they can be utilized—accounted for the preference of service-oriented deputies to deal personally (at least initially) with most problems and personalities within their provinces.

Active deputies reported that at least two-thirds and in some cases as much as 80 percent of all cases could be handled at the local level and did not require intervention in Saigon at all. In only one type of case, removal of province chiefs for corruption, did the deputy start at the national level. But a deputy's success in constituent service at the local level depended upon the type of problem and also upon the prior experience a deputy had within the province. Those deputies who were former provincial officials relied heavily upon their ability to get things done locally and reported the greatest success. Such deputies also tended to be more successful at the national level and often would work in conjunction with provincial officials in making application to the central ministries for assistance in development and public works projects. Confining constituency problems to the local level was also appreciated by provincial officials whose behavior, as a result, was less subject to criticism by the Saigon ministries. This tended to constitute the primary incentive on the part of the local official for taking some positive action on constituency problems presented by Lower House deputies for their consideration. In addition, despite the friendships that many of the service-oriented deputies had with American advisers in their province, they tended to rely upon the advisers to a lesser extent as Lower House deputies than they had as provincial officials. Many American advisers interviewed noted with surprise that the Lower House deputies avoided asking them for assistance where previously they would not have hesitated. The deputies in turn responded that they believed their government had sufficient means of its own and that they ought to concentrate not upon making Americans more responsive to the problems of the population but, rather, the GVN.

The constituency problems that required deputy intervention were remarkably similar from province to province. Almost without exception, the service-oriented deputies interviewed noted that most of the problems they handled were related not to the war but to the government's ineptness in dealing with the population. The Lower House deputy acted in response to a vision of what government ought to be like and of the ways people could be linked to it. Ironically, however, it may well be that just such a response and the philosophy underlying it—in contrast to the responses engendered by the rhetorical urgency of US tactics designed to "win the hearts and minds" of the population or to "root out" the Viet Cong infrastructure—will have had the most significant impact on resolving problems related to government incapacities. Despite the fact that the war has had an uneven impact that varied from province to province, the government tended to administer each province in the same way. As one editorial writer characterized the bureaucracy's relationship to the population: "The Vietnamese term for public administration is *Hanh Chanh*. To my knowledge *Hanh* has at least three meanings: to travel, to cause suffering to, to execute. The second meaning applies very well to the public servants: they are supposed to serve you, but while doing this they make you suffer a great deal. For a little piece of business you have to visit the same office several times. Each visit involves, among other inconveniences, a lot of waiting. And the longer you stay in government offices, the more you realize that they are lacking in cleanliness."[10] American advisers who served in provinces that had experienced the most war and the most peace also noted the same basic lack of concern for and response to the problems of the population in both types of provinces. Table 8-4

Table 8-4 Constituency service cases in order of frequency of problems mentioned[a]

Problem	Primary level of intervention	Percent of case load
1. Injustices related to the Phoenix program including illegal arrests made by police and security forces, torturing of suspects, imprisonment without charge or trial for longer than two months, imprisonment under substandard living, dietary, and sanitary conditions	Local	40
2. Injustices of the GVN administration including delays in relief assistance applications, failure to provide authorized assistance to refugees, illegal drafting of youths, failure to provide lawful allowances to war widows and orphans, unlawful removal of elected officials, failure to provide authorized agricultural assistance, and selling supplies at black market prices	Local and national	30
3. Public works projects including the construction of schools, roads, rural electrification, bridges, markets, water control and supply facilities, harbors, housing, and assistance to local businesses and industries	Local and national	15
4. Assuring that adequate food supplies and other materials are earmarked for and maintained within the province warehouses	Regional	10
5. Anticorruption cases usually resulting in calling for the removal of those officials implicated	National	5

[a]Based on interviews of a total of sixty deputies.

summarizes the five types of cases handled by service-oriented deputies, indicates the rough proportion they represented of the average (200-300 per year) case load, and the primary administrative levels where such problems were usually handled.

The Lower House as a body was not particularly swift in linking deputy constituency service work to its own development as an institution, and, until the Tet offensive of 1968, little attention was paid to this aspect of the legislature's role in either floor debates or in the organizational structure of the House as it was formulated in the bylaws. Until Tet, there were few procedures established for deputies to channel complaints originating in their constituencies to a ministry in Saigon. In the absence of such procedures, deputies either made their case known through their personal friendship with a minister or simply wrote to the appropriate ministry for action. Now all complaints can be channeled through the Speaker's office though deputies still prefer to seek action on a personal basis if they can. The Lower House secretariat has also organized a People's Aspiration Office under the direction of the Administrator General of the House (a civil service appointee) which has developed a case load of its own and has handled more than 2,000 cases.[11] Since Tet, moreover, the House has made official delegations to more than half of the provinces to investigate particular crises and distribute relief materials and money to war victims. In the summer of 1968, at the suggestion of service-oriented deputies, the minutes of the meeting discussing the general nature of constituency problems were sent to the executive.

Deputy Huy of DaNang expressed the theme of the session and observed that, to most of the population, the government appeared not as one institution but as having many distinct faces. Huy pointed out that government policies could only work effectively if cadres and the entire governmental infrastructure carried such policies out effectively. The session minutes would be forwarded to the executive, therefore, to inform him of the general situation in the countryside and of Lower House deputies' assessment of problems involved in the execution of public policies. It was hoped, as one deputy pointed out, that a close and sincere cooperation would develop between the executive and the legislature as well as among individual deputies and provincial, district, and village governments.

The major problems mentioned in the subsequent debate fell under three categories. The most frequently mentioned problem concerned the execution of the Phoenix program, to be discussed in Chapter 9. A second problem was the corruption of government officials. Deputies read into the record detailed cases, including the names of officials in their provinces engaged in corrupt activities. The anticorruption campaign, it was observed, was aimed at the wrong level. The current effort, they argued, was a pruning exercise that left the roots of corruption intact. Deputies sought not only to indict individuals but also to present an outline of the entire system of corruption that had been established in their provinces.

Based upon subsequent interviews, it would appear that the presentation of problems in detail at this meeting and later through articles in opposition newspapers was an indication of the limited ability of Lower House deputies to deal with the problem of corruption locally. Corruption was so ingrained that the deputies felt nothing short of the removal of an entire set of officials would remedy the problem. In most cases involving a single official, the deputies pursued a policy that could best be described, as one put it, of making "as big a stink as possible over the official in Saigon in the hope that the government would be obliged to move the official to another province in order to quiet things down." Removal campaigns, when seriously launched, were usually long and fierce and involved exchanges of abuse, countercharges of corruption, and press statements by each party. A removal campaign is distinct from tactics used by many deputies who were not active in their constituencies and who tried to compensate for this by making scathing statements in the province against the local officials, but without taking any official action to have such officials replaced.

A removal campaign is more involved and sustained. A corrupt province chief is confronted with documented evidence distributed with a locally written letter from the deputy to the constituents requesting their support. In Saigon, the charges are read into the congressional record and usually are published in one of the opposition's daily papers with supporting editorials. The deputy also presents his evidence to the Americans and throughout the campaign tries to get American advisers to bring pressure on Saigon to have the province chief removed. After the initial evidence is presented, countercharges are then made by the province chief who may use a respected citizen to write a letter to the population casting aspersions on the deputy to offset the charges made against the province chief. Prominent individuals have often been coerced into writing such statements, and this has been subsequently and openly admitted. The purpose of such letters is not to sway the local population but rather to present to Saigon a clear indication that respected members of the community support the province chief rather than the Lower House deputy. In response to this tactic, the deputy will often organize a petition and present it to the Minister of Interior. Thereafter another round of letters and counterletters are circulated with increasing arguments *ad hominem*. At this point, the province chief has usually received an indication of support in Saigon, and he will either seek to avert further clashes by firing some subordinate and blaming all the corruption on him or he will begin to harass local supporters of the deputy through the police.

In order to understand the dynamics of a removal campaign, it is necessary to understand the politics surrounding the tenure of province chiefs. A province chief is a military officer appointed to his position by the Minister of Interior. The position is usually a reward, based upon the outcome of political struggles between Vietnamese generals. When Thieu sought to diminish the power of Ky, for example, the province chiefs replaced during an "anticorruption" drive were all Ky supporters. A province chief's position and, ultimately, his success do not depend upon his performance as an administrator in the province except in a negative sense. As one deputy who had himself been a province chief prior to his election observed: "The government has a disease called 'official reports.' If a province chief knows how to write good ones, he will be promoted. But the writing of good official reports takes much time, and the province chief is left with little time for the population. If a province chief devotes most of his time to the people, then he has no time to write good official reports, and he will not be promoted." Another deputy pointed out that, "Official reports in this government do not have to reflect what is really going on; they only have to report that 'progress' has been made. If a province chief can say to his superiors that the programs in his province are making progress, then everybody is happy; the government officials can tell this to the Americans, and the province chief can keep his promotion." In addition, a province chief will not be penalized for doing a poor job unless he receives too much attention or publicity. A province chief can be corrupt, a poor administrator, or heavily favor one group versus another, for example, as long as this is not seriously challenged in Saigon.

The position of a province chief can be challenged if the particular general to whom he owes his appointment falls from power. Or, American advisers in the province can oppose the province chief and, if supported by their superiors in Saigon, can bring pressure to bear upon the appropriate generals to have the province chief transferred to another province or assignment. Little is known about either of these processes although all political actors in Vietnam are aware of their existence. Many American advisers interviewed noted that their greatest problems involved getting a corrupt official removed because such a request had to go through a hierarchy of channels. One adviser observed that, in order for him to get a corrupt district official removed, he had to go through the senior American district adviser who, in turn, presented the case to the senior American in the province. The Senior Provincial Adviser, as the latter is called, had to go to the Corps Senior Adviser who then took the case to Saigon where it went through a similar series of channels. As one adviser summarized the net effect of the process: "By the time it comes to a ranking American official in Saigon, the case appears too trivial a matter for Bunker to threaten his relationship with Thieu." Given this hierarchy and its inherent limitations, the Lower House deputy views American support as only marginally useful.

Finally, the position of a province chief can be challenged by a local political movement against him. This process has involved Lower House deputies in well-documented and well-publicized campaigns against corrupt province chiefs. The average length of a removal campaign initiated by a House deputy ranges from three to six months, and four of these campaigns have been launched. During the normal course of a removal campaign the province chief has little means to silence the deputy's charges and must rely entirely upon retaining the favor and support of the general who secured his appointment as province chief. While the deputy can continue to denounce the province chief and even may be able to do so in conjunction with American provincial advisers, the basic decision to remove or transfer a province chief is political rather than administrative, and it is made in Saigon.

Some of the removal campaigns have been surprisingly successful. In two particularly bitter ones, American advisers noted that the subsequent performance of the province chiefs actually improved as a result of the campaign. It was reported that they had reduced their corrupt activities substantially and, in one case, had even transferred some officials involved to another province while the province chief had begun to act more responsibly toward his duties and the population.[12] All of the deputies interviewed noted that campaigns against corrupt officials should be approached with extreme care. During the course of the campaign, it was suggested, the ill will roused among officials makes intervention for constituents practically impossible and, unless the official in question is removed or can be reformed, constituency work becomes impossible at the local level. This caution explains, in part, why there have been so few removal campaigns conducted by active deputies.

For a majority of the service-oriented deputies, intervention on behalf of constituents is the politics of the possible. The relationship between a deputy's feelings of personal success and efficacy and his selection of those problems most amenable of solution is a strong one, fostered by the maxim that requests their constituents to be reasonable in terms of what they seek and what the governmental authorities are able to provide. The principal purpose of the careful investigation that deputies try to make before handling a particular case is not only to establish the validity of the constituent's complaint but also to assess the chances for success. The administrative level where intervention is started, thus, reflects the deputy's assessment of those levels that have the greatest potential and authority to resolve the particular problem. Underlying constituency service, too, is the deputy's assessment of the various incentives government officials may have to resolve a problem once it is known that the Lower House deputy is interested in it. Essential to the deputy's strategy in a particular case is the need to keep the constituent fully informed of what is being done so that the constituent can gain understanding of how the government works and what his civil rights are. Constituency service, thus, has functioned both to solve specific problems as well as create clearly defined channels through which they can continue to be resolved in the future.

The Impact of Constituency Service
on Province Government

Until the involvement of Lower House deputies in constituency service, a virtual monopoly on decision making was maintained by the province and district chiefs in Vietnam. Under these high-level officials existed a network of lesser officials whose appointments, like those of their superiors, were due to political connections cultivated within the provincial services or the ministries in Saigon. In both cases, the constituency of the provincial officials was rarely the population they were appointed to serve. Since they had little impact upon the professional and political careers of these officials, the population also had limited means to seek relief from the decisions (or lack of them) of the government bureaucracy.

So also the government has had little means of relating itself to the population or responding to its needs. With the appearance of the Lower House deputy on the provincial scene, both the population and the government have been brought into a closer working relationship.

Based upon the cases observed, the development of working relations between the deputy and the province government required, first, that each actor know the other. In some cases of working relations, the deputy had previously been a ranking civil servant assigned to the province or a military academy classmate of the province chief. In cases of previous assignment at a high level within the province government, the deputy also benefited from the friendship and respect he had gained from a variety of lesser officials. Second, since the mandate of the deputy and his legal place in local government was ambiguous, working relations depended upon advice given by independent observers of the province scene to both parties that it would be in their mutual interest to cooperate.[13] The major incentive suggested to the province chief was that such cooperation would forestall deputy criticism that could be troublesome in Saigon. It was also pointed out that the Lower House deputy could provide a useful means of communication between the province chief and the local population, and, similarly, it was pointed out to the deputy that he would have the ear of the province chief, making the former more receptive to resolving constituency problems. In most cases it was reported that this independent advice served to reinforce what each actor had believed the potential of a working relationship to be, and it indicated, more importantly, the values and mood of the local political community toward conflict and cooperation. Such advice was essential for those deputies who wished to remain firm in their antigovernment orientation in the eyes of the local population but who also wanted to develop their influence and power within the provincial government. Whether accurate or not, the conclusion drawn from the advice of independent observers by the deputy was often that it would be possible to cooperate with the provincial government and still be regarded as independent from it. A third element that tended to favor the development of working relations can be termed the crisis factor: to the extent that in a time of crisis the province chief realized a positive benefit from the Lower House deputy, the chief was thereafter inclined to participate wholeheartedly in establishing good working relations.

Despite obvious incentives for the development of working relations, most province chiefs were initially cool to the idea. There was little need for them to communicate effectively with the population, and the relationship appeared one-sided. The deputy had all the problems, but also reaped all the political benefits from getting them solved. A crisis focuses national attention upon the province and, consequently, upon the performance of the province chief. For most province chiefs, the Tet offensive of 1968 was such a crisis. Deputies were called upon by province chiefs to assist in calming the population in the wake of the attacks and to urge the population to obey the province chief and to cooperate with the police. In areas where Viet Cong units had established themselves in populated quarters, often the deputy and the province chief would oversee the ouster of the Viet Cong. In one case, for example, during the 1968 offensive a deputy and the province chief were both working in a refugee area when a squad of Viet Cong opened fire from a cluster of ten or fifteen houses. The province chief called for more troops, and a pitched battle was begun to dislodge the Viet Cong. Soon the province chief was faced with the need to shell the entire settlement which housed four hundred or five hundred families. The chances were great that many houses would be destroyed, and the province chief asked the deputy if there was any way that this could be avoided.

The deputy called together those families who lived where the Viet Cong had positioned themselves. The heads of the families decided that they could sneak back into the cluster, set the houses on fire, and smoke the Viet Cong out provided that those families whose homes would be destroyed would be guaranteed construction materials at the official government price and that there would be no delays in their application to the government for reconstruction loans and assistance. The deputy got on-the-spot agreement from the province chief that the conditions would be met, and the villagers proceeded with their plan. The houses were set ablaze, and the Viet Cong were dislodged.[14]

In addition, the province chiefs also called upon the deputies to use their influence to speed up and seek supplements for relief assistance due the province through intervening with the national agencies in Saigon. The Tet offensive provided province chiefs inclined toward the establishment of working relations with the first clear example of its worth. Subsequent attacks such as occurred in May 1968 and the winter and spring of 1969 saw the further development of deputy-province chief cooperation. More-over, as new government regulations were issued to the provinces, the province chief would call upon deputies to help explain the more unpopular ones to the population. While in large measure it appeared to be the crises that the war produced which helped to cement effective working relations between the deputy and the province chief, interviews with both revealed that working relationships were viewed as part of a philosophy of government that each had in mind as they pursued their functions, but there had been little incentive in the past to put it into practice.

Although a majority of twenty-three cases observed fell under the category of working relations, two other patterns of interaction between Lower House deputies and province governments can be identified. One type can be termed reformed relations. In this type the deputy and the province chief usually began with either neutral or openly hostile attitudes toward each other. With war-related crises acting as a catalyst, reformed relations were instituted on the basis of a mutual recognition by both parties of the advantages inherent in cooperation. The province chief, often as a result of his witnessing the demise of one of his colleagues in another province during the course of a removal campaign launched by a Lower House deputy, recognized that cooperation with the deputy would assure that no trouble would be made for him at Saigon, and the deputy realized that he would be able to get more done for his constituents if he cooperated with the province chief. One deputy described the development of reformed relations in the following way, which was typical for the other cases observed:

> I entered office with the belief that it was my job to intervene for the population, and I organized a local office to assist me in doing so. At first I was very critical of the province chief, and our relationship was one of hostility towards each other. I realized, however, that, if such a poor relationship were to be maintained, the province chief would spend all of his time doing administrative work to avoid being charged with corruption and to insure that he would receive no bad reports from Saigon. I would also spend all of my time criticizing the province chief. The result would be that the people would be harmed rather than actually helped, and the cause of the communists would be advanced. I decided to see the province chief, explain my feelings to him, and suggest that we both make a common cause against the communists.

> Now we work very closely together. I have agreed to alert the province chief to any problems that I discover concerning local officials and local programs as an aid to making the province government more effective. In return, the province chief agreed to assist me in solving the problems brought to me by the people. And now we both work together on provincial problems that require action from one of the ministries in Saigon.

A third pattern of deputy relations with the province government can be characterized as hostile relations. In this pattern the deputy and the province chief were continually at odds with one another, there being no possibility of any effective working relations. The province chief regarded the deputy with disdain, often as an opportunist interested only in stirring up trouble for what the former perceived to be a smoothly functioning administrative machine. The province chief was also generally supported in this attitude by his American counterparts who also had no great regard for the Lower House deputy. The deputy regarded the province chief as an inefficient administrator, out of touch with the population, and corrupt. In most cases observed, hostility surfaced over the issue of corruption, and the deputy has waged a continual campaign to have the province chief removed.

These three patterns of relationships between the service-oriented deputy and the province government have tended also to determine the relationship between all deputies in those provinces where more than one was elected. The service-oriented deputy set the tone for his less active colleagues. In those provinces where a requested public works project was originally called to the province government's attention by an active deputy, the application to the Saigon ministries has increasingly come to bear the name of all the deputies and the province chief. In those provinces where an active deputy launched a removal campaign, similarly, he tended to enlist and receive the support of his colleagues. In this sense the service-oriented deputy has functioned not only to forge links between the population and the government, but he has also transmitted a mode of behavior to others in the house, paralleling at the local level the coalition of interests developed within the Lower House itself. Indeed, the fostering of coalitions within the province was, in part, responsible for the emergence of coalitions in the House.

As a new element in provincial government, the potential for the role of the Lower House deputy to grow into a valuable asset to both the population and the administration is great. One deputy province chief for administration pointed out that the deputy can serve as an important link in the process of government in Vietnam:

In our province, for the first time, the people have a direct and visible link to the province chief; the deputy is a voice that cannot be overlooked. But also for the first time the province chief has a direct link to the population. And because of the good working relations which exist between the deputy and the province chief, the province has been able to get more of its projects approved by the ministries in Saigon. This year, for example, our public works allocation will be larger because the deputy and the province chief collaborated to develop several new projects. The Lower House deputy then used his influence to get Saigon to approve them. This is the first time we have had any success in getting new projects funded.

More generally, one Lower House deputy suggested: "The government lacks intermediate levels through which the people can be assisted and the decisions of the government explained. The people have no means to effectively complain to the provincial government and the people." These statements suggest both the working relations that can develop between the Lower House deputy and the provincial authorities and the need for such a relationship to be created. Such relations are based upon the development of mutual respect by each of the actors for the other and a recognition of the ways that cooperation can aid each in the performance of his job. In those cases where effective working relations have been established, both the deputy and the province chief have realized that each can supplement the other's power, and in the process the population can be linked more closely to the government and provided with a voice and a source of influence traditionally lacking in local and provincial governments. Demands, thus, are transformed into interests.

Constituency Service and the Creation of National Interests

As the foregoing discussion makes clear, South Vietnam does not lack problems needing government response; rather, it lacks a responsive government. Institutions respond to pressures when it is perceived as being in their interest to do so.[1] But the provincial bureaucracy in Vietnam does not respond to the needs of the population as embodied in their requests for relief and assistance because neither the survival of the civil service nor the tenure of its officials is affected by such demands. The province chief, similarly, does not pay particular attention to the way his staff treats the population because his tenure and future career do not depend upon it. So also, President Thieu does not respond to the demands of political organizations for participation in the government because his tenure depends not on how the base of the government can be broadened but on how it can be narrowed and effectively controlled.

Lacking such incentives, the demand of one family or of many for governmental assistance or for the release of a relative imprisoned without trial as a Viet Cong suspect provides no incentive for government response. In themselves, popular needs and demands do not exert sufficient pressure on the government to reduce corruption or to implement the system of due process outlined in the Constitution. What is required is for demands to be transformed into political interests that the government cannot afford to ignore. To the Lower House deputy such a transformation is what is meant by broadening the base of the government; fundamentally, it is a call for governmental reform rather than a political revolution. As a legislative body, the Lower House has worked to create the legal framework for such reform. It has drafted legislation to decentralize the government, reform the civil service, and establish a system of due process. But, by the end of 1969, the deputies also realized the limited efficacy of such efforts unless they were also linked to an effort to create a basis upon which more effective political organizations could develop. Thus, the deputies realized that, unless a process of politics were established and more effective political organizations were to emerge, the political reform of the government would continue to be frustrated. The diffused demands of the population for deputy intervention on their behalf had to be transformed and organized into a set of national interests to which both the government and political organizations would respond.

Responding to constituency problems has been viewed as an important way to link the functioning of the Lower House to the population; taking the initiative on restructuring government and politics to make them more responsive to popular and political aspirations is viewed as a means of gaining the initiative in legislation that formerly was solely the prerogative of the executive to propose. The focal point of the discussion that follows is the question of the establishment of due process. The selection of this issue highlights the importance placed on reform. Unlike the more popularized issues of the recent past such as land reform, due process legislation originated within the House itself, a product of its struggle with the Thieu government.

The Case of the Phoenix Program

Internal wars and the tactics employed to prosecute them tend to abridge and abuse civil rights. Only through the abuse and abridgment of civil rights, however, has an awareness of their existence developed. The arrest of certain villagers as suspected Viet Cong agents is not a new feature of life in rural Vietnam,[2] but the advent of the Phoenix program has produced arbitrary arrests on so large a scale that reaction, both in Vietnam and abroad, could hardly have been avoided. This abridgment of civil rights has also presented the Lower House deputy with, as one described it, a "natural" in terms of constituency service work.

Of all the problems that concern the service-oriented deputy, none involves him more deeply in constituency service as those related to the injustices of the Phoenix program. Without exception, service-oriented deputies reported that this program generated most of their case load and required the greatest amount of personal attention. The program was instituted by executive action in late 1967 and promulgated in July 1968 by executive decree under the authority of Article 4 of the April 1967 Constitution, which provides in its first section that "The Republic of Vietnam opposes Communism in any form." The program, a national project to coordinate the efforts of the military and the civilian intelligence agencies in eliminating the Viet Cong infrastructure, was fully implemented in the wake of the Tet offensive of 1968 after years of American requests for such a program. With the aid of captured documents and interviews from Viet Cong defectors, the government security agencies developed a rather detailed picture of the Viet Cong infrastructure[3] and constructed a theoretical estimate of the number of Viet Cong cadre that staff it. Consequently the fundamental problem involved in "rooting out" this infrastructure has been the problem of identifying those individuals at the local and provincial levels who are members of the Viet Cong.

The Phoenix program was designed to coordinate the intelligence collected by all security agencies about Viet Cong cadres in order to identify specific Viet Cong suspects. As one observer of the program in operation has noted, "The eighth or ninth of such projects, the Phoenix program had the originality to centralize all intelligence and all powers of execution in the person of a single army or police officer in each district and province headquarters."[4] The government estimated that in 1969 there were 98,763 members of the Viet Cong in South Vietnam and claimed that it developed dossiers on 53,936 specific individuals.[5] These individuals are classified in the following way:

> Type A: all Communist Party members and party elements holding positions at any level in the Viet Cong hierarchy;
>
> Type B: cadres who are in charge of training and recruiting others but are not Communist Party members;
>
> Type C: elements of the population whose activities benefit the Viet Cong.

Each province is assigned a quota, based on intelligence estimates, of Viet Cong suspects of each type that must be arrested each month. Each province has an appointed Security Committee, membership consisting of the province chief who acts as chairman, a judge of the local court, the ranking military commander in the province or his representative, a province councillor, the chief of the national police field force, and the chief of the Internal Security Service who acts as the committee's rapporteur. The committee meets once a week, reviews the case against Phoenix suspects, and determines a verdict. Type A suspects can be imprisoned up to two years, Type B suspects from between one to two years, and Type C suspects for less than one year. All sentences can be reduced, although they seldom are, through probation. The decision of the Security Committee can be reviewed (whether at the defendant's request or not is unclear) by a Committee on Pacification composed of the province chief, the commander of the operational military forces in the area, the chief of the national police, the chief of military security service, and the chief of province's military intelligence adviser. This committee is the only one empowered to release suspects, and it is to this body that Lower House deputy interventions are aimed.

The principal problem with the Phoenix program concerns its arbitrariness. Arrests can be made by elements of either the national police field force, the military security service, or any military unit assigned to the province as its tactical area of responsibility. While it is probably true that dossiers can be constructed on members of the Viet Cong infrastructure, a positive identification is difficult to make. Viet Cong cadres usually operate under a variety of assumed names and have been noted for the deep cover they are able to develop. By habit and training they are not likely to reveal themselves carelessly. And herein lies the problem: Viet Cong are hard to identify. Often the security force must rely upon testimony from others who can describe a suspect's activities. In some cases, moreover, a suspect's specific link to a Viet Cong cadre has not been established; he may still be but a suspect rather than a confirmed cadre or party member. And it has not been unknown for a person to denounce another as being a Viet Cong for personal rather than patriotic reasons: "In one village in An Giang province a woman came to the GVN officials with the story that her brother-in-law had tried to persuade her husband to pay taxes to the Viet Cong. Though her brother-in-law turned out to be an old man with heart disease whom the woman disliked, the district intelligence cadre had within the week arrested and tortured him as a 'Viet Cong tax collector.' In another village a conscientious village official discovered that many of the peasants were selling whatever gold and jewelry they had to pay blood money to the local Phoenix agent in order to prevent their being harassed and arrested by the agent. When he attempted to tell the district chief about it, the agent fingered him as a 'Viet Cong suspect' and had him fired."[6] Cases of such abuse as the ones presented above are typical throughout Vietnam where Phoenix officials have turned the threat of arrest into a moneymaking scheme. It is significant, moreover, that the particular example cited by Fitzgerald occurred in An Giang, the most secure province in Vietnam, but one still required to meet a monthly quota.

A second major problem concerning the functioning of the Phoenix program involves the quota system itself. Each province is given a monthly quota of Viet Cong infrastructure to neutralize. The failure to achieve this goal reflects poorly upon the province government. Consequently there is tremendous pressure on officials and security agencies to capture people for the sake of fulfilling their quotas (in some cases exceeding them in order to demonstrate "progress"). One of the major sources of "Viet Cong suspects" are military operations that move into a Viet Cong area and pick up all the civilians they encounter. This method is called the "snatch" and on official reports the suspect is "linked" to the Viet Cong because he was found in an insecure area. Given the fact that few of the army's operations actually achieve surprise, it is reasonable to expect that Viet Cong cadres in the area have been forewarned by the local population or by the notorious lack of secrecy surrounding such operations and have fled by the time the operation begins. Many persons with no proven link to the Viet Cong end up as Phoenix suspects. The net effect of the program in some provinces has been to create new Viet Cong rather than to "root out" established operatives. As one deputy remarked in an interview: "The current program is actually creating eighty new Viet Cong for every ten that are in fact discovered."

A third problem with the Phoenix program is the opportunity it provides for corruption. Persons arrested to reach or exceed the monthly quotas are detained indefinitely until a bribe is paid (the most frequent figure mentioned was $5,000.00VN or about $25.00US) to local officials. In 1968, the government estimated that 17,996 Viet Cong cadres were eliminated, and, of that number, 2,524 were listed as killed in action, presumably before they were interrogated, while fleeing from an army operation or caught in its cross fire. From January to May 1969, another 18,577 were reported eliminated. The difficulties of identification, coupled to the pressure placed on local officials for results and the corruption that has come to characterize the program, have probably resulted in very few Viet Cong being captured, a fact acknowledged by American officials who have worked with or observed the program in operation.

The Phoenix program has been a major concern of Lower House deputies. They are called upon by the families of their constituents to seek the release of those detained, and often the deputies are the only nonmilitary personnel allowed to visit suspects in the province jail. Frequently, they are simply asked to carry food to the suspects to augment the meager diet of prison life. At the local level active deputies have generally tried to work through the province security committees in order to speed up the investigation and screening process. When the deputy is alerted to a constituent's arrest, it would appear that most have adopted the rule of thumb whereby they seek to have someone they know personally vouch for the victim and then, in turn, vouch for the victim before the security committee.

In May 1969, the abuses of the program were given national attention as the result of an inspection visit made to Vinh Binh province by a Lower House delegation consisting of the chairmen of the Judiciary, Information Chieu Hoi, Anticorruption, and Revolutionary Development Committees. The report of the investigating committee on the condition of the Vinh Binh jails and the corruption of the program resulted in a House petition, signed by eighty deputies, requesting an interpellation of the Ministers General of Justice, Interior, and Defense.

The principal theme of the interpellation was that the Phoenix program constituted a violation of the due process guaranteed to all citizens under the April 1967 Constitution. The constitutional case against the Phoenix program is based upon Articles 7 and 8 of the April 1967 Constitution. They provide that each citizen is entitled to a speedy and public trial and is protected from arrest and detention without a duly issued legal order presented prior to his arrest (except in cases where a person is caught flagrantly violating the law, that is, "in the act"). The accused and his next of kin must be informed within twenty-four hours of the charges made against him, and the Constitution specifically forbids the extraction of information by torture. Every defendant also has the right to legal counsel during every phase of interrogation and investigation, the right to bail, the right to sue for damages, if wrongly or unjustly accused, the right to privacy in the home unless a legal order is obtained, and defendants are presumed innocent until proven guilty. In theory the Phoenix program must conform to these basic guidelines and, as the then Minister of Interior (and now Prime Minister) Tran thien Khiem observed before the Phoenix program, there had been no clearly articulated standards governing arrests for suspected communist activities.

The Ministry of Interior maintained during the interpellation that only those caught in the act were arrested. In the cases of those suspected of communist activities or denounced by letter, the police could not arrest them for investigation; they could only invite the suspects to appear for questioning. Within twenty-four hours the particular suspect's case had to be brought before the Security Committee, which acted as a grand jury. Those actually arrested had to have their case heard in a public court within twenty-four hours. In insecure areas, the time limit could be extended to seventy-two hours. Further extensions of this limit, however, were permissible, and a suspect could be detained up to one month by a decision of the Security Committee. Thereafter specific authorization was required from the Ministry of Interior. Searches of private property required the approval of the local court, but in case of emergency two witnesses could be substituted for the search warrant provided the local court were subsequently notified. Suspects could not be tortured, and the detention center had to provide adequate sanitary and other facilities. Relatives were allowed visiting privileges twice a week to bring food.

In practice, the principles set forth by the Ministry have not been followed. The practice of due process is not an established one in Vietnam. The civilian court system is weak and understaffed in the provinces, particularly the rural areas, in contrast to the highly developed system which exists in Saigon. Moreover, of less than two hundred lawyers in Vietnam perhaps 90 to 95 percent practice in either Saigon or the other autonomous cities. What due process there is has been further undermined by the development over the years of a special military field court system. In the areas that have experienced both the most insecurity and the greatest stability during the course of the war, these courts have been the primary institution of justice for the rural population, for, under a variety of decrees, they have been authorized to handle all cases involving minor and serious offenses against national security. The trial personnel of the courts are military officers appointed by the executive. Little preliminary investigation is conducted, civilian defendants are usually not afforded counsel, and decisions are final since no appeal is permitted.

Guarantees of due process have also been weakened by the extensive powers of police and security forces. The Military Security Department established in 1951, for example, is empowered to arrest anyone without the prior approval of the civil courts although no reason is required to be given as to the charges against those arrested. Similarly, the army units can make arrests during operations without the approval of local civil courts. Indeed, as one deputy observed, "Local institutions that could protect citizens have in practice virtually no power [over the security services]." As a result, the guarantee implicit in the prior notification and approval principle has hardly been a curb to the powers of the police. In the Phoenix program alone, the government reported, more than 34,590 persons have been arrested under the auspices of the military security department and army intelligence units.

During the course of the interpellation, the deputies told of cases that suggested the program had violated almost every guarantee presented in the due process section of the constitution. Suspects have been tortured, beaten by the presiding military judge for speaking out on their own behalf, detained for periods of between five and sixteen months without trial, forced to pay bribes to local officials, treated as if they were presumed guilty rather than innocent, arrested based on letters of denunciation that were subsequently proved to have no basis in fact, and denied public trials. In some cases it was pointed out that the local security committees themselves had not met for extended periods so that captured suspects were imprisoned indefinitely. Noting the high proportion of military members of the security committees, one deputy suggested that its membership be expanded to include more popularly responsive persons. This and other suggestions for changing the administration of the program were consistently answered by the argument that, before Phoenix, the situation was much worse and that the program must be given a chance. Indeed, the tenor of the interpellation can be summed up in the remarks of one deputy who observed: "Why is it that I as the fifteenth speaker, to be followed by others, will say that the good intentions of the program are being harmed by your subordinate staff and still you refuse to believe it?" Finally, many deputies also noted that defendants were refused the benefit of counsel for their trial. In response, the Minister of Justice, Le van Thu, noted that, while Article 7 of the constitution states that a lawyer can be present at all stages of the proceedings against an individual, "this is only written in the constitution. In order to apply it, there must be rules and regulations promulgated and applied. This has not yet been done." And while an interministerial committee had been formed to develop such rules, it had made no progress by the end of 1969.

In addition to the constitutional case against the Phoenix program as it presently operates, subsequent interviews with the leaders of the floor debate during the interpellation and those deputies who participated in the investigation made in Vinh Binh revealed considerable concern about the program as a national strategy designed to counter the communists. While most of the individuals interviewed acknowledged that a program to eliminate the Viet Cong infrastructure was necessary, they believed it must clearly differentiate the government from the Viet Cong. Deputies advancing this argument maintained that incumbent governments in Asia, when faced with an internal war, have historically been torn between two opposing traditions best summarized by the following proverbs: *Bat nham mot nguoi hon la tha lam mot nguoi* ("Capturing the wrong person is better than releasing the wrong person"), as opposed to *Tha lam mot nguoi hon la bat nham mot nguoi* ("Releasing the wrong person is better than capturing the wrong person"). These proverbs are well known among Vietnamese, and for those living in the South they have come to represent the fundamental difference between the philosophies of communism and their republic. The first proverb represents the position that most people think is taken by the North Vietnamese government and by the Viet Cong since Tet 1968. The second proverb is said to describe a strong, just, and benevolent government of the kind that Vietnam should have. One deputy observed that the best example of this kind of government was that of the Khong Minh period of approximately 2,000 years ago, when enemies were released seven times in order to provide them the maximum benefit of the doubt. It is thought that any program aimed at the elimination of the Viet Cong should be based upon the second principle since the majority of the population views it in those terms. That the government can defeat the Viet Cong is only part of the struggle; it must also prove that in doing so it is more deserving of popular support than its opponent. Even if the wrong persons were released, such a demonstration of government concern for individual liberty might encourage more Viet Cong to defect. Thus, while the necessity of the program was recognized, opponents of the Phoenix program in the Lower House argued that the government must strictly control itself and, above all, use the objective of winning the war as a reason to safeguard rather than abuse individual rights and liberties.

In the context of constituency service the Phoenix program illustrates the way deputies not only serve the process of government but also create it. Intervention on behalf of those arrested was conducted as a constitutional matter, rather than as simply a matter of pressure politics involving influence relationships between the deputy and local government officials. At the local level the deputies' activities on behalf of constituents arrested under Phoenix operations, including their appeals to the local security council, are couched in constitutional as well as human terms, and such appeals are viewed as having begun the process of education for local officials about the guarantees of the Constitution. At the national level the Lower House has considered the program and its injustices in terms of the question of due process and how it can be achieved under conditions of internal war. More than any other problem in the range handled by service-oriented deputies, the injustices of the Phoenix program have become an institutional rather than merely an individual concern of members in the Lower House.

Legislating National Interests:
Establishing a System of Due Process

The primary legislative priority of the Lower House is, as one deputy aptly stated it, "limiting the authority of those officials who carry guns." A journalist who had himself spent four years in prison observed: "*Anyone with a gun can make arrests.* This is not just a cynical Saigon remark. While such a law cannot be found in any body of legislation, it is part of an unwritten code that Vietnamese civil servants at all levels understand and apply."[7] The concern of deputies, reflected in their legislation to establish due process and to reform local governments and administrations, is directly related to the belief that the legislature is the only public institution which can work toward the goal of changing the government system by changing its policies. For the Lower House deputy the public interest has joined the institutional interest of checking the power of the executive and the military. One service-oriented deputy summarized the current situation. "Today anyone who carries a weapon can arrest anyone who does not. Those who are arrested have no recourse to the law because in many cases it has simply not been drafted yet or the only legal system available is the one the military maintains in the countryside. The establishment of the due process system outlined in the Constitution would certainly benefit these people, and it would benefit those of us here in the House who realize the need to take away power from the military." Indeed most deputies interviewed would agree with the observation that, while the principles of due process are explicitly guaranteed in Article 7 of the Constitution, "the Administration still acts under the influence of feudalism."[8]

Most deputies reasoned that if the government required the support of the population in its effort to defeat the Viet Cong, then it must protect rather than abridge their civil and human rights. Commenting on this question one party journal expressed a view shared on a theoretical level by all organized political groups represented in the Lower House: "only in extremely necessary instances, owing to reasons of national security, may the rights of a citizen be limited. This limit must be established by a law stating clearly the sphere of applications [that is, the instances in which civil rights may be limited]."[9] The need to preserve and enforce a system of due process through the drafting of new laws is related also to the right of political groups to organize, a right that has in the past been abridged in the same ways that individual civil rights have been abused. But, as will be subsequently discussed, the rights of those engaged in political activities and the penalties they paid for it were never of national or public concern. Relatively few people were engaged in politics, and those that were, more often than not, had been both hurt and helped by the arbitrary actions of the police. To question political rights as a national institutional concern might have occasioned even greater retribution. Due process as a national issue was a most innovative way to avoid such problems and yet still provide benefits to all political groups. If a system of due process could be established to protect citizens as individuals and for relatively apolitical reasons, then the freedom of political organizations could also be better protected.

Today, South Vietnam has two systems of justice, separate but unequal.[10] One system of justice is relatively old and has been well established in urban areas; the other system of justice is a relatively recent outgrowth of the war and exists as virtually the only legal system in the countryside. The urban system is largely civil in character and personnel, while the rural is almost entirely under the control of the military. "Formal legal institutions as such really exist only in the urban areas of Vietnam. Rural areas are hardly touched by these more organized institutions and instead follow various forms of tribal and customary law. The peasant majority is almost totally unfamiliar with the law, the courts, and the values of the formal legal system."[11] While this statement is substantially true and underscores the important element of popular unfamiliarity with the legal system that exists, it does not take into account the role that the military have increasingly come to play in the administration of justice in the rural areas.

The system of military courts developed over the years in the countryside is in some senses an extension of Vietnamese legal traditions, as are the civil courts that developed in the urban areas. Prior to colonialization, Vietnamese courts did not distinguish between civil and criminal offenses, and the court system was a unitary one. "The principle of separation of powers in administrative and judicial matters did not exist. Administrative officials also assumed the role of judges because they represented the power of the king, and, like the king, were considered as 'The Father and Mother of the people.' "[12] While the French sought to change the legal system through the introduction of their own judicial personnel and the Napoleonic code, the administration of justice in the province and the rural areas remained essentially unchanged, and the thrust of most legal reforms and changes in Vietnam has been directed at the urban areas.

Courts in the provinces were presided over by the French province chief, and his administrative service chiefs served as prosecuting officers. Even after the period of reform in the early 1900's and until the termination of France's colonial hold over Indo-China, "the organization of the Vietnamese judicial system still presented many shortcomings, with no definite distinction between the administrative and judicial hierarchies, with no special magistracy. Within the court[s], there [was] no separation of the functions of prosecution, investigation, and trial, all of these being entrusted to a single official."[13] And the period regarded as the "renaissance" of Vietnamese legal history (1945 to the present) has not substantially changed the situation in the rural areas. What development and changes in the court system have taken place in reaction to the unitary nature of the court system before 1945 have been confined largely to the urban and metropolitan areas. Paralleling the development of civil and commercial law in the urban areas has been the growth of the jurisdiction of the military and the extensiveness of its courts in the rural areas.

To many rural inhabitants the military constitutes not only the government but also its justice. The growth of the military's role in rural justice is a consequence of its growth as a major institution of government. Just as military officers generally constitute the ranking officials in the provincial and district administration, so also military courts and tribunals often constitute the ranking judicial authorities in the countryside. The presence and capabilities of the military courts in the countryside are considerably more extensive than those under the authority of the Ministry of Justice. At present there are only two district-level courts presided over by a Justice of the Peace, and one is located in Saigon. Nine provinces have a Court of First Instance which functions as the basic provincial judiciary, and twenty-two provinces have courts organized by Justices of the Peace with Extended Jurisdiction who act as courts of first instance. Two regional Courts of Appeal in Saigon and Hue try cases referred to them by the provincial Courts of First Instance. One Court of Cassation exists to which complainants may appeal decisions of the lower-level Court of Appeal, and other more specialized courts have been established to deal with such questions as labor law, housing, minority customs, and land reform disputes.

By mid-1967 there were less than two hundred civilian officials to staff this court system, and that number has not substantially increased. In addition, there are less than two hundred civilian lawyers, of which fewer than fifty practice outside Saigon. The impact that the thinness of the court structure has had upon the civilian judicial system has been described in the following terms:

> There have been many difficulties in equitably applying the law. Distance between courts is often great and sometimes imposes an insurmountable burden on people seeking relief through the law. For example, to seek cancellation of an administrative decision by a province chief in Quang Tri or An Xuyen, a petitioner has to make the long trip to Saigon to file his petition. There, so far removed from the people and circumstances involved, the administrative judge, no matter how experienced or how rich in jurisprudence, may find it difficult to truly render justice. This adds to the problems of developing in the residents of more remote areas a strong belief and confidence in justice.[14]

The Ministry of Justice has attempted to deal with such problems through the creation of mobile civil courts and circuit riding judges, but such practices have not been noticeably effective. During 1969 the military court system handled approximately four hundred civil cases while almost no civil cases were handled in the civil courts. Indeed, justice more often came to rural inhabitants in the uniform of an army officer.

The tradition of establishing military courts in the countryside and the streamlining of their procedure (that is, the concentration of examining and deciding powers in a single military officer) dates from the necessity for such courts during the final days of the government of Bao Dai. Since that time two types of military courts have been developed. As an extension of its predecessors under the Diem government,[15] a regular military court exists in each of the four tactical zones under the auspices of the Directorate of Military Justice in the Ministry of Defense. Each court is endowed with broad and substantial powers of trial and punishment. "The martial court tries all crimes committed by military personnel, and all political, minor or serious offenses prejudicial to national security committed by military personnel or civilians. The Military Code has clearly defined the circumstances in which civilian offenders are brought to the Martial Court. Sentences of the Martial Court are final and can only be appealed to the Court of Cassation."[16]

The competency of the Military Court system, while broad, is by no means clearly defined. More than a dozen overlapping decrees exist, empowering it to try civilians. The basic procedural handbook used in the administration of military justice does not contain a clear definition of offenses "prejudicial to national security." One military judge observed that the rule of thumb used by himself and most of his colleagues was that whoever the police or security agencies brought to his court for trial came under his jurisdiction and had committed de facto crimes against the national interest.

The Mobile Military Field Court constitutes the other major branch of the military court system. As initially conceived, the courts under this system were designed only to try cases involving defendants caught in the act of endangering the national security, and their procedure is rapid and direct. Except in cases where the death penalty is decided, which automatically requires review for clemency by the President, the decision of the Field Courts is final. In practice, these courts try virtually any case brought before them. The trial personnel of the Field Court consists of five military officers, none of whom are required to be lawyers but, rather, are selected for the post by the President. Defendants may have the benefit of counsel appointed by the court, but such counsel need not be a practicing attorney. The Military Field Court is an institution designed to make a rapid response to threats to the national security during an internal war. It may meet at any place and at any time with little preliminary investigation of the case. The significance of its flexibility and power was noted by one civilian judge in a province where the Field Court had been most active: "My job is to try and 'beat' the Field Court to the case. I have been in the province five years and have established a regular circuit that I ride, but I am dependent upon the military for my transportation. By the time they agree to transport me to an area the Military Field Court has already been there, and all that is left for me to do is handle trivial matters such as the registration of births, deaths, and marriages."

The establishment and protection of a system of due process depends both upon the provision of adequate laws that define its principles and punish those who would violate such principles and upon the power of a public institution to enforce those laws. From a constitutional point of view, due process depends upon the construction of an independent and autonomous judicial system, the establishment of an agency empowered to discipline those who would violate its principles, and a framework of laws and regulations that govern its interpretation. But, given the Vietnamese context, the question of due process is also a highly politicized one. To those who violate or abridge a citizen's right to due process, it must be demonstrated that not only is such action unconstitutional but it is also politically unwise. In Vietnam, the burden of proof lies with the proponents of due process, and the significance of due process is directly related to the significance its violation presents as a political issue. A principle of the Constitution must have political as well as legal importance, and it must prove more costly to violate than not to violate such a principle in order for it to be established in practice.

The arrest and detention of political opponents as a device to forestall and weaken such opposition is part and parcel of Vietnamese politics. One opposition deputy, whose brother-in-law was a prominent Buddhist monk arrested for allegedly aiding Viet Cong activities in Saigon, led the campaign to get the monk released, declaring that the arrest was purely a matter of politics. This was, perhaps, somewhat of an overstatement. "When Prime Minister Huong was running for the presidency and before 1967 he had asked for the support of [this particular] Buddhist monk. The monk had always refused. Thus, when Huong became Prime Minister he sought the most immediate opportunity to arrest the monk. We know the order for the arrest came from the Prime Minister's office and not the President's." When the deputy was questioned as to whether the release of the monk was the result of Lower House pressure, he replied that this was partly correct although the monk's freedom was achieved through a presidential grant of amnesty rather than by a reversal of the verdict rendered by a military court against him—an outcome short of what various House petitions advocated. "The real reason the monk was released was because Huong is no longer Prime Minister." To the professional or semiprofessional politician the intrigues of such vendettas and such explanations of political events involving arrests are commonly offered and sincerely believed. In addition, those who are arrested often consider their sacrifice symbolic despite the very real specter of torture and deprivation that characterizes most Vietnamese prisons, and they readily point to the fact that the future of North Vietnam was planned by its greatest revolutionary as a political prisoner.

Outrage at lack of power rather than lack of due process has characterized the response of opposition groups when their members are imprisoned by the government. Concern about the treatment of political opponents within the context of Lower House legislation has not until recently focused on the abridgment of due process. By itself, the treatment of the political opposition would not necessarily have led legislators to turn the issue of due process into one of institutional concern. Indeed, the primary feature of the Lower House's initial concern for those arrested for political offenses against the government was to get those imprisoned released rather than to attempt to abolish the system by which they were arrested.

Initially, the House appeared to assume that a legal framework did exist to guarantee due process and that the Ministry of Justice was effectively supervising its implementation. Experience with the Phoenix program, however, suggested that such initial confidence was misplaced. Moreover, a survey of the editorial comments made on the arrest of prominent political and religious figures in Vietnam over the past few years reveals a lack of similar explicit concern for changing the system under which political activists can be arrested. The rash of editorials that appeared in opposition papers demanding the release of the Buddhist monk referred to earlier, for example, did not, with only one exception, question the abridgment of due process that the monk's arrest and trial represented. The following editorial, written by a Lower House deputy is fairly typical in its first part of many that have appeared in connection with similar cases in various Saigon newspapers:

> But only to cancel the Thien Minh verdict is not sufficient to show the spirit of conciliation and solidarity of the government. Many others are in the same situation as Ven. Thien Minh—students who demonstrated for peace, a number of reporters, non-Communist political figures contacted by the Communists, and so forth. These also deserve the government's tolerance, if it is true that the present regime wants to prove it has chosen the path of tolerance.

> Tolerance toward Venerable Thien Minh only will bring no praise from the people, but will be regarded as an act of injustice—they will think that influential persons are under another law than a common one.[17]

The oblique reference to the constitutional question is significant in a number of respects. The author of the editorial was chairman of a special committee organized in 1967 to seek the release of seventeen students drafted into the army for their demonstration against the outcome of the 1967 presidential elections. As chairman of the committee, Deputy Chung did not pursue the matter along constitutional grounds, and, after the students were released, he recommended that the committee's functions not be extended. By the end of 1969, however, the attention of the House once again focused on questions relating to the abridgment of due process by the executive, but such concern was not of a more permanent and enduring nature.

The growth in the number of people affected by the Phoenix program in the provinces and the scandal it created, rather than the increase in the number of political and religious leaders arrested and imprisoned in the

Saigon metropolitan area, stimulated for the first time a deeply rooted concern for the establishment of the guarantees of due process. Ironic as it may seem, the relatively apolitical significance of the arrest of rural citizens, rather than the politically significant arrest of organizational and religious leaders, transformed the question of due process into a political issue intimately tied to the House's perception of the public interest and its own.

In the formative days of the Lower House, when confronted with problems involving the illegal arrest or summary trial and detention of civilians, the House tended to take a narrow view of its role in the matter. The primary objective of any House intervention that was proposed aimed at obtaining the release of those imprisoned, and participants in such intervention activities tended to believe that the new constitutional system would require time to "shake down," in general, and that due process, in particular, would be instituted by ministerial decrees and reforms. According to this evolutionary view of how civil rights would be established, the House's fundamental role was that of a watchdog. The dominant sentiment expressed by those deputies who participated in the early debates over the issue was that the system of laws existing in 1967 and the guarantees of due process in the Constitution were adequate although it would take some time before procedures could be established to assure their full implementation. Such an evolutionary view, moreover, was not seriously challenged by conditions requiring urgent action. During the last quarter of 1967 and the first quarter of 1968, the ramifications of the Phoenix program were not yet apparent, the level of overall repression of young student leaders was not noticeably high or symbolically unacceptable, and the potential for making a cause célèbre out of the arrest, summary trial, and detention of presidential candidate Truong dinh Dzu was practically nonexistent due to Dzu's rather unsavory commercial background. In addition, delegations of deputies had had some success in working with the executive on the question of political repression.

Consequently, the debates that took place over the issues involved in the arrest of students demonstrating against the election of Thieu or of demonstrators who participated in the Buddhist Struggle Movement of 1966 were characterized by considerable groping and hesitancy on the part of deputies to declare that the House had a particular role in regularizing the administration and execution of justice. Deputies' concern for the nature and the form of due process to be established by law developed gradually and tended to parallel the apparent and perceived decline in executive-legislative relations, the increase in repressive tactics used by the Thieu government to silence political opposition, and the extension of overt repression to a sizable proportion of the countryside. Indeed, the development of concern for due process and related questions of civil rights went through three almost distinct phases. The initial concern of the House was to use its institutional pressure to seek the release of those illegally arrested. In the second phase, while the desire for the release of those arrested was still dominant, considerable concern was also manifest for the constitutional role that the House should play in safeguarding and guaranteeing due process in the absence of an executive proclivity to do so. During both stages legislative output was low and what laws were made were promulgated by executive decree. In the third and current phase, due process has been viewed primarily as an issue linked to the very existence of the House itself vis-à-vis the executive. It has prompted active deputies within the House to initiate through legislation fundamental reforms in the nature of government and administration. Concern for the establishment of due process in this current phase has been linked to the general imperative that the power of soldiers and police must be limited at all levels of government.

The House's first involvement with the question of due process came shortly after its inauguration in 1967. On 2 October 1967, members of the Saigon Students Union organized a press conference to make known their position with regard to the outcome of the presidential election. Five days later the national police arrested seventeen of the leaders of the demonstration and held them in detention until 30 October. On that day they were "released," drafted, and sent to a nearby military training facility. The House formally considered the matter in the middle of November at the request of a number of deputies who had petitioned the Speaker to put the question on the agenda. The leaders of the floor debate, deputies who later were active in the investigation and denunciation of the Phoenix program, tended to denounce the practice of drafting youths who opposed the government into the army as being detrimental to the morale and effectiveness of the army. The army, they argued, could become a place of punishment rather than an agent of national service. While concern was expressed that such tactics on the part of the executive might "create a habit of disregard for constitutional rights"[18] and debate was premised upon the fact that the Constitution guarantees the right of opposition by legally constituted organizations, of which the Saigon Students Union was one, the substance of the debate concerned the way in which the House could most effectively respond to the students' plight. After three sessions that dealt almost exclusively with the procedure to be adopted, it was decided on 16 November 1967 to establish two special investigatory committees, one to deal with the specific matter of the arrest and drafting of the seventeen students and another to investigate the general nature of "political verdicts" under which persons had been jailed since the time of Diem. The second of these committees was to be set up after the House had organized a permanent committee structure.

Two weeks after the "Special Committee on the Students' Verdict" had been established, its chairman reported on its activities to the house. In a meeting with the Prime Minister the committee presented six points to which it subscribed.

- the holding of a press conference is an exercise of "free democratic rights";
- draft deferment is a privilege prescribed by law which cannot, therefore, be revoked by executive whim;
- if the executive believes students are guilty of a particular offense, then such guilt should be established in a court of law;
- the history of Vietnam demonstrates the value of national reconciliation and compromise (that is, leniency in this case) and that it generates more support for the government;
- students should only be drafted "in the natural course of events" (that is, when their deferments expire);
- the work of the committee was not designed to draft new laws but to see that the students were justly treated and that their situation would be regularized.

The chairman of the committee concluded his report by expressing his confidence that the problem would be rapidly and satisfactorily solved and that the manner in which it had been handled had laid the framework for cordial and meaningful executive-legislative relations.[19] By the end of December five students had been released from the army, and their student deferments were restored. The cases of the other twelve still awaited decision, although it was expected that they would also be returned to civilian life and to their studies.

The deputies' concern for the way political questions should be treated, rather than concern solely for the substance of the case at hand, is also reflected in their treatment of the issues involved in the range of "political verdicts" and decisions under which participants in various political events had been arrested and detained. Shortly after progress had been reported in the case of the "students' verdict," the House was confronted with the question of how it should respond to the people arrested and still detained as a result of the Buddhist Struggle Movement of 1966. Deputy Nguyen dai Bang of Hue city reported to the House in plenary session on 13 December 1967 that he had received a letter from a delegation of families representing those who had been arrested for their roles in the movement. The letter stated that twenty-six persons would be tried on 19 December before a Mobile Military Field Court and that these persons had been denied due process. The letter denounced the government and called the forthcoming trial an act of revenge against the Buddhists and evidence that the government was too weak to stabilize the political situation in central Vietnam by means other than repression.

The substance of the debate over the significance of the letter during that session and in succeeding ones, however, was focused largely on the question of whether or not such matters were constitutionally ones on which the House had competence to speak. The question of due process was a matter for the judiciary, it was argued, and, if the House discussed the matter or took specific actions in the particular case, then the House would have violated the separation of power prescribed in the Constitution. The separation of powers argument was subsequently rejected as specious by a majority of the members present largely because the dominant interpretation of the Vietnamese constitution is that the utility of separation of powers lies in the fluidity it permits rather than in the distinct lines between branches that it draws. It was argued, moreover, that in reality the administration of justice was even wholly independent from the executive and, therefore, if House intervention could help to make it more so, then such intervention would not constitute a violation of separation of powers but serve as a means to promote it. After two days of debate on the issue of the House's competence to deal with the question raised by Deputy Bang, it was decided to establish a special committee on "political verdicts" that would draft a provision for amnesty for all those arrested and in jail for their participation in political events since November 1963 and coordinate with the executive for the promulgation of this amnesty as well as in the case of the people to be tried before the military court.

The tenure of the Special Committee for Political Verdicts was not characterized by any significant successes. When its term had ended, the chairman recommended that it not be extended (although the House voted to the contrary). The committee had few meetings with representatives of the executive and received less and less encouragement from the latter that the question of "political verdicts" was one where a meaningful executive-legislative dialogue could be established. One member of the committee observed the lesson of the committee's experiences: "The reason the executive refuses to release the students [involved in the Struggle Movement of 1966] we have intervened for, in my opinion, is that the executive wants to give our legislature a lesson that you [the House] should fulfill your legislative duty and that this problem is an executive matter, and we [the executive] do not accept your intervention [in it]."[20] The waning of this committee's functioning and effectiveness represented a significant break with past legislative traditions and behavior in Vietnam. It marked the end of the use of special committees and delegations as a primary means of dealing with the executive. From this point until the end of 1969 the tendency for sensitive political issues raised in plenary sessions to be handled between the two branches by means of a delegation was replaced by the increasing reliance upon the interpellation of government ministers in open and closed sessions. The interchanges which took place during these interpellations tended to be symbolic and formalistic. Each side presented its own view repeatedly, but neither side exchanged views. Legislative-executive relations were at a low ebb.

The decline in executive-legislative relations paralleled a marked increase in the tendency for the House to assert its institutional independence from the executive. In the area of due process, this independence grew out of concern for the ambiguities in the body of decree laws promulgated prior to the Constitution of 1967 that provided the executive with substantial emergency powers. As a direct result of experiences within his constituency and based upon his study of the then current body of laws regulating and empowering the executive to abridge civil rights under "emergency procedures," Deputy Khieu thien Ke of DaNang introduced a draft bill in June 1968 that would affirm by its promulgation the existing state of war in South Vietnam but substantially limit the grant of power to the executive that previous "State of War" decrees had provided. The intent of Ke's bill was to abolish a 1965 ordinance that gave the executive virtually unlimited authority to restrict individual liberty, a grant of authority that, Ke maintained, was now not in keeping with the spirit of the Constitution. Under the Constitution of 1967 only the legislature could make such a grant to the executive.

The controversial 1965 ordinance provided in its second article that

"The Central Executive Committee [of the ruling junta, meaning the executive] is delegated the authority during the entire period of a state of war to apply appropriate measures to preserve the territory [of the Republic of Vietnam] and public order and security." The purpose of the revision was to delineate clearly the power of the executive and the specific action that it might take to protect public order and national security during the war. The specific actions that were enumerated, moreover, were clearly defined by existing laws that, in the author's view, contained adequate safeguards of individual civil rights. The measure was also intended to serve as a signal to the executive that the due process described in the Constitution rather than the "due process" that had grown up in connection with the military court system had to be followed. Finally, the bill was aimed at making it clear to the executive that all grants of power affecting the rights of citizens must come from the legislature. The dominant opinion of the House committee that reported the bill to the floor was that the importance of the bill lay in the signal it would represent to the executive, and the final House version did not include any specific enumeration of executive emergency powers but, rather, declared that the 1965 decree was abolished and that the 1967 Constitution was the major guideline to be used to determine what was within the power of the executive. The committee's view was that sufficient legislation already existed to delineate executive power and protect the people's rights. The bill was transmitted to the Upper House for its consideration at the end of June.

The Upper House did not share the Lower House's view of the draft bill as either a signal to the executive that only the legislature could authorize grants of emergency power or that existing legislation was sufficient to guide the executive and protect the people's rights during the war. The version of the bill returned by the Upper House for reconsideration in October 1968 contained an enumeration of nine specific executive actions that were authorized during a state of war:

—Control over the distribution of foodstuffs;
—The search of private homes at any time;
—Determining the place of residence of elements considered dangerous to national security;
—Prohibition of all labor strikes and strikes by market vendors;
—Prohibition of all demonstrations or gatherings considered harmful to national security and public order;

—Prohibition of the distribution or possession of all printed matter harmful to national security;
—Prohibition on the possession and use of arms;
—Control and restriction of communications and travel as determined by security requirements;
—The ability to proclaim martial law depending upon the security condition of a particular area.

In addition, the Upper House version preserved the broad power of jurisdiction for the military court system: "All violations of the law related to national security fall within the jurisdiction of the Military Field Courts which will try them in accordance with emergency procedures." In transmitting the new version of the bill, the Upper House made clear that, while it agreed that the 1965 decree was too general a grant of power and had to be changed, existing legislation was not adequate to clearly delineate the power of the executive and that, if the present bill did not do so, a harmful vacuum would exist and the executive would, as one senator put it, "take advantage of the people's rights."

In response, Lower House debate on the Senate version of the bill stressed that the specific grants of power it contained were as harmful as the vacuum that the earlier version, according to the Upper House, would create. The emergency procedures of the Military Field Courts, it was suggested, were "dictatorial and ruthless" and their continued existence or any legislation that tended to prolong such an existence was harmful to the establishment of an independent judiciary. Debate over the Upper House version lasted two days, but the outcome favored the Upper House version. Not enough votes in the Lower House could be mustered by those who opposed the changes that had been made to override the new version, and it was passed on to the President who promulgated it in November 1968.

In comparing the Upper and Lower House versions of the bill both are not striking for the protection of the people's rights they contain. Indeed, the vacuum left by the Lower House bill which relied upon existing laws to delineate executive power is almost as sweeping as the specific grants of power made in the Upper House bill. The significance of the differences between the two bills lies in the intent of each of the institutions that passed them. The Lower House wished to use the bill as a signal to the executive that the ultimate source of authority for all branches was the Constitution and that each branch must operate within the framework of the principles prescribed. The absence of any clear delineations of executive power in the Lower House version, however, reflected the uncertainty and lack of consensus among Lower House deputies about the extent of its own power and that of the Constitution. A generalized statement kept the situation fluid and maximized the House's ability to investigate further and test its role and powers vis-à-vis the executive. To the Senate, particularly supporters of a strong executive within the Senate, the bill represented an encroachment upon the powers which a majority of that body felt the executive needed and would demand of them. Some members of the Senate recognized the groping nature of the Lower House's involvement in the question of civil rights and due process and, thereby, also recognized that because of such groping the bill came at an opportune moment to assure the provision of adequate powers to the executive.

The groping that characterized the drafting of legislation concerning the promulgation of a state of war was in large measure a reflection of individual deputies' initial groping for their role vis-à-vis the executive. Indeed, the rather superficial nature of the Lower House's early legislation contrasts sharply with the legislation that was subsequently drafted.[21] So also the attitude of the House has changed substantially with regard to the adequacy of existing legislation and decrees covering a multitude of civil and administrative problems. The increase in the scope of the activities of the Lower House is a result of two distinct phenomena: namely, the threat to the institution's existence posed by the continued growth of the power of the executive, and the increasing involvement of deputies in the problems, politics, and government of their constituencies. The growth of the power of the executive as manifest in its increasing disregard for legislative opinion, reliance upon third parties to influence legislative behavior, and arbitrary administration of justice through the military courts has stimulated the growth of a spirit of independence within the legislature and its concern with due process as both a political and a constitutional issue. The Lower House has sought to gain the initiative in defining the terms by which certain key governmental and administrative reforms can be made. And, more important, a variety of deputies agree that the existence of the House as an independent institution depends upon its ability to shape governmental reform. The issue of due process and its establishment became linked to the whole question of the nature of local and provincial government. Taken together, these two concerns—both aimed at limiting the authority of the military—comprise the major legislative activity of the House as it entered its 1969-70 session.

The legislation drafted thus far makes the intent of the House clear. First, Lower House legislation aims at clarifying the status of persons jailed for political crimes. Two draft bills have been submitted concerning the fate of those imprisoned for their role in the following "political events":

— the revolution of 1 November 1963;
— the reorganization of 31 January 1964;
— the demonstration of forces on 13 September 1964;
— the coup d'etat of 19 February 1965;
— the coup d'etat of 20 May 1965;
— various demonstrations aimed at overthrowing the governments of Nguyen Khanh, Tran van Huong, and Phan huy Quat (1964-65);
— the FULRO event [the rebellion of the Montagnards].

One of the draft bills provides for the establishment of a civilian Council for the Consideration of Political Cases to review the cases of those' imprisoned for the above events; the other bill simply declares all judgments against such prisoners null and void and orders them returned to freedom. In order to cope with the problem to due process posed by the growing authority of the military court system, draft legislation has been proposed that would limit the jurisdiction of the regular military courts and authorize funds for the extension of the civilian judicial system by providing for more judges and more courts throughout South Vietnam. In addition, draft legislation has been submitted that aims at assuring the right of counsel to any citizen arrested by any arresting agency and which promises a speedy investigation and decision in the case of those captured by the Phoenix program, thus seeking to limit the time that a suspect can be detained without access to legal counsel and without his case having been acted upon.

Legislation has also been submitted that would substantially reduce the power of the Military Field Courts. This legislation fixes the duration of the court's existence, and requires that trial personnel have legal experience and be appointed by the Supreme Court rather than the President. Most important, the draft legislation would limit the jurisdiction of the Military Field Court to only those cases involving persons "caught in the act" rather than to any case involving national security as it is now empowered to try. Finally, individual deputies have acted to extend the bases of civil courts within their constituencies and have suggested the establishment of a system of civil district courts to facilitate the handling of civil disputes and the consideration of cases that too often fall to the military courts for lack of any comparable civilian court system at the local level. In their request to the Chairman of the Supreme Court, the deputies noted that they had the support of the province chief and in interviews suggested that this had been one of the outcomes of establishing working relations with the province government. The deputies also noted that, should the district court system work in the first trial province, they were prepared to work with other service-oriented deputies to pave the way for its adoption throughout Vietnam.

The struggle to establish a system of due process has also involved the Supreme Court and provided it with major occasions to assert its independence from the executive and associate its decisions with what emerged as a growing demand to have military tribunals declared unconstitutional. In the spring of 1970, twenty college students were arrested for "violating national security" by their participation in a series of demonstrations against the Thieu government and were scheduled to be tried before the Saigon Mobile Military Field Court. The court heard their cases on 20 April and, rather surprisingly, accepted the argument of their attorneys (one of whom was a deputy) that the constitutionality of the court was in question, and, in compliance with the Supreme Court law, forwarded the matter to that body for decision. In the meantime, the military court granted provisional liberty to ten of the twenty defendants. On 29 April the Supreme Court heard the arguments on the case and decided that the military courts were unconstitutional since its judges were not appointed by the Supreme Court but by the executive and that its procedures violated the due process guarantees of the Constitution. Less than a month earlier, on 5 May, the Court affirmed its earlier decision by reiterating in the case of the prosecution and trial of Tran ngoc Chau that the military courts were unconstitutional. The changes which the proponents of due process had hoped for as a result of these decisions appeared to have been secured, and the Ministry of Defense announced shortly after the decisions that it was preparing to cease the operations of the Military Field Courts.

Later, however, the legislature in joint session on 16 June voted to reinstate the Military Field Courts on the grounds that they were essential to national security. The significance of this action is difficult to judge although it is clear that the consensus achieved in the Lower House over the issue of due process was not matched by a similar commitment on the part of the Senate. As such, it illustrates the limits on effective reform action that is based largely within only one house of the legislature. This realization, coupled to the recent Senate elections, may suggest to the deputies that, unless greater cooperation can be fostered between houses as well as within them, the ability of the legislature to curb the powers of the executive will remain limited. The ambiguous note upon which this assessment of the relationship between constituency service work and the functioning of the House as a political institution ends strikes the theme of the next and concluding chapter of this study: political leaders in South Vietnam have just begun to discover that the bases of political community are the bases also of effective political action.

Chapter 10

The Bases of Political Community in South Vietnam

A political settlement and an end to the war depend upon the creation of political community between the nationalists and the communists in South Vietnam.[1] The prospects for both are linked to the creation of an arena where the current military struggle between these two forces can be transformed into political competition. For such a political solution to be practicable, however, the noncommunists and the Viet Cong will have to face each other as political opponents and this, by the end of 1969, the Saigon government was unprepared to do. A politically weak government would never agree to compete with the Viet Cong, and as long as it remains weak it will never have the incentive to seek an end to hostilities. Consequently, efforts to end the war require that Vietnam's politics and not its armies be strengthened. The purpose of this study has been to describe the creation and development of the Second Republic and the sources of conflict and accommodation that exist within its legislature as a micropolitical community.

Peace depends upon the achievement of political community in South Vietnam. Unless nationalist political forces are able to organize themselves effectively, they will not be able to compete politically with the Viet Cong; nor will they be strong enough to influence the Thieu government to seek a political settlement. In a very real sense the Lower House has begun to do that which the Viet Cong mastered quite early: link the population to government. Whether this process has in fact gone far enough or deep enough is not clear, but the farther and the deeper it goes, the Vietnamese would suggest, the more practicable becomes the notion of ending the war.

The elections that inaugurated the Second Republic selected an elite reflecting the political diversity of the polity at large but also containing important bases for accommodation. The challenges the Lower House faced during the period from 1967 to the end of 1969 in its dealings with the Thieu government, coupled with the growing involvement of its members in the problems of their constituencies, tended to provide incentives for political cooperation rather than political conflict among the deputies. The discovery of common interests both at the local and the national levels, in turn, led to the expansion of the scope of the House as a political arena where private demands could be transformed into public interests, interests designed to achieve a fundamental alteration both in the process of government and in the nature of politics. Such developments suggest a trend in Vietnamese politics that has been notably lacking in the past; they point, even if only tentatively, toward the beginning of political coalescence.

Coalescence must precede community, and formidable obstacles exist for those who seek it. First, cooperation and accommodation at the elite level must be transplanted to the polity at large. Second, sufficient incentives must exist for national political forces to cooperate on a truly national scale. Third, a relationship between government and political organizations and the population has to be developed where the people can realize tangible and meaningful benefits for participation in and support of their government. The extension of intraelite cooperation to the political milieu from where it was drawn has moved slowly, and only recently have issues developed into interests that stress a common cause among political forces. Even cooperation on such issues as the need to curb the power of the Thieu government, the preservation of legislative autonomy, or the necessity of reversing the direction of the Phoenix program does not necessarily mean that all conflict between political organizations can be either resolved or effectively controlled.[2]

Another principal obstacle to the achievement of a nationalist coalescence is reflected in the concern of some deputies that such an effort would require political incentives that do not presently exist. A coalescence of political forces, according to this view, would threaten the Thieu government's power base. While Thieu may recognize in theory the need for the support of the population in order to win the war, in practice he is faced with the more immediate problem of his own political survival. And for Thieu this does not depend upon the political mobilization of the population or upon the support of its organizations but upon his ability to dominate and control the military. One deputy observed: "The achievement of a nationalist coalescence depends upon the fate of Vietnam's social and political revolutions. So far the country has had neither, and as long as the generals are in power and the US is in Vietnam there will be no incentives for the generals to seek either the mobilization of the peasants or the renovation of society and government by establishing a regime based upon social justice." The Thieu government can do much to prevent such a coalescence from occurring, should such a development appear threatening to the regime. Indeed, to most Vietnamese the only development that would foster a coalescene in the short run is the inclusion of the Viet Cong in the political system.

To Vietnamese political leaders, therefore, confrontation with the Viet Cong in the political arena could prove worthwhile. All acknowledge that at the present time they would be unable to do so, but the present period is viewed as one of preparation for that eventuality. Such preparation is sorely needed. The Thieu government must learn to live with political forces and develop a relationship with the population that has hitherto been absent in government and politics in Vietnam. At the end of the 1960's the nationalist government in Vietnam existed as a military and an administrative entity, but not as a political force. While military developments, particularly those occurring after the Tet offensive in 1968, appear to have limited substantially the ability of the Viet Cong to dominate South Vietnam, the government has been unable to link the population to its cause. As one editorial writer summarized the situation:

> As the year 1970 begins, we can say that throughout the country military security has been considerably improved. But, as we are familiar with political warfare and Communist techniques, we cannot be over-optimistic because occupying land and controlling the people do not necessarily mean we have the people on our side. . . . what achievement has the government made after months of beating the drums for "political competition with the Communists?" None, alas. If we let opportunities go by, if we permit the Viet Cong to succeed in "neutralizing the people" [that is, creating the conditions whereby those not directly under Viet Cong control will also not directly support the government], the military security long built up will be like a "corpse without a soul" because, by sitting on the fence, the people never actively lend the Administration a helping hand in its anti-Communist struggle.[3]

Indeed, to most Vietnamese engaged in politics it appeared that the Thieu government was not at all inclined toward such political mobilization; it was headed, instead, in a direction disturbingly similar to that of the dictatorships of the past.

To the opposition, President Thieu's governance seemed the very antithesis of its declared goals, a parody of itself, in a country inclined toward strong or even dictatorial governments.

How should people understand President Thieu's statement that he risks unpopularity in order to protect the nation, while two years ago he launched the "Build Democracy" slogan to win his election? Indeed, how can democracy be built since the people are not the ultimate object of political activities? ... We will welcome the "severe measures" he promised if he has to take them for the people's sake.

We have chosen freedom and democracy, and we have rejected Communism because we don't want to follow the Communist path—the end justifies the means. Therefore, if no distinction is made now between ends and means how can we get out of the rut? By choosing democracy we have ostensibly considered the people as the masters of this land. Vox populi Vox Dei. Take for instance the problems of austerity and self-reliance. The people will endorse such policies unless they are mere slogans. Those who usually protest and exert pressure here are not the majority, nor do they represent anybody. If the President only pays attention to this minority, he will not move any nearer to his set goals, namely ending the war, building democracy and reforming society.

We are ready to tolerate dictatorship but a clear-sighted one for the sake of the people and not that of the regime.[4]

To the moderate supporters of the government, denied participation in the process of decision making or without means to influence it, frustration at the direction of President Thieu's political activities was as great as in the case of declared members of the opposition. As one editorial representing the progovernment point of view observed,

While President Thieu categorically confirmed that he would not indulge in politics, and while his six-party Political Front remains inactive, his government formulated a new political organization called the Inter-Ministerial Committee for Political Propaganda. This committee, headed by the Prime Minister himself, was motivated by the imperative need of defeating the Communists politically this year, through "mobilization of public opinion to challenge them."

Such an initiative is very interesting in principle. It would mean, however, "politicizing the whole government apparatus, civilian as well as military," that is, transforming civil servants and military men into political cadres. Two indispensable conditions would then be needed: First, the President and his government must have at their disposal competent core cadres able to play the role of "political instructors." Secondly, the President and his Prime Minister must define their political position vis-à-vis that interministerial committee which will become a kind of "Central Politburo."

Are the President and the Prime Minister courageous enough to follow this "political course?" Otherwise, a third hypothesis might be raised, contrary to the government's assertion that "the Inter-Ministerial Committee for Political Propaganda was not directed against national ranks." Indeed, that committee may tacitly be a propaganda tool of the Administration, a weapon to fight political opponents within nationalist ranks, exactly as the government radio and television stations are currently doing.[5]

Rather than link the population to the government or support organizations that could promote such an objective, by the end of 1969 the Thieu government still appeared preoccupied with consolidating its power base and limiting the potential of all political forces to mobilize the population.

In contrast, the attitude of political organizations during the period studied changed considerably. In 1967 political leaders interviewed tended to feel that their enemies were principally each other; in 1969, they had come to view their principal opponent as the Viet Cong. There were perceptible signs within long-factionalized organizations of progress toward resolution of factionalism and initiation of efforts to redefine the relationship between political groups and the population. Political organizations had begun to create interests by developing service relationships with their supporters that resembled closely the constituency service of Lower House deputies. Perhaps the most dramatic example of this change appeared within the militant Buddhist political organizations. As one leader, also a Lower House deputy, observed of the process: "The principal problem that we as Buddhists face is the reconstruction of our communities that have been ravaged by the war, by the Viet Cong, and by the repressive policies of the Thieu government. This is also a political task because we wish to instill in our people a sense of their identity. But to do this we have to gain the trust of the people. That is why the principal objective of the political organization we will construct will not be like the older Struggle Movements, but will be linked to what the needs of the people are and how, through their organizations, we can help to meet those needs. Politics must be made to serve the people and only in that way will the people come to trust political organizations."

As a consequence, Buddhist organizations within provinces and regions have increasingly come to emphasize social welfare services as essential to changing their image and relationship to the population. All of the members of the 1966 Struggle coordinating committee, for example, were, by 1969, the principal leadership for Buddhist social welfare services. All expressed the hope that such organizations would accomplish what the more issue-oriented movements of the past had failed to do, that is, the secularization of Buddhist participation in politics, and would provide a basis for the continuing involvement of the population in organizations of more enduring character than those previously created. In addition, most Buddhist leaders at the provincial and regional levels reported that they had come to deemphasize the importance of the split in the Saigon hierarchy between the moderate Quoc Tu and the militant An Quang factions.[6] As one leader observed: "While we are mindful of events and personalities in Saigon, we exist here in our own small world and are responsive by and large to local needs and pressures. And within this world we must get along with the government." To this end, the operating principle, both of social welfare organizations in particular and of local Buddhist hierarchies in general, was the promotion of cooperation between their forces, the government, and other religions as well. Propelled to seek cooperation by the magnitude of problems within their provinces, Buddhist leaders acknowledged that the patterns of such cooperative relationships were often established by Lower House deputies.

While the elections held in 1967 did not result in the creation of new political organizations, participation in the emerging framework of politics of the Lower House appeared to provide new organizational incentives and to suggest new patterns of cooperation and political action between and within political forces. The signs of new directions in politics are beginning to emerge, but the phenomena are so recent that an assessment of their impact on politics in general is not yet possible. It is clear, however, that activities of the Lower House deputies are increasingly being linked to the functioning of the House as a political institution that could both mediate between diverse interests and organize them into new sources of support for both the government and nationalist political organizations.

In addition, constituency service can serve as an important ingredient to strengthen the support for, and broaden the base of, such institutions and the political organizations they represent.[7] Deputy involvement in constituency problems can be translated to the political organization he represents or seeks to construct, producing both a new image for the organization and a link to the population. Development of effective means to represent the interest of the population, too, is likely to prove decisive for GVN efforts to foster the loyalty and support of the population. Without doubt, the failure to respond to local grievances has contributed to the success of the Viet Cong in mobilizing the population.[8] Constituency service functions to redress grievances that have long separated the population, the government, and noncommunist political organizations. At an earlier point in the war one counterinsurgency expert noted that, "I remember saying to General Khanh [the leader of the ruling junta at the time] that when I heard of a case of a peasant suing the government for a buffalo killed by the army during operations and being paid that compensation, we would be winning the war."[9]

Constituency service can also increase the scope of support for, thereby strengthening, the legislature vis-à-vis the executive. To the extent that a legislature serves as an arena where political forces can discuss their problems and organize effectively around the resulting issues, a legislature can demonstrate to the executive that it represents the interests of political forces the regime cannot afford to ignore. In the case of South Vietnam, representation involves not only the serving but also the creation of political interests. The creation of political interests may lead to the development of more effective political organizations and, in turn, more responsive government and administration. The experience of the Lower House, however, also suggests limitations beyond which such an institution cannot go without also developing a party system to support it. Cohesion among legislators can substitute for that which ought to exist among political forces, but only temporarily; intraelite cooperation is a prelude to the emergence of a party system, not a replacement for it.[10] Parties are the basic instruments of mobilization. Unless political organizations effectively mobilize the population, the Lower House, or any other institution for that matter, is unlikely to be successful in creating a political community where even nationalist political forces, let alone those represented by the Viet Cong, can participate.

Within Vietnam the achievement of political community is likely to be hastened not by the development of strong, progovernment political organizations but by the organization of opposition forces. The development of party systems depends upon the existence of meaningful polarities,[11] and to most Vietnamese the absence of effective opposition to the government is regarded as the principal cause for the government's increasing isolation from the people and its apparent disinterest in mobilizing their support. Only when the opposition emerges as a force to be reckoned with do the people feel that Thieu will take the necessary steps to organize a base of support for the government within the population at large. As one political leader, who expressed the consensus of many, observed during the summer of 1970:

President Thieu will only pay attention to demands of those political forces that are organized and have popular support. Right now, no party in Vietnam has such support, and Thieu has no need to pay much attention to either the political parties which exist or the recent demands made by those who have demonstrated for such causes as veteran's benefits, the release of political prisoners, or an end to the war. Thieu also does not listen to those of us who have always been supporters of the government; like the opposition, we are also weak in Thieu's eyes because we lack popular support for our parties. But even should we develop such support Thieu will still not regard us as important unless there also exists an organized opposition to make an organized progovernment party significant.

The emergence of an organized and effective opposition is essential to changing the bases of politics in Vietnam. Only with that development will the Thieu government take the steps necessary to organize its supporters. Until that is done, no coalescence among nationalist political forces can be expected, and without that coalescence no suitable means can be devised to regulate political competition between the nationalists and the communists. The achievement of political community requires political institutions both to foster coalescence and to regulate competition. As Huntington has perceptively observed: "In a society of any complexity, the relative power of the groups changes, but if the society is to be a community, the power of each group is exercised through political institutions which temper, moderate, and redirect that power so as to render the dominance of one social force compatible with the community of many."[12] In Vietnam this community of the many depends upon the scope of their organization and the institutions they support; so also does peace.

Implications for Young Legislatures and Old Regimes

Praetorian regimes thus far have not proved transient phenomena; they encompass many if not most of the eighty or so countries which gained independence after World War II. Though such regimes are narrowly based and generally have weak governmental systems, praetorianism is emerging as an incredibly persistent political order. The coups and countercoups of Africa and Latin America, and even attempts at social revolution in Southeast Asia, have thus far had remarkably little effect upon transforming praetorian polities into political communities. It is in such a

Table 10-1   Strategies for young legislatures versus old regimes

Issue in legislative development	Strategy for the young legislature	Strategy for the old regime
Power	Do not compete with executive; and	Share power with legislature; or,
	Trade-off legitimation of regime's policies for freedom to operate at the local level	Keep it occupied with legitimation functions: give it staff and keep members involved in the capital
Party development	Keep it separate from legislative activities; and	Sponsor a multiparty system that can be dominated; and
	Avoid making legislative blocs into parties	Gauge need to develop a progovernment bloc by the growth of the opposition
Governmental reforms	Concentrate on local reform packages, and be prepared for the long haul	Share legislature's reform objectives and, thus, preempt them
Executive dominance	Use threat as a basis for promoting cooperation between diverse groups	Use harassment of individuals to demonstrate the limits of the legislature's capacity to challenge political order

milieu that the young legislatures of most developing countries exist. In the table above I have tried to generalize from the Vietnamese experience some principles of behavior that young legislatures and old regimes might draw.

The sources of political power for young legislatures should be consciously differentiated from those of the regime. Too often, legislative politicians have sought to imitate the organizations of the regime and compete with them, bringing about dissolution of the assembly or incarceration of its members. Such politicians fail to see that the incubation of political organizations and the creation of power ought to take place in a milieu where the regime is weakest by creating links between the urban population and peasantry, so notably absent in most praetorian regimes. This is a prime site for the political activities of legislators as long as such activity is carried on outside the capital. In constituency-based assemblies, particularly, such activities are more appropriate at the local level, and keeping them there protects against premature exposure of relatively weak, but promising, organizations to the regime. Succumbing to the increasing pressure of both scholars and intergovernmental advisory groups alike to give the legislatures more to do and more staff might be wise counsel for the regime. If legislatures were busier and their members faced such formidable legislative tasks as is the case, for example, in the United States, perhaps both the perception of the need to create power and the organization this would require at the local level could be delayed or obviated altogether.

The internal organization of the legislature should not consciously reflect the political structure of the polity; nor should legislative leaders seek to use the blocs as if they were national chapters of regional and local organizations. When the internal organization of the legislature is least congruent with the prevailing political structure, old divisions among political, ethnic, or religious groups are minimized. Indeed, the legislature should be used to discover new bases for intergroup cooperation rather than to reinforce old divisions and enmities. Effective political parties require power; to create parties when power is in such short supply fosters cliques and factions instead of parties. The regime, of course, can preempt this process, ending the threat it ultimately would represent to the stability of praetorian rule. To do this, however, the regime is left with few long-range alternatives, other than becoming itself the sponsor of a political party system. But whether praetorianism would simply mature or, in the process, be transformed is yet unclear. Such uncertainty indicates the need for a chapter in comparative studies thus far unwritten: legislative development, as it is now unfolding in Vietnam as elsewhere,[13] lies at the very heart of politics and political change, not at the periphery.

Chapter 1. Political Community and
Political Order in South Vietnam

1. Vietnamese political leaders have also recognized the effect created
by this scene, and in January 1970 members of the progovernment bloc in
the Lower House petitioned the government to have the soldiers' statue
removed. The Fine Arts School at Hue was commissioned to make a statue
of the Emperor Le Loi to replace it. One of Vietnam's most famous
heroes, Le Loi founded the dynasty bearing his name, which lasted for
more than three centuries, drove out the Chinese invaders, modernized the
country's public administration, and was dubbed the "Peacemaking King"
for his efforts. No more appropriate replacement for the soldiers' statue
could have been found.

2. See Samuel P. Huntington, *Political Order in Changing Societies*
(New Haven, Conn., Yale University Press, 1968), pp. 1-92.

3. Jean Chesneaux, *Contribution a l'historie de la nation vietnamienne*
(Paris, Edns Sociales, 1955), p. 99.

4. See John T. McAllister, Jr., and Paul Mus, *The Vietnamese and
Their Revolution* (New York, Harper and Row, 1970), *passim*.

5. See Huntington, *Political Order*, pp. 192-263.

6. *Ibid.*, p. 262.

7. For a suggestion for such a political solution, see my "The End of
the War as a Setting for the Post-War Development of South Vietnam,"
Asian Survey, 11 (Apr. 1971), 341–351. A discussion of North and South
Vietnamese views of how the war will end and the kind of political
competition each expects to face is contained in *After the War, What? A
Report to the U.S. Department of State on Alternative Political Outcomes
Affecting the Participation of International Organizations in the Recovery
and Development of North and South Vietnam* (Washington, D.C., 1972).
For background descriptions of the political organizations and social
forces, see my "Government and Countryside: Political Accommodation
and South Vietnam's Communal Groups," *Orbis,* 13 (Summer 1969),
502-525; "South Vietnam: Neither War nor Peace," *Asian Survey,* 10 (Feb.
1970), 107-132; and "The Political Implications of Rural Problems in
South Vietnam: Creating the Public Interest," *Asian Survey* 10 (Aug.
1970), 672-687.

8. See, for example, Eugene Webb, "A Review of Social Science
Research in Vietnam with Procedural Recommendations for Future

Research in Insurgent Settings," *Institute for Defense Analysis Research Paper, P-450* (Dec. 1968).

9. Samuel P. Huntington, "Social Science and Vietnam," *Asian Survey*, 7 (Aug. 1967), 503-506.

10. See, e.g., the statements contained in Thich nhat Hanh, Ho huu Tuong, Tam Ich, Bui Giang, Pham cong Thien, Dialogue: [*Letters Addressed to*] (*the Rev.*) *Martin Luther King, Jean Paul Sartre, André Malraux, Rene Char, Henry Miller* (Saigon, La Boi, 1965). At a less philosophical level, the stories contained in Ly qui Chung, ed., *Between Two Fires: The Unheard Voices of Vietnam* (New York, Praeger, 1971) provide an excellent description of daily life during the war.

11. Elsewhere it has been suggested that most Vietnamese believe that the end of the present war will signal only that the conflict between the nationalists and the Communists has been shifted to a political arena. See my "South Vietnam: Neither War nor Peace," pp. 110-112.

12. Robert Scigliano, *South Vietnam: Nation Under Stress* (Boston, Houghton Mifflin, 1963), p. 161.

13. For an empirical analysis of the war's impact on Vietnamese society, see Committee on Foreign Relations, US Senate, *Impact of the Vietnam War* (Washington, D.C., 1971).

14. Political mobilization complements social mobilization. If social mobilization, according to Deutsch's classic formulation, denotes that process by which "major clusters of old social, economic and psychological commitments are eroded or broken and people become available for new patterns of socialization and behavior," political mobilization refers to the process by which the people thus affected are redeployed into politics. Political mobilization involves the organization of social forces and their assimilation into politics. While social mobilization may create new demands upon governmental processes regarding the distribution of social and economic valuables, political mobilization involves the transformation of these demands into interests, the aggregation of interests into organizations, and the development of strategies to influence the way in which the distribution of such valuables are arrived at. See Karl W. Deutsch, "Social Mobilization and Political Development," *American Political Science Review*, 55 (Sept. 1961), 494. See also the discussion of political mobilization in Guy Hunter, *Modernizing Peasant Societies: A Comparative Study in Asia and Africa* (New York, Oxford University Press, 1969), *passim*; and Huntington, *Political Order*, pp. 397-461.

15. Indeed, it has been suggested in the Greek case that the legislature functioned not to promote political participation but to limit it. See Heinz Eulau, "Changing Views of Representation," in Ithiel de Sola Pool, ed., *Contemporary Political Science: Toward Empirical Theory* (New York, McGraw-Hill, 1967), p. 61.

16. "Few who swear by the principles of democracy know that Buddha blazed a trail in setting up democratic institutions in India. 'It may come

as a surprise to many to learn [as one European scholar has written] that in the Assemblies of the Buddhists in India two thousand and five hundred years ago are to be found the rudiments of our own [i.e., European] parliamentary practice of the present day.' The work of the Buddhist Sangha . . . today is conducted on just the same principles on which the Buddha founded the Order.

The Speaker, the leader of the House, the quorum, the ballot, the order of the day, the discussion or debate, the passing of a bill after three readings and the sending of a vote from afar [i.e., the proxy], all these are still valid in conduct of the meetings of the Sangha . . . in many Buddhist countries. Nguyen thang Thai, "Buddhism and Democracy," *Vietnam Guardian* [26 Aug. 1969], p. 3.

17. In most European polities the emergence of representative assemblies was succeeded by their decline into a "junta of the servants of the Crown [rather] than an assembly of the representatives of the people." See Robert Luce, *Legislative Principles: The History and Theory of Lawmaking by Representative Government* (Boston, Houghton Mifflin, 1930), p. 60. See also, Hugh Tinker, *Ballot Box and Bayonet: People and Government in Emergent Asian Countries* (London, Oxford University Press, 1964).

18. George McT. Kahin, "Postrevolutionary Indonesia: The Period of Parliamentary Democracy," in Kahin, ed., *Major Governments of Asia* (Ithaca, Cornell University Press, 1963), p. 591.

19. Tinker, *Ballot Box*, p. 57.

20. As Huntington has characterized the process: "Historically, political institutions have emerged out of the interaction among and disagreement among social forces, and the gradual development of procedures and organizational devices for resolving those disagreements. The breakup of a small homogeneous ruling class, the diversification of social forces, and the increased interaction among such forces are preconditions for the emergence of political organizations and procedures and the eventual creation of political institutions." (Hungtington, *Political Order*, p. 11.)

21. M. J. C. Vile, *Constitutionalism and the Separation of Powers* (Oxford, Eng., Clarendon Press, 1967), p. 2.

22. See Frederico Mohrhoff, *La dissolution des assemblées legislatives dans les constitutions modernes* (Rome, C. Colombo, 1953), *passim*.

23. See Huntington, *Political Order*, pp. 12-24.

24. See Jean Blondel, *et al.*, "Legislative Behaviour: Some Steps Towards a Cross-National Measurement," *Government and Opposition* 5 (Winter 1969–70), 67–85.

25. See the criticism and its elaboration in Gerhard Lowenberg, *Parliament in the German Political System* (Ithaca, Cornell University Press, 1967).

26. Samuel C. Patterson, "Comparative Legislative Behavior: A Review Essay," *Midwest Journal of Political Science,* 12 (Nov. 1968), 602. See also John C. Wahlke, "Behavioral Analyses of Representative Bodies," in

Austin Ranney, ed., *Essays in the Behavioral Study of Politics* (Urbana, University of Illinois Press, 1962), pp. 173-190.

27. Andre de Blonay (for the Inter-Parliamentary Union), *Parliaments* (New York, Praeger, 1962), p. 298. A similar "decline" in significance has also been noted for the election process itself. See Eric A. Nordlinger, "Representation, Governmental Stability, and Decisional Effectiveness," in J. Roland Pennock and John W. Chapman, eds., *Representation: Nomos X* (New York, Atherton, 1968), pp. 123-127.

28. Bernard E. Brown, *New Directions in Comparative Politics* (New York, Asian Publishing House, 1962), p. 40. This is not to say that individual legislators do not remain powerful but that the institution to which they belong has declined in its standing vis-à-vis the executive. See also Huntington, *Political Order*, p. 115.

29. Walter H. Mallory, ed., *Political Handbook and Atlas of the World, 1966* (New York, Harper and Row, 1966).

Chapter 2. Government versus Politics: Traditional
Political Institutions and the Absence of Political
Community in Vietnam

1. For a description of this tactic see my "Government and the Countryside: Political Accommodation and South Vietnam's Communal Groups," *Orbis,* 13 (Summer 1969), 502–525.

2. A description of this failure in the past can be found in the most recent edition of Robert Shaplen's *The Lost Revolution* (New York, Harper and Row, 1966) and in Robert Scigliano, *South Vietnam: Nation Under Stress* (Boston, Houghton Mifflin, 1964). Current policies of the Thieu government will be discussed in Chapter 5. See also my "South Vietnam: Neither War nor Peace," *Asian Survey,* 10 (Feb. 1970), 107–132, and "The Political Implications of Rural Problems in South Vietnam: Creating Public Interests," *Asian Survey*, 10 (Aug. 1970), 672–687.

3. Whether or not such a village system existed in reality appears to be a moot question in Vietnamese political discourse, which stresses the attributes of the "village system" (i.e., its solidarity and political mobilization functions) rather than its historical validity. Indeed, these attributes of the village system are the ones which most Vietnamese hope will be elaborated in national institutions and in this sense the village council traditions described below constitute an embryonic legislative tradition. For a discussion of the empirical as opposed to the ideal characteristics of the village system, see Samuel L. Popkin, *The Myth of the Village* (forthcoming).

4. Paul Mus, "Vietnam: A Nation Off Balance," *Yale Review,* 41 (Summer 1952), 527.

5. The corporate nature of the village in the system of government in Vietnam is briefly discussed in Dennis J. Duncanson, *Government and*

Revolution in Vietnam (London, Oxford University Press, 1968), pp. 57-58. More extensive treatment of this subject appears in Nguyen huu Thang, *La Commune annamite* (Paris, Recueil Sirey, 1946); Abbé P. Lemonnier de la Bissachère, *Etat actual du Tunkin, de la Cochinchine, etc.* (Paris, Galignani, 1812); and more recently in Alexander Woodside, *Vietnam and the Chinese Model* (Cambridge, Mass., Harvard University Press, 1971).

6. Maurice Dausse, *La Civilisation annamite et le protectorat français* (Bordeaux, F. Pech et cie, 1919), pp. 30-31. Although the formal governing role of the councils has changed much in Vietnam, the character and political significance of the village council has changed little as one classic study in Long An province in the mid-1960's makes clear: "A group of older men, many of whom had served on the council laughed heartily when one noted that the people used to be the servants of the village council, now the village council is the servant of the people." (See Gerald C. Hickey, *Village in Vietnam* [New Haven, Conn., Yale University Press, 1964], p. 185.)

7. In theory, however, this institution was to be part of a government system based upon the following four ideals adapted from traditional proverbs:

- Justice knows no partiality;
- The people matter most, next the national institutions, and lastly the King;
- The power of the emperor stops at the village gate; and,
- If a King has seven good censors his dynasty will be long-lasting.

The government system thus prescribed included the development of rudimentary (albeit in-house) opposition (i.e., the Censorate which provided a check upon the Emperor), the independence of branches, official responsibility, and selection of a legislative institution (the Imperial Court) based upon merit. Even though the Imperial Court was appointed by the King, proponents of this view of Vietnamese tradition suggest that since those who might qualify for appointment had to pass a national examination which was open to all, the Court would be chosen from all strata of the population. The power of the central government, finally, would be checked by the autonomy of the "village republics," as they were characterized, and require the former to actively recruit their support.

8. Ralph Smith, *Vietnam and the West* (London, Heinemann, 1968), p. 60. See also Nguyen van Thai and Nguyen van Mung, *A Short History of Vietnam* (Saigon, Times Publishing Co., 1958).

9. See Jean Leclerc, *De l'évolution et du développement des institutions annamites et cambodgiennes sous l'influence française* (Rennes, Edoneur et Ruesch, 1923), p. 99. See also Vu quoc Thong, "Concerning Decentralization of Power in Provinces: Creation of Provincial Councils under French Domination," *Administrative Research* (Journal of the National Institute of Administration, Saigon), III (Oct. 1959), 13-50.

10. Leclerc, *De l'évolution*, p. 121.

11. A discussion of the functions of these councils is contained in *ibid.*, and in Nguyen khac Ve, *Les institutions représentatives des intérêts des habitantes de l'Indo-Chine* (Paris, Jouve Eds., 1922).

12. Little data exists in detail on the functioning of the municipal councils and the Vietnamese interviewed who were elected to them as representatives of some of the extremist groups of the 1920's and 1930's tended to regard them as less significant than the Colonial Councils. The Trotskyists elected to the Saigon Municipal Council, for example, suggested that, while it was useful as a forum in which to air their grievances, the opposition movement was so fragmented and factionalized that even the propaganda aspects of council participation were undermined by the overwhelming French presence and also by the fact that the more dynamic elements of the party were either underground or irreconcilably opposed to any who participated in the council's deliberations. Efforts to uncover additional data on the municipal councils of this period were unsuccessful, and the brief descriptions found of them in general volumes on modern Vietnamese politics reflect by and large the slim packet of materials which exists in the library of the National Assembly. See, for example, the comments contained in Robert Scigliano, *South Vietnam: Nation Under Stress* (Boston, Houghton Mifflin, 1964), pp. 69-74, *passim*; Joseph Buttinger, *Vietnam: A Dragon Embattled*, 2 vol. (New York, Praeger, 1967), *passim*; and I. Milton Sacks, "Marxism in Vietnam," in Frank N. Traeger, ed., *Marxism in Southeast Asia* (Stanford, Calif., Stanford University Press, 1964), pp. 102-170.

13. Virginia Thompson, *French Indo-China* (New York, Macmillan Co., 1937), p. 399. A similar assessment can be found in John C. Donnell, "Politics in South Vietnam: Doctrines of Authority in Conflict," (unpub. diss., University of California, 1964), p. 17 and *passim*.

14. As will be discussed in this chapter and in Chapter 4, participation in the French governmental or political system required the adoption of French cultural values (such as religion by the Vietnamese elite, which served to erode their legitimacy for the mass of the Vietnamese population). While those Vietnamese who actively participated in the French system may have possessed elite status before their commitment, the adoption of elements of French culture had the effect of culturally alienating the elite from the population with the result that they could no longer be considered the natural and legitimate cultural leaders of the society.

15. Vietnamese voters are required to be at least twenty-five years of age, registered on the tax rolls where they reside, and fall into one of the following categories:
- a landowner that paid a specified minimum in annual taxes;
- a merchant or business owner who had a license for at least three years and who paid a specified minimum in annual business taxes;
- a graduate of a French secondary school or university;
- a member of a local council such as the Saigon Municipal Council or any of the provincial councils;

       —   a retired or inactive civil servant with at least five years of active duty;

       —   a district or province chief with at least three years of active duty, a duly recognized village notable, or a retired village chief; or,

       —   a holder of certain specified French military decorations.

Each of these categories actually defined the occupational and social division among the ethnic Vietnamese elite and spurred competition among them to organize as a bloc. Most councils tended to be dominated by the Vietnamese members of the Chambers of Commerce and Agriculture in Saigon.

16. In 1922 the membership of the council was enlarged to include ten councillors of ethnic Vietnamese and French citizenship each and four additional French councillors elected from the membership of the Chambers of Commerce and Agriculture in Saigon. A description of these two bodies can be found in Walter Langlois, *André Malraux: The Indochina Adventure* (New York, Praeger, 1966), pp. 98-99.

17. The term of the council was four years, and it met for only twenty days of public sessions per year at a time fixed by the governor-general to discuss an agenda prepared by him. During the interim when the council was not in session a seven-member permanent commission (established in 1910 by decree) was elected from the members of the council at the close of each regular session of which only two were required to be ethnic Vietnamese. The governor-general also appointed the president of the council and its secretary (usually the eldest and the youngest of the body, respectively). In 1922 the governor-general divided the council's electorate into specific constituencies to assure each of the seven categories of voters some representation on the council. Those categories that on the basis of their registered voters qualified for more than one representative were presented with lists of candidates for election and voted for the list rather than for each member separately.

18. Ve, *Les institutions*, pp. 33-34.

19. This was particularly true during the 1920's and a good description of the governor's role can be found in Langlois's summary of Malraux's writings on the subject (*André Malraux*, pp. 163-180).

20. *Ibid.*, p. 23.

21. Leclerc, *De l'évolution*, p. 120. The deliberations of the council centered around five basic issues which the French undoubtedly used to legitimate the actions they believed ought to be taken in the economic affairs of the colony. The council was empowered to set personal property taxes, to vote on the budget of the colony and associated public works projects presented by the governor-general, and to take action in the name of the colony unless the governor-general did it himself in such matters as the signing of treaties. In addition to these regulatory and ceremonial legislative tasks the council had generalized power to advise, consent, or draft laws relating to the method of taxation and the disposition of public

properties that were to be executed by the governor-general. But even in these matters the legislation drafted and passed reflected the heavy hand of the governor. Finally, the council was empowered to give advice when so asked by the governor-general on all questions of economic or social significance to the colony. The Consultative Chambers of Tonkin (established in 1886) and of Annam (established by imperial edict in 1920), although similar in most respects to the Colonial Council, lacked any legislative authority. Despite even these limitations, political debate proved too troublesome to the French and in 1908 the governor-general, fearing that the council would become a "*union* of agitators and loud [i.e., obnoxious] theorists, expounding unrealistic demands," replaced it with a purely consultative commission (composed of the elected members of the council plus one-quarter more councillors chosen by the administration and a like number of notables elected by the appointed district chiefs).

22. The election of a Trotskyist slate in 1939 to the Colonial Council reflected not a continuation of the reform-oriented programs of political movements of the 1920's but rather their increasing estrangement from such an ideological line. In any case the Trotskyists were elected to the council at a time when any influence they might have had on the French administration would have been shortly overtaken by events. See, for example, the discussion continued in Sacks, "Marxism," pp. 111-115; Scigliano, *South Vietnam*, p. 70; and Buttinger, *Dragon*, Vol. I, *passim*.

23. R. B. Smith, "Bui Quang Chieu and the Constitutionalist Party of French Cochin-China, 1917–1930," *Modern Asian Studies,* 3 (1969), 136.

24. *Ibid.*, p. 147.

25. Ve, *Les institutions*, pp. 25-26.

26. Leclerc, *De l'évolution*, p. 120.

27. See Ve, *Les institutions*, p. 40; also Virginia Thompson, *French Indo-China* (New York, Macmillan Co., 1937), p. 62.

28. See Bernard Camilli, *La Representation des indigènes en Indo-chine* (Toulouse, Fournier, 1914), pp. 110-123.

29. Quoted in Langlois, *André Malraux*, pp. 163-164.

30. The essential similarity in backgrounds between the co-opted Vietnamese and the revolutionaries is suggested in Thai and Mung, *A Short History*, pp. 300-314, and in Donald Lancaster, *The Emancipation of French Indo-china* (London, Oxford University Press, 1961), p. 74.

31. Smith, *Vietnam*, pp. 63-64. See also Thai and Mung, *A Short History*, p. 246.

32. Smith, *Vietnam*, p. 21.

33. US Department of State, Office of Intelligence Research (OIR), Division of Research for Far East, *Political Alignments of Vietnamese Nationalists, OIR Report No. 3708 (1 October 1949)* (Washington, D.C.: US Dept. of State, 1949), p. 81.

34. *Ibid.*, p. 82.

35. That is, between the inauguration of the DRV National Assembly on 25 February 1946 and the beginning of its second session on 28

October, the number of deputies had been reduced from approximately 370 to 291 and thereafter to 242 on 9 November when the DRV constitution was formally approved by a vote of 242 to 2. The ranks of the assembly had, in effect, been purged of virtually all non-Viet Minh members. Of the two deputies who voted against the constitution, one was subsequently arrested and the other went into hiding. Between 23-27 October, Philippe Devillers reported that some 200 leaders of opposition groups were arrested (*Histoire du Viet-Nam de 1940 à 1952* [Paris, Editions du Seuil, 1952], p. 312) and during the session itself it was reported that those remaining were under the constant surveillance of the police and subsequently were either arrested or assassinated (Buttinger, *Dragon*, Vol. I, pp. 404-412.)

36. See the report of this meeting in Democratic Republic of Vietnam, *Against U.S. Aggression* (Hanoi, Foreign Language Publ. House, 1966), *passim*.

37. From an address delivered on 23 April 1955 and reported in Embassy of Vietnam, *News from Vietnam*, 1 (29 Apr. 1955), 1.

38. Kim Lang, "Editorial," in *Hoa Binh [Peace]* and quoted in *ibid*. (23 Sept. 1955), p. 4. Emphasis added.

39. The latter had not taken office when the coup d'etat occurred.

40. Robert Scigliano, "The Electoral Process in South Vietnam: Politics in an Underdeveloped State," *Midwest Journal of Political Science*, 4 (May 1960), 157.

41. Nationalist opposition groups declared a boycott of the 1956 and subsequent elections and issued the demand that the electoral system be changed to proportional representation.

42. Donnell, "South Vietnam," p. 47. One scholar of the Diem era observed of her activities that "It has been said that Mme. Nhu is charged by the Ngo family with keeping the National Assembly in line with the wishes of the Executive and her activities in support of her own bills tend to reinforce the validity of this supposition . . . " Donnell also reported that many of the National Assembly deputies claimed that all candidates had to sign an undated letter of resignation from the body should the President find their activities offensive to the policy of the regime (*ibid.*, p. 307), although in interviews conducted with a number of former deputies in 1969 this was disputed. During the fall of 1969, a communiqué of the Saigon Students Union referred to this practice and speculated that the current Lower House and Senate deputies probably had to sign a similar document for President Thieu. One former deputy denounced the students' charge as "absolutely false" and said that if that had been the case, then it would have been publicized and denounced when the Diem regime was overthrown.

Unfortunately, only scattered records of the proceedings of the Diem era National Assemblies are extant in Vietnam. In the days following the 1962 coup, police agents had gathered up and destroyed more than half of the total holdings of the Congressional Library in Saigon and confiscated all documents and debates in the possession of members.

Donnell's comprehensive thesis is the only secondary source in which the actual deliberations of the assemblies are discussed.

43. Secretariat of State for Information, Republic of Vietnam, *The Constitution* (Saigon, Quoc Hoi Viet Nam, 1956), p. 4. These remarks of President Diem, of course, cannot be read today without a sense of irony in that, at the cost of parliamentary democracy, Diem established the very type of rule he criticized above.

44. For a discussion of Diem's control over the bureaucracy see John T. Dorsey, Jr., "The Bureaucracy and Political Development in Vietnam," in Joseph La Palombara, ed., *Bureaucracy and Political Development* (Princeton, N.J., Princeton University Press, 1963), pp. 318-359.

45. Donnell, "South Vietnam," p. 421. The Diem government's reaction to existing political forces no doubt reflected the perception of the threat to the regime that a number of organized and armed parties could pose.

46. Duncanson, *Government*, p. 226. What opposition did ultimately emerge to the Diem government had thus to demilitarize in the sense that criticism of policy could be tolerated as long as its exponents were powerless to enforce changes.

47. Scigliano, *South Vietnam*, pp. 153-154. See also Donnell, "South Vietnam," p. 323, where he notes that even a rudimentary sense of identification with the constituencies had been largely replaced by a sense of identification with the institution of the Assembly itself.

48. Quoc Hoi Viet Nam (Congress of Vietnam), *Nien-Giam Quoc Hoi Viet Nam* (Yearbook of the Congress of Vietnam) (Saigon, Quoc Hoi Viet Nam, 1956), p. 26.

49. Fifteen Can Lao party members had been elected to the Assembly, but had run on other tickets such as that of the NRM. See Donnell, "South Vietnam," p. 233.

50. Robert Scigliano, "Political Parties in South Vietnam Under the Republic," *Pacific Affairs*, 33 (Dec. 1960), 341.

51. The only account of this debate can be found in the summary which appears in *News from Vietnam*, 3(19 Dec. 1956), 3-4. The record of the debates of the Diem assemblies was destroyed by the police in the wake of the 1963 coup d'etat. Former members reported in interviews that their personal copies were confiscated and many of those kept on file in the parliamentary library were destroyed by a fire in which five thousand volumes of material perished. Thus, the principal sources of information about the proceedings of the National Assemblies are contained in a few brief references in the South Vietnamese embassy's newsletter, several chapters of the Donnell thesis, and in the summary of the activities of the Congress found in the 1956 and 1959 yearbooks.

52. Many deputies speculated that Diem believed that the existence of two blocs would further enhance the semblance of democratic procedure that he wished the Assembly to represent.

53. See the description of this philosophy and its practice in Vietnam in Donnell, "South Vietnam," *passim*.

54. The manifestos of both blocs are reprinted in Congress of Vietnam,

Nien Gaim Quoc Hoi Viet Nam, *Quoc Hoi Lap-Phap Nhien Khoa Hai* (Saigon, Quoc Hoi Viet Nam, 1959), pp. 24-33.

55. Adrian Jaffee and Milton C. Taylor, "A Crumbling Bastion: Flattery and Lies Won't Save Vietnam," *New Republic*, 144 (19 June 1961), 17.

56. Scigliano, "The Electoral Process," p. 153.

57. For a description of the bills see Donnell, "South Vietnam," p. 201.

58. *Ibid.*, p. 311.

59. Secretariat of State for Information, Republic of Vietnam, *The Constitution*, p. 40.

60. *Ibid.*, p. 10.

61. Duncanson, *Government*, p. 227.

62. An excellent discussion of the entire budgetary process under the Diem government can be found in Robert Scigliano and Wayne Snyder, "The Budget Process in South Vietnam," *Pacific Affairs*, 33 (Mar., 1960), pp. 48-60.

63. Negative votes were not recorded if a measure passed.

64. The assembly passed numerous resolutions condemning communism and the Geneva agreements, sent "messages of solidarity" to the population, endorsed the government of Diem, created a new national flag and anthem, scheduled parliamentary delegations to other countries, voted to place a symbolic casket of soil from North Vietnam in the anteroom of the chamber to indicate its position on unification, and ratified all treaties that the government had negotiated.

65. In summarizing the accomplishments and characteristics of the legislature on the eve of its second term, Scigliano observed that "the National Assembly is still an institution largely of form, hardly of power. In its original guise as a constituent body, the legislature was called on to do little more than ratify a constitution prepared in the main by other hands. It has enacted only a small number of bills, only a handful of which were of any importance, and these were drawn by the executive. No bill has been modified to any important extent in the National Assembly, and little serious debate has issued from it. Although the National Assembly has been divided into majority and minority blocs, these blocs constitute verbal not factual distinctions of legislative viewpoint. The President of the Republic not only dominates the legislative process, but he also exercises broad policy on his own."

66. Donnell, "South Vietnam," pp. 322-323.

67. *Ibid.*, pp. 309-310.

68. *Ibid.*, p. 310.

69. Scigliano, "The Electoral Process," p. 158.

70. Donnell, "South Vietnam," p. 314.

71. The summary presented above is based upon Donnell's discussion of the memorandum, *ibid.*, pp. 316-319.

72. Military Revolutionary Committee Direction Board, "Declaration of 25 August, 1964."

73. Provisional Leadership Committee, "Decree of 8 September, 1964."

74. *Ibid.*, Article 2.

75. Armed Forces Council of the Republic of Vietnam, "Decision of the Armed Forces Council, December 20, 1964."

76. General Nguyen Khanh, "Creation of the National Legislative Council: A Decision of the Armed Forces Council," 17 February 1965.

77. Major General Nguyen van Thieu for the Armed Forces Council (as its secretary-general), "Duties and Organization of the Armed Forces Council, 15 March 1965," and published in USOM, *Public Administration Bulletin, Vietnam*, No. 22 (1 Apr. 1965), pp. 1-5.

78. National Leadership Committee, "The Formation of the Council of the People and the Army," Decree Law No. 020/66, 10 June 1966, and published in USAID, *Public Administration Bulletin, Vietnam*, No. 29 (1 July 1966), pp. 35-37.

Chapter 3. Elections and Political Participation in South Vietnam

1. Samuel P. Huntington, *Political Order in Changing Societies* (New Haven, Conn., Yale University Press, 1968), p. 402. See also Harry Eckstein and David Apter, "The Impact of Electoral Systems on Representative Government," the editors' introduction to *Comparative Politics: A Reader* (New York, Free Press, 1963), pp. 247-248.

2. See Stein Rokkan "The Comparative Study of Political Participation: Notes Toward a Perspective on Current Research," in Austin Ranney, ed., *Essays on the Behavioral Study of Politics* (Urbana, Ill., University of Illinois Press, 1962), p. 52.

3. Based on data and analyses in Bruce M. Russett *et al.*, *World Handbook of Political and Social Indicators* (New Haven, Conn., Yale University Press, 1964), pp. 84-90, 270.

4. See Douglas W. Rae, *The Political Consequences of Electoral Laws* (New Haven, Conn., Yale University Press, 1967).

5. It was not possible to write a parallel account of the Viet Cong experience with elections although an interesting view of the process can be found in Robert A. Kaiser, "Defector Relates VC Odyssey: Describes 1969 Forest Congress," *Washington Post* (18 June 1970), pp. 61, 64, which suggests that Viet Cong elections emphasize just the reverse: low levels of competition are designed to foster high levels of political mobilization.

6. Despite the stringent controls of the screening process to assure that no Viet Cong would be elected to the assembly, it appeared that some deputies of strong leanings in that direction were elected nonetheless. Interviews with deputies about their relatives in the north or in the Viet Cong revealed that as many as thirty had actively maintained such family ties. See also the discussion of the Chau case in Chapter 6.

7. For a description of the administrative aspects of holding elections, see my "Notes on the Administration of Elections in South Vietnam," in

Southeast Asia Development Advisory Group Papers on Problems of Development in Southeast Asia, No. 25 (4 December 1967) (New York: The Asia Society, 1967). The elections referred to include the following: village and municipal councils (January, June 1953; Bao Dai government); provincial councils (October 1953; Bao Dai government); national referendum (October 1955; to replace Bao Dai government); National Constituent Assembly (March 1956); second term for National Constituent Assembly (August 1959); presidential (April 1961); third term of National Constituent Assembly (1963); local (for forty-four provincial councils and five municipal councils; May 1965); Constituent Assembly (September 1966); village councils (April 1967); hamlet chiefs (May-June 1967); presidential and Upper House (September 1967); Lower House (October 1967).

8. Giovanni Sartori, "Political Development and Political Engineering," in John D. Montgomery and Albert O. Hirschman, eds., *Public Policy, 17* (1968), 276-277. See also Stein Rokkan, "Electoral Systems," in *International Encyclopedia of the Social Sciences*, Vol. 5 (New York, Macmillan, 1968), 6-19.

9. Robert Scigliano, "The Electoral Process in South Vietnam: Politics in an Underdeveloped State," *Midwest Journal of Political Science, 4* (May 1960), 156.

10. *Ibid.*, p. 147.

11. See David O.D. Wurfel, "The Saigon Political Elite: Focus on Four Cabinets," *Asian Survey*, 7 (Aug. 1967), 527.

12. United States of America and the Government of the Republic of Vietnam, "Declaration of Honolulu," 8 Feb. 1966.

13. Reported in "A Question of Survival," *Newsweek* (18 Apr. 1966), p. 27.

14. At that time it was estimated that between 4,000 and 5,000 Buddhists had been arrested in the wake of Struggle Six. See Robert Shaplen, "Letter from Saigon," *New Yorker* (20 Aug. 1966).

15. As will be suggested in subsequent chapters, particularly in Chapter 4, the military officer corps was and remains far from cohesive in its politics or monolithic in the kinds of national figures its members chose to support.

16. Text of Letter from General Ky to the head of the Vien Hoa Dao, government radio broadcast.

17. Giovanni Sartori, "Constitutionalism: A Preliminary Discussion," *American Political Science Review*, 56 (Dec. 1962), 860 *et passim*.

18. Jumper and Normand, "Vietnam," in George McT. Kahin, *Governments and Politics of Southeast Asia*, 2nd ed. (Ithaca, N.Y., Cornell University Press, 1964), p. 423. A discussion of earlier Vietnamese constitutions can be found in Francis J. Corley, "The President in the Constitution of the Republic of Vietnam," *Pacific Affairs*, 34 (Summer 1961), 165-174, and J.A.C. Grant, "The Vietnam Constitution of 1956," *American Political Science Review*, 52 (June 1958), 437-462.

19. Speech of Deputy Ngo van Nham, reported in *Bien Ban Phien Hop Cua Quoc Hoi Lap Hien [Minutes of the Constituent Assembly Meetings]*, 12 December, 1966 Session, p. 45.

20. The term opposition as it is used here refers to the coalition of independent deputies who had been in the past outspoken critics of the Ky government, some with reputations established for their opposition to the Diem regime. As such they did not represent political organizations but the opinion of the urban and religious intellectuals.

21. The leaders of the debate over the constitution also sought to avoid taking sides via the constitution in the development of the Thieu-Ky conflict. Supporters of each of the generals sought to write a provision in the constitution that assured their candidate of election as president. The controversy centered mainly around the provisions for the age of the presidential candidates. Thieu supporters favored making the minimum age forty in order to automatically disqualify Ky and based their arguments on the need for a mature leader of the government. Ky supporters opposed this provision, and the opposition deputies favoured the inclusion of both candidates with the hope of splitting the military vote into two factions, increasing thereby the chances that a civilian ticket could win the election. In response to the issue of maturity the opposition deputies argued that many men such as Jesus Christ were brilliant public figures while still in their thirties and that by thirty-five (the proposed minimum age) a man is considered fully matured in the physical sense.

22. Nguyen huu Thong, "Ly-Tuong Truyen-Thong Cua Dan-Toc" [The Traditional Ideals of the People], in Quoc-Hoi Lap-Hien [Constituent Assembly], *Thuyet-Trinh ve Hien-Phap* [Briefing on the Constitution] (Saigon, Administrative Office of the Constituent Assembly, 1967), p. 2.

23. See the general discussion of these aspects contained in Ivo D. Duchacek, "National Constitutions: A Functional Approach," *Comparative Politics*, 1 (Oct. 1968), pp. 91-102.

24. Robert Shaplen, "Letter from Saigon," *New Yorker* (7 Oct. 1967), p. 149.

25. Reported in "Ky is Said to Term Aims of U.S. Selfish," *New York Times* (1 Apr. 1968), p. 11.

26. S. M. Lipset, *Political Man: The Social Bases of Politics* (Garden City, N.Y., Anchor Books, 1963), p. 183.

27. See the discussion of this process in Sartori, "Political Development," p. 273, and in Rae, *Political Consequences*.

28. The term "party system" as used above needs to be qualified in the Vietnamese case. It refers to the diverse collection of political organizations and movements associated with a specific declaration of principles, a flag, and a central executive committee and more precisely denotes participants in what could be termed the Vietnamese "political organizational system." It constitutes at best a weak organizational system but one which nonetheless comprises all identifiable interest groups in the society. In discourse, Vietnamese generally refer to the older organizations of the

1920's and 1930's, such as the *Dai Viets*, VNQDD, and Hoa Hao Social Democratic party as political parties and to the organizations founded after the war against France as movements (*phong trao*). Neither generation of organizations, however, has demonstrated their capacity to carry out the three predominant characteristics of modern political parties: namely, to mobilize the population, to create and aggregate interests, and to link the social forces they represent to the governmental process. (See Huntington, *Political Order*, p. 91). Rather most political organizations in South Vietnam have demonstrated characteristics of factions and not political parties.

29. Sartori, "Political Development," p. 280.

30. William N. Chambers, *Political Parties in a New Nation* (New York, Oxford University Press, 1963), p. 20.

31. Sartori, "Political Development," p. 281.

32. As suggested in the previous chapter, the election of candidates from the Constitutionalist party of the 1920's did not represent the participation of activists who were basically opposed to the French but those who sought to achieve reform within their system.

33. The principal exception to this general finding is found in the cases of the contests in Saigon and Gia Dinh which, despite their substantial politicization, had among the lowest voter turnouts in the House elections.

34. The magnitude of the decline in voter turnout between two separately scheduled elections is by no means unique to Vietnam. Declines of ten percent are generally regarded as normal, for example, in US national elections.

35. The significance of the Viet Cong as a political threat changed, however, as time and events occupied a more prominent role in doctrines of political organization that most groups espoused. See Chapters 7 through 9 for a discussion of this transformation.

36. "Who to Vote for Whom?" *Saigon Daily News* (20 Aug. 1967).

37. See James Q. Harrison, "Elections and Revolution: An Analysis of the Fall Elections in South Vietnam," Woodrow Wilson School of Public and International Affairs, undated, unpub. MS., pp. 59-60.

38. This finding is also suggested in Harrison's paper which reported "no significant relationship between [government] control and the performance of any of the candidates," *ibid.*, p. 41.

39. See, for example, Bernard Weinraub, "South Vietnam's No. 1 Dove," *New York Times Magazine* (8 Oct. 1967), pp. 43, 110-115.

40. Only two parties practices a strategy designed to appeal to the mass of the population. The *Toan Viets*, for example, sought to create a national political organization with appeal to Cao Dai, Hoa Hao, and VNQDD voters. Its campaign was apparently well organized in half of the country's provinces by an extensive cadre system and the membership of the lists of the coalition contained the largest number of candidates with diverse backgrounds drawn from a substantial number of provinces. The leaders of the coalition predicted that they would receive at least half of

the votes in seventeen provinces and close to that figure in fourteen others due to the organization of their campaign. While the *Toan Viet* slates placed in the top twenty, none of its lists were elected, and, while it had broader support than most other lists (the *Toan Viet* slates polled better than average votes in sixteen provinces), it lacked sufficient support in the urban areas, which was essential to election success. The other broadly based slate of the newly formed "Farmer, Worker, Soldier Movement" (*Nong Cong Binh*), however, registered the greatest success of all other slates and received significant support in twenty-one provinces.

41. Calculation of probability is based upon Rae's formula for the calculation of the probability of diadic disagreement in which the fractionalization of the system is Fe = 1 − the sum of party shares squared or

$$Fe = 1 - (\sum_{i=1}^{n} T_i^2) = .82$$

in the case of Upper House election. See Rae, *Political Consequences*, p. 50.

42. John C. Grumm, in "Theories of Electoral Systems," *Midwest Journal of Political Science*, 2 (Nov. 1958), 375, notes in fact that "Experience has shown that majority and plurality elections produce glaring inequities and are inappropriate when associated with a multiparty system. To a much greater extent in a multiparty system than in a two-party system, wide disparities exist between the distribution of the vote and the distribution of seats among the parties. The election gamble becomes one in which the odds are almost completely indeterminate, since the number of winning candidates that a party might have will bear a very uncertain relationship to its total vote."

43. Indeed, as will be suggested in Chapters 6 through 9, such coalescence comes not as a consequence of electoral strategies in a fragmented, praetorian polity but rather in the interaction between elites over the question of defining public interests and national and institutional goals.

44. The government undertook to finance the propaganda and leaflet printing for each candidate. This support was limited to multiple copies of one poster with the candidate's photograph, slogan, and symbol, a biographical statement, and a summary of their legislative programs. Most candidates, however, realized the necessity of spending their own personal funds on the campaign. The largest single item requiring personal funds reported by all candidates interviewed was the cost of per diem allowances for their campaign cadre which ranged from figures of 200-500 piasters per day for between several dozen to several hundred campaign workers. Costs for these services had to be borne by the candidate's family or from contributions that, in the case of those withdrawing for personal reasons, could not be secured. Militant Buddhists claimed that many candidates were disqualified from running in the election owing to their antigovernment stands. But analysis of those candidates that were disqualified tends

to contradict the charge made by the Buddhists. Approximately 116 candidates withdrew from the campaign between the first posting and the publication of the final candidates' list, and data is available on the reasons for withdrawal in the case of 108. Forty-eight candidates listed "personal reasons" for withdrawal. Interviews with some of these candidates revealed either family pressures over the cost of the election campaign or concerns described by one candidate as "purely personal and without pressures from anyone." Thirty-eight candidates were disqualified by the local election commissions for failure to submit the required documentation, and two were disqualified for being convicted of misdemeanors that resulted in their dismissal from the civil service. Thirteen candidates were unable to run because of failure to obtain leave from the military service, and one candidate was similarly unable to run because he could not get a leave of absence from his teaching post. Only three candidates were disqualified because of suspected links to the Viet Cong, and one candidate withdrew protesting that the elections would not be fair. Of the remaining two candidates, one withdrew from the race in one province to run from another constituency, and one was disqualified for failure to fulfill his military service obligations. In no case of a candidate's withdrawal from the campaign was government pressure charged or declared either in interviews or in the vernacular press. Moreover, militant Buddhist participation in the election did not appear to be significantly affected by the withdrawals as only one militant candidate withdrew.

45. Ethnic Vietnamese deputies who received clear majorities were Nguyen van Chuyen, 67 percent, attributed to the support of local Phu Bon Catholic organizations; Dan van Cong, 52 percent, supported by "Three Star" Hoa Hao faction in Chuong Thien; Le min Chieu, 81 percent, supported by local Hoa Hao in Kien Tuong.

46. See Huntington, *Political Order*, p. 147.

Chapter 4. Representation as Participation:
Bases for Conflict and Accommodation

1. S. M. Lipset, "Party Systems and the Representation of Social Groups," *European Journal of Sociology*, I (No. 1, 1960), 51. See also the views presented in Carl J. Friedrich, *Constitutional Government and Democracy* (Boston, Little, Brown, 1941); Harold D. Lasswell and Abraham Kaplan, *Power and Society* (New Haven, Conn., Yale University Press, 1950), pp. 111ff.; Kenneth Prewitt and Heinz Eulau, "Political Matrix and Political Representation: Prolegomenon to a New Departure from an Old Pattern," *American Political Science Review*, 63 (June 1969), 428.

2. Hanna Pitkin, *The Concept of Representation* (Berkeley, University of California Press, 1967), p. 209. (Emphasis in the original.)

3. See, for example, Leonard D. White, *The Jacksonians* (New York, Macmillan, 1954); Myron Weiner, *Party Building in a New Nation: The Indian National Congress* (Chicago, University of Chicago Press, 1967);

Richard Park and Irene Tinker, eds., *Leadership and Political Institutions in India* (Princeton, N.J., Princeton University Press, 1959); Jean Grossholtz, *Politics in the Philippines* (Boston, Little, Brown, 1964); Frederick W. Frey, *The Turkish Political Elite* (Cambridge, Mass., MIT Press, 1965); and Marshall R. Singer, *The Emerging Elite: A Study of Political Leadership in Ceylon* (Cambridge, Mass., MIT Press, 1964).

4. A good discussion of this model is contained in William B. Quandt, "The Algerian Political Elite: 1954-1967," (unpub. diss., Massachusetts Institute of Technology, 1968). See also Lewis Edinger and Donald R. Searing, "Social Background in Elite Analysis: A Methodological Enquiry," *American Political Science Review*, 61 (June 1967), 428-445.

5. The best portrait of the membership of local council and elected bodies is found in Gerald C. Hickey, *Village in Vietnam* (New Haven, Conn., Yale University Press, 1964).

6. The 1969 local elections do suggest that future village politics may reflect the participation of a younger generation. Between 5 and 15 percent of those elected in 1969 were members of the locally based Rural and Popular Forces, but whether or not this trend will last or that the numbers of these individuals in politics will increase remains to be seen.

7. In other politics it has been observed that even when those elected are not drawn from a distinctive social elite, their very election serves to differentiate them from the rest of the population and such status differentiation tends to be preserved thereafter. See Heinz Eulau, "Changing Views of Representation," in Ithiel de Sola Pool, ed., *Contemporary Political Science: Toward Empirical Theory* (New York, McGraw-Hill, 1967), p. 80.

8. See Dankwart A. Rustow, "The Study Of Elites: Who's Who, When and How," *World Politics*, 18 (July 1966), 690-717.

9. Samuel C. Patterson, "Comparative Legislative Behavior: A Review Essay," *Midwest Journal of Politics*, 12 (Nov. 1968), 602-603. Patterson both reviews five recent works and cites thirteen other studies of individual countries in which this finding is suggested.

10. Religious differences, while classified here as a political variable, are a borderline case.

11. The third term of the National Assembly under Diem, elected in October 1963, is not treated here since that body did not formally deliberate for any substantial period of time. There is, however, little reason to suspect that its membership differed substantially from that of its two predecessors. Data on those elected to the 1963 assembly are incomplete and less detailed than that which is available for the deputies of the first and second assemblies. A comparative analysis of the three assemblies is now being done by Professor Wesley Fishel at Michigan State University, and Fishel's preliminary tabulations suggest that the known characteristics of those elected in 1963 do not differ in any significant way from those of their predecessors.

12. For a general statement of the theory, see Edward Shils, "The

Intellectuals in the Political Development of the New States," *World Politics*, 12 (Apr. 1960), 320-330. The most comprehensive work on the relationship between elites, the educational process, and politics has been done on the Middle East. Frederick Frey, *The Turkish Political Elite* (Cambridge, Mass., MIT Press, 1965) both contains a summary of this research and relates it to his own study of legislative institutions in that polity.

13. This distinction was part of the cultural heritage people were socialized to accept. Particularly in the northern portion of the country (Hickey argues that education in the South was not a necessary determinant of the elite status as it was in the North but rather that it was coincidental with the attainment of wealth by the local gentry. [*Village in Vietnam*, pp. 233-247]). Under colonialism the criteria did not change but the educational system did as the French sought to introduce their own educational system to supplant the traditional Vietnamese system. For a detailed discussion of education under colonialism in Vietnam, see Vu tam Ich, "A Historical Survey of Educational Developments in Vietnam," *Bulletin of the Bureau of Social Service*, University of Kentucky, 32 (Dec. 1959), 1-143, esp. 72ff. The French reform of the Vietnamese educational system was aimed at preparing future civil servants to replace those elder mandarins trained in the Confucian tradition. See Le thanh Khoi, *Le Viet-Nam: Histoire et civilisation* (Paris, Editions de Minuit, 1955), p. 354.

Education formed the basis upon which the social pyramid was constructed. The *Si* or intellectual was located at the top followed by the farmer, the artisan, and then the tradesman or merchant. The basis of the pyramidal classification was education while its articulation depended upon the professions and occupations of those who had education versus those who did not.

14. Speech of Deputy Nguyen van Sam reported in the Minutes of the Constituent Assembly session of 12 December 1966, p. 17.

15. In contrast, locally elected civil servants tended to have little nonpartisan involvement in community affairs and most of those elected were members of established local political organizations. Teachers in the Upper House tended to be university-level instructors or local teachers who had risen to administrative posts in the Education Ministry. Civil servants in the Upper House, similarly, while they had some service at the province level, generally tended to be Saigon officials or represented that class of civil servants who received their appointments through political involvement with Diem's Revolutionary League of Civil Servants in the late 1950's.

16. During the Diem era, conversion to Catholicism was viewed as a prerequisite for advancement within the military and in civilian politics, and some generals have claimed that many of their colleagues converted primarily to improve their standing with President Diem. Others have also suggested that Diem would not trust officers with command assignments who, in addition to their absolute political loyalty, were not also Catholic.

Most of the officers who converted to Catholicism did so in the later years of the Diem regime and explained in interviews that, while Diem tended to view Catholic officers favorably, their decisions were all personally motivated. No clear evidence exists, however, to corroborate these observations, although it is likely that conversion was motivated as much by political considerations as it was by personal convictions since, unlike most Catholic converts, those in the army have been only nominal practitioners of the faith at best.

17. See Charles Joiner, "Patterns of Political Party Behavior in South Vietnam," *Journal of Southeast Asian History* 8 (Mar. 1967), pp. 83-98.

18. A survey of the strengths of some of the more prominent of these groups can be found in the appendix to my "South Vietnam: Neither War nor Peace," *Asian Survey*, 10 (Feb. 1970), 124-131; see also Peter King, "The Political Balance in Saigon," *Pacific Affairs*, 44 (Fall 1971), 401-420.

19. For a summary of the major Vietnamese and Western interpreters of it, see Milton Osborne, "The Vietnamese Perception of the Identity of the State: Absolute Ideals and the Necessity to Compromise," *Australian Outlook*, 23 (Apr. 1969), 7-17, and Gerald C. Hickey, "Accommodation and Coalition in South Vietnam," *RAND Corporation Papers, P-4213* (Jan. 1970).

20. See my "Government and the Countryside: Political Accommodation and South Vietnam's Communal Groups," *Orbis*, 13 (Summer 1969), 107-132.

21. Eight deputies had actually served in the Viet Minh prior to 1954 and eighteen deputies had been political prisoners during that conflict with the following breakdown:

— three were arrested at least once by the French and the Viet Minh
— seven were arrested at least by the French or the Viet Minh
— eight were arrested at least once by the Viet Minh.

Nineteen deputies had served in the two republics' legislatures while another twenty-one were in its prisons: seventeen were jailed for their opposition to the Diem regime, and four had been imprisoned for their opposition to the juntas that came to power in the wake of the 1963 coup d'etat.

22. Whether or not a deputy's perception of his elite status resulted in creating a gap between elite and mass and the divorce of the politics of the one from the politics of the other appeared to depend upon the motivation for seeking office and the difficulty in relating to their constituents (see Chapter 8). Ironically, those intellectuals who appeared to understand the Viet Cong's ideology best and who professed sympathy with it also believed that their elite status was a bar to engaging in political mobilization of the masses.

23. Refers to those deputies associated with the Movement for the Renaissance of the South discussed in Chapter 7.

24. While role characterization appears similar to those described in J.D. Barber, *The Lawmakers: Recruitment and Adaptation to Legislative Life* (New Haven, Conn., Yale University Press, 1965) and John C. Wahlke, Heinz Eulau, William Buchanan, and LeRoy C. Ferguson, *The Legislative System: Explorations in Legislative Behavior* (New York, John Wiley, 1962), the concept is not derived from role theory. Rather, role characterization reflects the level of deputy involvement with their constituents, blending both the consequences of their motivation for seeking office and the scope of their activities once elected into a single concept.

25. See Chapter 7.

26. Equivalent to a province chief in an autonomous city.

27. See Chapter 9.

28. Too often these deputies felt new structures and public facilities had been built for rather than by the people. When it came time either to use or, more important, to defend schools, such support was not forthcoming.

29. An accommodative attitude appears to be a product not only of the political milieu from which the deputies were drawn but also a more general outcome of the legislative process. Such a development, for example, has been noted in the case of American state legislatures where it was found that "evidence from several directions points to the conclusion that a central function of the American state legislature is the accommodation of interest-group demands in the legislative process. Experience in the legislature tends to produce in individual legislators, whatever their previous background and experience, the attitudes most appropriate to this function ... [and that] ... legislators' role concepts lead them to seek accommodation of group interests not by direct embodiment of group demands in public policy (either as group agents or as unwilling pawns) but by attempts to conciliate and harmonize them into an authoritative decision meeting legislators' criteria of the public interest." (See John C. Wahlke *et al.*, *Legislative System*, pp. 311-342, esp. 342.)

Chapter 5. Government under the Second Republic: Consolidation versus the Creation of Political Power

1. See Gerald C. Hickey, "Accommodation in South Vietnam: The Key to Socio-political Solidarity," *RAND Corporation Papers, P-3707* (Oct. 1967); I. Milton Sacks, "Restructuring Government in South Vietnam," *Asian Survey*, 7 (Aug. 1967) 515-526; Samuel P. Huntington, "Vietnam: The Bases of Accommodation," *Foreign Affairs*, 46 (July 1968), 642-656; Duong van Minh, "A Question of Confidence," *Foreign Affairs*, 47 (Oct. 1968), 84-91; Nguyen manh Conh, *Hoa Binh:Nghi-gi Lam-gi [Peace: What Do We Think? What Do We Do?]* (Saigon, Khai Tri, 1969).

2. Duong van Minh, "Viet Nam: A Question of Confidence," *Foreign Affairs*, 47 (Oct. 1968), 85. Since his return from political exile, Minh

himself has been suspected of such plotting. On the anniversary of the 1963 coup, Minh made a series of interesting and much-distorted public statements which implied that he believed the government must make a new effort to relate itself to the people. Minh declared, in a definitive text he circulated on 13 November 1969 to clarify the distortion of the press reports, that "when the people's aspirations are known and respected by the government, they will then provide sincere and total support to the government," and that "this country needs true and greater unity for its survival." To those ends, Minh advocated the organization of "a means of seeking the people's views as a measure to aid the nationalist side in winning the war by gaining the people's support and confidence." The political implications of such remarks were left open to much speculation, and some newspapers declared that Minh was organizing an opposition force of his own. What was more likely, however, was that the remarks of General Minh reflected his sincere belief that the GVN must win the confidence of the people and that they constituted an extension of his statements in the *Foreign Affairs* article quoted above at least as much as it could have been construed as an announcement—however vague—that he would not object to opposition groups rallying around his flag. Throughout his short-lived candidacy for the presidency in 1971, Minh did not vary from this passive conception of leadership. See Allan E. Goodman, "South Vietnam and the New Security," *Asian Survey*, 12 (Feb. 1971), 121-137.

3. David O. D. Wurfel, "Backgrounds of South Vietnamese Cabinets," *Asian Survey*, 7 (Aug. 1967), p. 527.

4. *Ibid.*

5. "Restructuring Government in South Vietnam," *Asian Survey*, 7 (Aug. 1967), pp. 515-516.

6. *Xay Dung* (17 June 1968).

7. "Patch it Up," *Saigon Daily News* (14 June 1968).

8. Lee Lescaze, "South Vietnamese Cabinet Appears Weak," *Washington Post* (10 Nov. 1967), p. 21.

9. Tom Buckley, "Reforms Delayed by Thieu-Ky Split," *New York Times* (11 Jan. 1968), p. 1.

10. *Vietnam Press*, 30 Aug. 1968.

11. An excellent description of the atmosphere in which the ouster of Huong was executed can be found in Elizabeth Pond, "Vietnamese Politics: *Plus ca change, plus c'est la meme chose*—Maybe," in *Report from Saigon* (New York: Alicia Patterson Fund, Sept. 1969), and her "Vietnamese Politics: Longer Term," *ibid.* (Oct. 1969).

12. "Is It Intentional or because of Difficulties?," *Tieng Noi Dan Toc* (2 Sept. 1969). The use of the word "strangers" was intended to denote the lack of the cabinet's relation to popular political organizations and its introduction of former Diemists who had been both strangers to post-Diem politics and to the population they purported to represent. The editorial writer was making an oblique reference to the disrepute of the neo-*Can Lao Nhan Xa* party within the greater Catholic community.

13. For a description of the founding and organization of the *Nhan Xa*, see Allan E. Goodman, "South Vietnam: Neither War nor Peace," *Asian Survey*, 10 (Feb. 1970), 117-119.

14. Senator Nguyen van Ngai, quoted in Nguyen hoang Doan, "President Thieu Only Has Influence on a Minority in Congress," *Hoa Binh* [*Peace*, a Catholic daily] (11 Aug. 1969), p. 8.

15. See the distinction between political consolidation and reform made in Samuel P. Huntington, *Political Order in Changing Societies* (New Haven, Conn., Yale University Press, 1968), pp. 344ff. A most comprehensive discussion of recent American assistance programs in Vietnam can be found in Vincent Puritano, "Four Doctrines of Counterinsurgency and Their Implications in Vietnam," unpub. paper, John F. Kennedy School of Government, Harvard University, Jan. 1969. A discussion of the impact of efforts to achieve reform by development programming during the Diem era can be found in Allan E. Goodman, ed., "Lost Revolutions: Notes on the Experience of Political and Administrative Reform in South Vietnam," *Southeast Asia Development Advisory Group Reports* (1 Apr. 1968).

16. Minister of Information (Huong cabinet) Ton that Thien, "Town versus Country: A Basic Source of Tension and Conflict in Vietnam," mimeographed paper prepared for a conference at the University of Hawaii's East-West Center, 1967, p. 13.

17. A common theme raised in virtually every interview held with American officials was that the GVN appeared unable to absorb the range of development programs and goals that policy planners in Saigon and Washington had designed as essential elements for victory in "the other war" against the political and administrative infrastructure of the Viet Cong. The inability of the GVN to absorb American resources and programs, in the view of most officials, was linked primarily to the administrative difficulties such programs involved and particularly to the fact that a Vietnamese province chief is responsible for the administration of 386 programs. Such a view, however, assumed an identity of interest between the GVN and the American mission which, in fact, did not exist. Indeed, the Vietnamese, as suggested in my "The Political Implications of Rural Problems in South Vietnam: Creating the Public Interest," *Asian Survey*, 10 (Aug. 1970), 672-686, and in Jeffrey Race, "How they Won," *ibid.*, pp. 628-650, viewed the problems of rural development differently than their American counterparts and, consequently, the failure of the GVN to absorb American development programs was also related to a fundamental but tacit disagreement over their political significance.

18. Gerald Hickey, quoted in *Time* (28 Mar. 1969), p. 27.

19. George C. Lodge, *Engines of Change, U.S. Interests and Revolution in Latin America* (New York, Alfred A. Knopf, 1970), p. 365.

Chapter 6. The Executive versus the Legislature:
Political Competition and Institutional Imperatives

1. See the general description of this phenomenon in Samuel P.

Huntington, *Political Order in Changing Societies* (New Haven, Conn., Yale University Press, 1967), pp. 24-32.

2. Truong tien Dat, *Hien Phap Chu Thich [The Constitution Anno-tated]* (Saigon, 1967), pp. 191-192. (Ellipses in original text.)

3. See, for example, the discussion of the phenomenon contained in Michel Ameller, *Parliaments* (London, Cassell, 1966), pp. 133-135 *et passim*. Ameller points out that the only major exception in general grants of authority occurs in the case of the French Constitution of 1958 and that of three former French colonies in Africa (the Camaroons, the Central African Republic, and Senegal). By providing only a general grant of authority to the legislature, the framers of the constitution were making an astute political judgment. They realized that defining the scope of powers of an essentially new political institution would be premature and perhaps also unacceptable to the executive which had to approve their draft of the constitution. The framers recognized that the predominance of the executive could not be overcome by a grant of authority on paper, but would depend upon the growth of political power of the House.

4. Although initially the threat of executive dominance was by no means perceived by all deputies, gradually an awareness developed in response to a series of events that, by the end of 1969, had come to affect a large enough proportion of the House membership to evoke widespread concern about the need for concerted action to preserve legislative autonomy. The increasing incidence of public demonstrations of executive contempt for the legislature, coupled to what was perceived as continual action on the part of President Thieu to subvert the legislative process served as the basis for deputies' concern and as rallying points for cooperative action. Each of the factors making for widespread concern about legislative autonomy suggested the nature of the legislative response required. Executive disdain for the legislature in public pronouncements signaled the need for the unified response from the legislature. And executive subversion of the lawmaking process indicated the need for the legislature to struggle to gain initiative in the formulation of policy and to develop means to control its implementation. By the end of 1969 it was clear to most deputies that the legislature would have to compete with the executive to obtain the place ascribed to it by the constitution.

5. Unfortunately, little detail is known about the workings and the precise composition of this group of influential deputies, and it was not possible to identify more than a handful of those considered its members. Interviews with the particular deputy in question, however, did not produce a substantial elaboration of the process characterized in the article, although several other deputies were mentioned who were regarded as similarly "helpful in working towards the organization of the House." Interviews with these deputies again did not reveal specific examples of their work although it became clear that an important part of the influential core were deputies affiliated with the New Society Group described in Chapter 7. Consequently, it must be assumed that at least part of the motivating force behind the influential deputies originated in the

doctrine of political organization of the New Society Group that stressed the need to discover the bases of cooperation between diverse interests. Translated into leadership terms, as one deputy observed, this meant that House leaders "must try to understand the tendencies and positions of various blocs and deputies in order to maximize the chances that a crisis can be anticipated and, through compromise, averted."

6. While it was hoped by the Constitution's drafters that the loose prescription of the separation of powers and functions would facilitate cooperation between branches it was also recognized that, in separating power, power also had to be created. "While the Constituent Assembly debated the draft constitution, the National Leadership Committee [of the military junta then ruling South Vietnam] sent it several letters requesting that it include in Article 3 the principle of equality between the public power agencies [i.e., the branches of government]. According to the National Leadership Committee's viewpoint, this principle would avoid mutual encroachment, and any predominance of one agency over the others. The National Leadership Committee did not agree that the legislature be given predominance as provided for in the draft constitution, for it considered that such predominance would jeopardize political stability, [and that] this would be a danger for the country, which at this moment needs a strong and stable government in order to cope with ever-changing conditions. The National Leadership Committee requested that, if predominance were given to the executive, at least the principle of equality of the three branches should be prescribed. . . . The members [of the Assembly] countered that this country had no use for the equality of power principle, which would only create a predominant position for the Executive. . . . A member (Dr. Phan quang Dan) compared the division of power in the constitution to the constitution of a kangaroo: this animal has two long and two short paws, but its body is balanced, its equilibrium lies in the very difference of its two pairs of paws. The predominance of the legislature as prescribed in the constitution, all things considered, does not impair the . . . balance in principle of the . . . branches. Among the three powers, the legislative is by nature the weakest for it is only the power of speech (*parlement*, from *parler*, meaning to speak). Compared with the power to execute, the power to speak is afflicted with every handicap and weakness. . . . Owing to this very specific weakness, even if the constitution gave to the legislature [such as the power to vote no confidence in the government], it would not imperil the principle of tripartite equilibrium." (Truong tien Dat, *Hien Phap* . . . , p. 80). The separation of power did not, for the drafters, also imply equality of power between branches.

7. Indeed the transformation of representation into political power appears to be a major variable in the power relations of executives and legislators. See, for example, the analysis presented in Samuel P. Huntington, "Congressional Responses to the Twentieth Century," in David B. Truman, ed., *The Congress and America's Future* (Englewood Cliffs, N.J.,

Prentice-Hall, 1965), pp. 5-31, and the more generalized findings of the Inter-Parliamentary Union, *Parliaments* (New York, Praeger, 1963), p. 203ff. The discussion of how such a transformation appeared to be undertaken within the context of the Lower House forms the focus of the remaining chapters of this study.

8. Evidence on this period will, perforce, have to form the focus of other analyses. For a preliminary assessment and one based only on the fragmentary data available in the US, see Allan E. Goodman, Randolph Harris, and John C. Wood, "South Vietnam and the Politics of Self-Support," *Asian Survey*, 11 (Jan. 1971), *passim*, and Allan E. Goodman, "South Vietnam and the New Security," *Asian Survey*, 12 (Feb. 1972), 121-137. A complete analysis of the significance of the 1971 elections is now in press as a result of a SEADAG Seminar in December 1971.

9. A detailed discussion of executive-legislative relations during the Constituent Assembly's tenure can be found in Cynthia K. Frederick, "The South Vietnamese Constitution of April 1, 1967: The Institutionalization of Politics in the Second Republic," unpub. diss., School of Oriental and African Studies, University of London, July 1969, pp. 57-81. Details of the Diem era can be found in John C. Donnell, "Politics in South Vietnam: Doctrines of Authority in Conflict," unpub. diss., University of California, Berkeley, 1964, pp. 316-319.

Virtually all of the major differences between the executive and the Constituent Assembly were handled through such committees. Perhaps a major element in the assembly's frequent choice for such committees was the participation of Dr. Phan quang Dan in their organization and dealings with the National Leadership Committee. Dr. Dan, a well-known figure in opposition circles since the days of Diem and an appointed Minister of State for External Relations in the Khiem cabinet, acted during the life of the assembly as one of the principal voices of moderation, though strongly in favor of the independence of the assembly. Despite frequent resorts to tactics such as press conferences to focus attention on the work of the assembly, Dan's objective was to keep the level of verbal and public acrimony low since, he believed, the National Leadership Committee could be dealt with more effectively in private. The tenure of the assembly, moreover, was short, and Dan reasoned that the National Leadership Committee was quite new at dealing with and accepting the authority of an elected body. In addition, interviews with members of the Constituent Assembly suggest that, as leader of the Directorate, Premier Ky recognized the need for a progovernment working majority in the assembly and regarded it as something that it was the responsibility of the government to build. To this end Ky met privately and regularly with members of the government bloc and gave them a number of secret briefings on constitutional and national issues. Ky's principal advisers also recognized the value of a working majority in the legislature and reinforced the Premier's personal efforts to keep bloc and legislative leaders informed. These advisers were an important channel of communication that functioned to keep the level of public conflict between the Assembly and the executive low.

10. Reported in *Chinh Luan* (19 Nov. 1969), p. 3.

11. Over time, the political diversity of the members of this committee has changed considerably. In the 1967-68 session only two members of the opposition were in the committee, while, by the start of the third session, the committee's membership included five opposition deputies and a large number of more moderate deputies who had increasingly come to demonstrate their independence from the executive. It remained to be seen whether the introduction of new members and the changed positions of some of the older ones would be able to revive the moribund power of the budget committee. But the general cause of legislative independence from the executive in fiscal matters had been aided by recent decisions of the Supreme Court discussed below.

12. The current Minister for Liaison, Cao van Tuong, described the functions of his office as, first, to coordinate within the executive branch all matters affecting the legislature, and, second, to serve as a contact point for deputies seeking action from various ministries on constituency problems. The latter function involves the receipt and disposition of approximately one hundred letters from congressmen each month. The bulk of the requests received concern proposed public works projects, petitions of relief and assistance, and requests for draft deferments. Deputies have had little success in getting favorable decisions from the executive on draft deferments, and Tuong noted that requests for public works projects and relief assistance depend upon the deputy's relations with the local governmental agencies concerned. Where there is agreement between deputies and local government, proposed public works projects have a greater chance of being approved by the Saigon ministries.

13. The appointment of the present minister, for example, has been regarded by opposition as well as moderate deputies as an indication of the executive's low regard for the House. While Tuong himself has a career background which parallels that of many deputies, his role in making the Diem National Assemblies "decorations" of the executive is taken as a clue of Thieu's actual intentions. From 1954 to 1956 he was the head of the social welfare directorate in the Ministry of Labour under Diem (another member of the Khiem cabinet, Le trong Quat, Vice-Minister of Information, was the director of the ministry). In 1956 he was elected to the National Assembly from Thua Thien province and served as its vice-chairman. Thuong was also one of the few Buddhist members of the National Revolutionary Movement of Ngo dinh Nhu and a member of the *Can Lao* party; currently he is a member of the *Nhan Xa* party. Tuong has served as an adviser to the Lower House committees on Social Welfare and the Judiciary and assisted in the drafting of the legislation which established the Inspectorate, the Special Court, and the Supreme Court.

Opposition and resentment to Tuong's appointment grows out of the fact that he was both a member of the *Can Lao* and vice-chairman of the 1956 National Assembly. The latter is regarded by most deputies as a rubber-stamp assembly, totally subservient to the executive, while the *Can Lao* and *Nanh Xa* parties are regarded by the Buddhist members of the House as anathema. The appointment of such a figure, obviously extremely sympathetic to the executive, it is maintained, is but another indication of the low regard the executive has for the House and the independence of the legislature.

14. Thang's formal resignation was in large part only a pro forma response to the public criticism his activities had engendered. After June 1969 there was no indication that his relationship with or influence upon President Thieu had substantially changed until his death.

15. Two weeks later the Palace was picketed by Theravada Buddhist monks who demanded to see the President. The initial visit was made by Khmer deputies of the Lower House who were concerned about the President's recent decision that the Khmer people would no longer be entitled to ethnic minority status.

16. See Robert G. Kaiser, "Corruption is Vietnam's Way," *Washington Post* (7 July 1969).

17. The crimes were mainly trading on the black market and a much-publicized discovery that one deputy returning from a visit abroad had sought to illegally import *Playboy* calendars into Vietnam for sale on that burgeoning portion of the black market devoted to pornography and vice. While the precise number of deputies involved in corrupt practices will never be known and the motivations behind the actions of those who readily came under the sway of Mr. Thang will similarly be a subject of much unresolved speculation, a breakdown of the deputies by their major activities probably can serve as a rough estimate of the number potentially suspect. See Chapter 8.

18. Quotations are taken from stories carried in *Hoa Binh*, 29 Oct. 1969.

19. By the time the interviews were conducted, the issue had been transformed into a major crisis about which most deputies were reluctant to speak.

20. Text of the interview reported in *Vietnam Press, Single Edition, No. 5034*, 27 Oct. 1969, pp. 4-7.

21. Chau's immunity was considered voided by the military court when a petition that contained the signatures of three-quarters of the deputies in favor of the action was transmitted to the President. The constitution, however, provided that immunity could only be revoked by an actual vote of the deputies, and the Supreme Court ruled that parliamentary immunity can only be rescinded by "the outcome of debate and vote in a plenary session of the House concerned." Deputies who supported the petition suggested that this method was chosen as an expedient means to quiet the protests and demonstrations taking place that would, in all likelihood, have invaded the House Chamber were the deputies to assemble for a vote. Opponents of the petition declared not only that it was unconstitutional but also that the signatures of some of the deputies were forged. Other deputies complained that, when they had reconsidered their action and

sought to have their names removed from the document, they were not physically permitted to do so although they were assured that their names would be removed. When the document was submitted to the President, however, deputies discovered that their names were still on the list. Still other deputies who had never signed the petition in the first place noted their surprise when they were told that their names were included in the list of signers.

22. The most complete account and interpretation of the Chau crisis can be found in Elizabeth Pond's *The Chau Trial* (New York: Alicia Patterson Fund, March 1970), a monograph that adds considerable detail and insight to her shorter articles on the crisis which appeared in the *Christian Science Monitor*. Other articles which present details and analysis of the crisis include the following: Joseph Kraft, "Thieu Line Blocks Speedy War Exit," *Washington Post* (5 Feb. 1970), p. 23; Robert G. Kaiser, "Thieu Authorized to Try 2 Deputies for Links to Reds," *ibid.*, p. 18; Kaiser, "Accused Saigon Deputy Blames U.S.," *ibid.* (18 Feb. 1970), p. 1; Ralph Blumenthal, "Saigon Deputy Seized in Assembly," *New York Times* (27 Feb. 1970), pp. 1, 2; Blumenthal, "In the End the Saigon Comedy was Not Very Funny," *ibid.* (1 March, 1970), p. E-3; Lee Lescaze, "Analyst Fears U.S. Accepts Viet Repression," *Washington Post* (4 Mar. 1970), p. 12; Terrence Smith, "Thieu and Chau: Prosecution of Opposition Deputy Viewed as Naked Display of Power," *New York Times* (6 Mar. 1970), p. 2; Robert G. Kaiser, "Ten-Year Term for Chau Fails to Settle Issues," *Washington Post* (6 Mar. 1970), p. 16.

23. That some opposition deputies signed the petition—and later denounced the document as false—also raises a question that other researchers might find significant: do legislators, when faced with what appears a better-than-equal chance that the legislature will be dissolved, tend to sacrifice outspoken but vulnerable members to ward off that event?

24. The latter is an advisory body to the Supreme Court on judicial matters and on the appointment, promotion, disciplining, and assignment of lower court judges. Under the 1956 Constitution this council was empowered to make authoritative decisions on the above questions, but its membership included the President of the republic or his representative.

25. Establishing the councils generated controversy over their functions and their powers in the Constituent Assembly. Some deputies questioned the practicality and expense of setting up so many councils, but such opposition has not prevented the councils from being legally established.

26. To date the Upper House has contributed the bulk of the legislation concerning the regulation of labor while the Lower House has contributed the remainder.

27. See Chapter 8.

28. Adherence to these attitudes has also paralleled the division between deputies on the basis of these activities within the House and within their constituencies. A more detailed description of the resulting divisions can be found in Chapter 8.

29. Speech of Deputy Nguyen khac Tan, *Minutes of the 47th Session of the Lower House*, 1 Mar. 1968, p. 26.

30. Speech of Deputy Tran duy Tu, *ibid.*, p. 31.

31. Extracted from the Court's mimeograph of its decision, 13 Aug. 1969. Unlike the Supreme Court decisions in the United States, the Vietnamese Court's decision is extremely brief and contains no summary of the arguments presented before it. Descriptions of the sense of the arguments summarized above and those to be presented below were based upon interviews with the participants in the process. Vietnamese Court decisions also are not generally characterized by obiter dicta; thus, any that may appear are generally considered extremely significant.

32. Within a few hours after the taxes were announced, goods had "disappeared" from merchants' shelves and were either sold to the black market to avoid the payment of taxes on stocks or hoarded to drive their prices up to offset the tax increase. Vietnamese who had rushed to buy up such needed items as milk and rice reported that shops which the previous day had been relatively full of such commodities were now empty or selling their wares at black market prices.

33. The Court, however, held that it was within the power of the President to increase the rates of taxes already in existence, in contrast to its decreeing into existence entirely new taxes such as those involved in the austerity taxes.

34. The Court's decision, however, was embodied in obiter dicta and, technically, was not a formal ruling on the case. The issue was initially brought to the Court by the President of the Senate who had acted on the advice of both his own body and that of the Lower House. Subsequently, for reasons which are not entirely clear, the President of the Senate refused to appear before the Court to argue the case, and the Court formally held that by so doing he had withdrawn his request for an interpretation of the constitutionality of the austerity tax decree. To most Lower House deputies, however, the President of the Senate's actions were the direct result of pressure that President Thieu and Nguyen cao Thang were rumored to have applied to have the case dropped. Neither party, of course, had apparently expected that the Court would be bold enough to offer the dicta that it did.

Chapter 7. Legislative Blocs as Political Participation: Doctrines of Political Organization and Competition in Transition

1. The organization and functioning of legislative bodies, except in polities where partisanship is not permitted, based upon blocs appears to be a universal characteristic of modern legislatures. See Michel Ameller, *Parliaments: A Comparative Study on the Structure and Functioning of Representative Institutions in Fifty-five Countries* (London, Cassell, 1966), pp. 97-122.

2. The deputies themselves were uncertain about the meaning of the two-bloc system. These blocs reflected no real differences in political thinking. In the Diem era, legislative blocs were an adjunct of the dominant party created by the regime as a convenient means of presenting legislation and controlling debates. At best, an uncertain tradition of bloc organization existed from the Diem era. In any case, since these blocs were organized and controlled by the government and supported the government, they had little experience in discovering ways to regulate partisanship or to develop their own autonomy.

3. Hung Nguyen, "Vai Nhan Xet Ve Ban Hien Phap Ngay 1-4-1967" ["Some Observations about the Constitution of 1 April 1967"], *Tan Dai Viet* (Jan.-Apr. 1967), p. 43.

4. For perceptive definitions of these two polarities in the spectrum of legislative organizations, see the discussion contained in William Chambers, *Political Parties in a New Nation: The American Experience, 1776-1809* (New York, Oxford University Press, 1963), pp. 21-27 *et passim*; Frederick Frey, *The Turkish Political Elite* (Cambridge, Mass., MIT Press, 1965), pp. 301ff.; Huntington, *Political Order in Changing Societies* (New Haven, Conn., Yale University Press, 1968), pp. 412ff.

5. The use of the term friendship association is particularly significant in the Vietnamese context. In sharp contrast to the dearth of mobilization-oriented political organizations at the national level, the society is criss-crossed with a nearly countless array of highly organized mutual aid associations at the local level. These organizations, proscribed from politics by national law and police regulations, perform nonetheless important political functions. They resolve conflicts among members and between other groups, they provide for the regular succession of leadership by means of elections, and they successfully mobilize even the poorest of their members to support programs sponsored by the group. Friendship associations are thus a trusted, stable, and primary form of participation completely lacking the fragmentation characteristic of the more visible parties and cliques usually identified by Western observers of the Vietnamese political scene. The first major study of these associations will appear in spring 1973 in Lawrence M. Franks, *The Role of Friendship Associations in Community Development*, unpub. thesis, International Urbanization and Public Policy Program, Clark University, forthcoming.

6. John Grumm, in his extensive studies of legislative blocs, for example, suggests that the basic criteria for analyzing blocs included the following:

- definition of the bloc's size, composition, purpose
- explication of its internal structure and the structure of interrelationships within the blocs
- measuring the cohesiveness of blocs and the relationship between blocs as relatively cohesive entities
- the nature of issues that engender a bloc response

— and the bases of the motivational factors salient to the behavior of the bloc and its members.

(See his "The Systematic Analysis of Blocs in the Study of Legislative Behavior," *Western Political Quarterly*, 18 (June 1965), 350-362.) To treat the blocs in South Vietnam with such a full inventory of analytical questions would be highly misleading since the process would impose a structure and a life upon the blocs that does not yet in fact exist. The approach taken here, instead, will focus upon only those features of the blocs which are relevant to their current political role in and significance to political participation in Vietnam.

7. See my "Government and the Countryside: Political Accommodation and South Vietnam's Communal Groups," *Orbis*, 13 (Summer 1969), 502-525.

8. The Alliance of Deputies (*Lien Minh Dan Bieu*) was predominantly a southern *Hoa Hao* and agrarian coalition, while the Movement for the Renaissance of the South (*Phuc Hung Mein Nam*) represented the young, southern Buddhist intellectuals who had been critical of the regime's predominantly northern and Catholic character. The Democratic Bloc (*Khoi Dan Chu*) was composed of the urban Catholic professionals throughout the country, and the Independents consisted of an older generation of Saigon politicians who declared as a group their individual autonomy from any of the other coalitions. This latter group, however, supplied the effective leadership for the assemblies' deliberations.

9. Senator Pham van Tam (alias Thai lang Nghiem), quoted in Robert Shaplen, "Letter from Saigon," *New Yorker* (7 Oct. 1967), p. 160.

10. *Ibid.*

11. Huntington, *Political Order*, p. 414.

12. Shortly after this conversation the respondent informed me that the group he represented had decided to leave Don's front.

13. Senator Le tan Buu, Secretary-General of the Republic Bloc, reported in *Vietnam Press* (morning edition), 20 Sept. 1969.

14. While failing to expand in the way the leaders would have liked, the Upper House blocs nevertheless emerged as relatively stable entities. Regular meetings were held to develop positions on particular issues and strategies to guide formal debates. These functions appear to have been aided by the growth of an esprit de corps within the Senate that was not manifest in either the Constituent Assembly or in the current Lower House. The blocs also established committees to deal with local and regional problems, although this function appears less directed to constituent service work than to conducting investigations of government policies at the corps level. The blocs have commissioned and assigned Senators to write special studies of particular national issues to serve as reference documents in debates. By and large the deliberations of the Upper House contrast sharply to those of the Lower House in terms of their efficiency and the quality of the arguments presented, a feature owing both to the

professional backgrounds of the average Upper House member and to the absence of representatives of the militant and radical religious and political groups.

15. Khoi Doc Lap [*Doc Lap* Bloc], "Nguyen-Tac Gan-Ban [Basic Principles]" (Saigon, the bloc, 1968), p. 6.

16. *Ibid.*

17. An explanation of why no An Quang bloc appeared in the Lower House is related to the reluctance or inability of the An Quang hierarchy to organize at that time a lay political group or party. See my "South Vietnam: Neither War nor Peace," *Asian Survey*, 10 (Feb. 1970), pp. 115-117.

18. As reported in a survey taken by the editors of *Chinh Luan* (16 Oct. 1969).

19. One bloc member, for example, advanced the idea that all graduates of the National Institute of Administration (NIA) be given one year of military training to enable them to serve as district and province chiefs. This particular deputy, having risen to where he could have competed for a province chief position if he had the military training, viewed this suggestion as an extension of his own experience and that of his colleagues. He also expressed views in basic sympathy with the *Cap Tien* party program, whose leaders have made the achievement of such a change one of their principal goals. The Khmer deputies of the bloc also suggested similar reforms to enable those Khmers who were properly trained to become province chiefs in areas where the minority make up a substantial proportion of the population.

20. In 1966, for example, the VNQDD explicitly ruled out such a coalition of forces with groups that had made overtures (including the MRS) for a united front in the Constituent Assembly elections. While over time this policy appeared to soften in the sense that no subsequent formal declaration of independence was issued, the VNQDD leadership was divided over the question of its relationships with other groups with potentially the same set of interests. In interviews, all VNQDD leaders, both at the national and the local levels, paid lip service to the concept, but in practice appeared to oppose such cooperative arrangements. Instead, the dominant opinion of the VNQDD was that the party's first priority was to resolve its own internal troubles and increase the base of its support. A similar sentiment and priority was expressed by the *Dai Viet* party.

21. A description of this archane movement can be found in Joann L. Schrack *et al.*, *Minority Groups in the Republic of Vietnam* (Washington, D.C., Department of the Army, 1966), pp. 808-824.

22. One of the more famous Catholic priests of North Vietnam who organized his entire parish and moved it south to avoid Communist domination.

23. An excellent and detailed, though somewhat dated, account of life in Saigon can be found in Marilyn W. Hoskins and Eleanor M. Shepherd,

Life in a Vietnamese Urban Quarter (Carbondale, Ill., Southern Illinois University Office of Research and Projects, 1965).

24. Doxiadis Associates, *Saigon Metropolitan Area*, 4 vol. (Athens, Doxiadis Associates, 1965), pp. 21-35, vol. 1.

25. Charles F. Sweet, "Political and Social Development in Saigon: Implications for American Communities," paper presented at the Southeast Asia Development Administration Advisory Group's Development Administration Seminar, Endicott House, Dedham, Mass., 16-17 May 1969, and quoted here with the kind permission of the author.

26. The logical counter to this attitude is to demonstrate that, through their work in the House, the deputies have been able to get more funds directed to the district. Such a strategy, however, had been ruled out by the overwhelming desire of those on the development council to avoid its association with politics and thereby not jeopardize its ability to work with the GVN. Since the deputies are still associated with the project, they have been bound by this attitude although they have nevertheless continued to work for the project's benefit in the legislature.

27. See Chapter 9.

28. At any given point in time between thirty and forty deputies in the House declared themselves independent as they moved from one bloc to another. Of the total number of deputies who were independent at the inauguration of the House, only three remained independent throughout the sessions ending in 1969. For those deputies who entered the independents group at one point or another, their independence constituted merely a jumping-off place while they awaited the formation of a new bloc or the transformation of an older one. Amongst these deputies, the only informal grouping discovered was the New Society Group. The departure of eight deputies to the *Xa Hoi* bloc left a total of twenty-six independent deputies by the end of 1969. It was not clear, however, if these deputies were soon to join other blocs or were waiting for the creation of new ones. Some suggested in interviews that they were generally disappointed with the blocs in the Lower House and consequently were not planning upon entering or forming a bloc. Deputies of this view tended to be those who characterized themselves as unsuited to be politicians. This did not necessarily mean, however, that they did not intend to run for reelection; rather they shared the feeling expressed by one deputy:"I intend to run for reelection based upon the respect I may have of the population. I am tired of promising to do things for the people which are of trivial significance such as settling a family dispute, getting someone's uncle a business license, or someone's son a visa or draft deferment. I think also that the people are tired of having to hear such promises. My job is to write laws, and this is the only thing I want to do." In other cases, deputies attributed their independent status to the lack of success that they had in convincing a particular bloc of the need to follow a specific direction on such issues as land reform or taxation. These deputies resigned in protest to disassociate themselves with bloc positions although

in interviews they did not rule out the possibility of cooperation with their former blocs in the future.

29. The absence of roll call voting, and the lack of any deputy's desire to ask for one, suggests that House members by and large are reluctant to have their positions a matter of public record. The constituencies from which they may thus be seeking to "hide" probably range from the most obvious, such as Thieu or the police, to a general concern that during such an uncertain period it is best to leave as imprecise a record of public activities as possible in order to avoid harassment or worse in the future (i.e., when parliamentary immunity is replaced with obscurity in the case of those not reelected or when a new regime might come to power with much hostility toward those who took an active role in the early days of the Second Republic).

30. That is, for the chairman and vice-chairman of each of the permanent committees. Committee membership was determined by the House rules which set proportions for each bloc which designated members to the committees and then volunteered their names to the Speaker.

31. For a full discussion of these problems in other polities see Ghita Ionescu and Isabel de Madriaga, *Opposition: Past and Present of a Political Institution* (London, Watts, 1968); and Robert A. Dahl, ed., *Political Oppositions in Western Democracies* (New Haven, Conn., Yale University Press, 1966).

32. Reference is made here to the Phoenix program described in Chapter 9.

33. For a discussion of what the inclusion of the Viet Cong into the political system might involve, see my "The End of the War as a Setting for the Post-War Development of South Vietnam," *Asian Survey*, 11 (Mar. 1971), pp. 341-351.

34. Indeed, were this view to prove correct, it could be said of the Buddhists as it was said of the Tories of the 1750's that "the opposition . . . to central authority . . . vanished wherever members of that class entered the orbit of government." See Sir Lewis Namier, *England in the Age of the American Revolution* (London, Macmillan, 1961), p. 183. See Chapter 10 for a concluding evaluation of the importance of an alternative to such co-optation.

35. Nevertheless, the term "opposition" has meaning to those deputies that consider themselves part of it. Deputies refer to their participation in the "Forces of Opposition" to denote both a generally critical posture toward the Thieu government's policies and a belief that for the legislature to function properly a clustering of deputies as effective and cohesive as progovernment blocs is required. These deputies consider themselves the representatives of those social forces which have struggled against the government in the past even though they now are reevaluating struggle politics and its possible replacement by a politics of accommodation. The primary arena within which such a reorientation is being worked out appears to be the legislature.

36. The term "mellowing" is used here to refer to the process by which the radicalism of the opposition was toned down to permit its cooperation with other political groups that were not committed to the same political goals or critical to the government to the same degree.

37. C. Wright Mills, *The Power Elite* (New York, Oxford University Press, 1956), p. 19.

38. Arend Lijphart, *The Politics of Accommodation: Pluralism and Democracy in the Netherlands* (Berkeley, University of California Press, 1968), p. 200. See also John C. Wahlke, Heinz Eulau, William Buchanan, and LeRoy C. Ferguson, *The Legislative System: Explorations in Legislative Behavior* (New York, John Wiley, 1962), pp. 216-235. In Vietnam, of course, such "overarching cooperation" has been largely splintered between professions where, for example, medical doctors with similar backgrounds but different political affiliations have been able to cooperate and where civil servants and military officers, similarly, who may have been sharply divided in terms of their personal political loyalties have been able to work toward common objectives. The scope of elite cooperation thus depends upon the existence of issues which tend to emphasize the commonality of objectives and deemphasize the salience of traditional political divisions.

39. Seymour M. Lipset and Stein Rokkan, "Cleavage Structures, Party Systems, and Voter Alignments: An Introduction," in Lipset, ed., *Party Systems and Voter Alignments: Cross-National Perspectives* (New York, Free Press, 1967), p. 5.

Chapter 8. Creating Public Demands:
Patterns of Deputy-Constituency Relations

1. Whether the development of such institutional interest articulation would result in the Lower House becoming a vehicle for interest aggregation in terms of the creation of national policy or a clientelist pattern of politics in terms of the sociology of Vietnamese politics or a mixture of both, Lower House deputies viewed each of these outcomes as acceptable. As has been noted in comparative studies, "The distinction between interest articulation and aggregation is a fluid one," and clientelist patterns of politics "may survive, quite functionally, very late into the development process." The former quotation is taken from Gabriel Almond's, "Introduction: A Functional Approach to Comparative Politics," in Gabriel Almond and James S. Colemen, eds., *The Politics of the Development Areas* (Princeton, N.J., Princeton University Press, 1960), p. 39, and readers are referred there to the discussion of interest articulation and aggregation. See also the discussion of public interests contained in Samuel P. Huntington, *Political Order in Changing Societies* (New Haven, Conn., Yale University Press, 1968), pp. 24-32. The latter quotation is taken from John D. Powell, "Peasant Society and Clientelist Politics," *American Political Science Review*, 64 (June 1970), 425, where this pattern of politics is perceptively discussed.

2. Nghiem Dang, *Vietnam: Politics and Public Administration* (Honolulu, East-West Center Press, 1966), p. 121.

3. For an empirical analysis of the phenomena, see my "Correlates of Legislative Constituency Service in South Vietnam," in R.C. Boynton and C.L. Kim, *Legislative Systems in Developing Countries* (forthcoming).

4. While many observers think that the low proportion of deputies active in constituency service (exactly 33 percent of the total membership) reflects the Lower House's lack of interest in the affairs of the country, it would appear that the "service-oriented" deputy is a rare commodity in any polity. In one study of American state legislatures, for example, out of more than four hundred legislators in four states that were studied only 27 percent "spontaneously mentioned what one may call 'service functions' as an important aspect of their legislative job, and not all of these functions are in the nature of 'service,' literally interpreted." (John C. Wahlke, Heinz Eulau, William Buchanan, and LeRoy C. Ferguson, *The Legislative System: Explorations in Legislative Behavior* [New York, John Wiley, 1962], p. 304.)

5. As sketchy as the data on this group of deputies may be, one could very well be led to suggest that the obverse of a constituency service orientation may well be a "puppet" one. Manipulation by a powerful executive may be as satisfying as conflict if it is viewed in terms of future career aspirations.

6. Similar to observations made in other countries, the tendency for legislators to "go to the people" with complex national or international issues is limited by the difficulty manifest in explaining such issues to a heterogeneous audience. See Malcolm Moor and Bertram Koslin, "Prestige Suggestions and Political Leadership," *Public Opinion Quarterly*, 16 (Spring 1952), 77-93.

7. A similar division of time, however, has also been observed in the work pattern of congressional staffs in the US Congress. See Samuel P. Huntington, "Congressional Responses to the Twentieth Century," in David B. Truman, ed., *The Congress and America's Future* (Englewood Cliffs, N.J., Prentice-Hall, 1965), p. 25.

8. Deputies receive an office allowance as part of their salary of $10,000VN per month, equivalent to about $50.00US at the unofficial but more realistic exchange rate of $200.00VN to $1.00US that existed throughout most of the period from 1967-1969. But all service-oriented deputies reported that this amount was inadequate. One of the most active deputies, for example, said that his monthly salary of $84,000VN ($420.00US) was spent in the following way:

$30,000VN: living allowance for the deputy while in Saigon
 30,000VN: living allowance for the deputy's family in their province
  7,000VN: salary for a clerk-typist

13,200VN: transportation for travel to and from his constituency
twice a month
 3,800VN: miscellaneous expenses
$84,000VN: Total expenditures

Considering that a clerk in civil service work in Vietnam today earns a minimum of $7,000.00VN and a secretary perhaps a little less, the maintenance of a professional staff must come in good measure from a deputy's private funds. But funding is only part of the problem. With the war and the general mobilization policy in force, it is difficult to find such talent free from military obligations. The small number of clerks that are free from the draft are avidly sought within the professional communities in all of Vietnam's major cities and provincial capitals. Thus, after an initial desire to hire a permanent professional staff, active deputies have come to rely either upon a member of their family or upon volunteer workers whose principal reward comes from what patronage may be available to the deputy within his particular province.

9. Elsewhere it has been noted that educational functions are a common trend in legislatures of developing polities where representatives have engaged in constituency service work; see Jean Meynaud, "The General Study of Parliamentarians," *International Social Science Journal*, 13 (1961), 514.

10. While the writer went on to describe the untidy atmosphere of most government offices, many also believed he was making an oblique reference to the corruption which pervades the bureaucracy by using the term "cleanliness." See Nguyen, "Needed: Cleanliness," *Saigon Post* (9 Aug. 1969), p. 1. Descriptions of governmental unresponsiveness to the problems of the population can be found in G.H. Fox and Charles Joiner, "Perceptions of the Vietnamese Public Administration System," *Administrative Science Quarterly*, 8 (Mar. 1964); Nghiem Dang, *Vietnam, passim*; and my "The Political Implications of Rural Problems in South Vietnam: Creating Public Interests," *Asian Survey*, 10 (Aug. 1970), 672-687.

11. By the end of the 1968 session the Speaker of the House reported that 2,200 letters requesting intervention were received by the office of the following types:

 −50   requests for amnesty for political prisoners
 −290 requests that suspects detained under the Phoenix program be released
 −450 requests for war damage compensation
 −200 requests for war widows, orphans, and handicapped veterans assistance
 −100 requests for draft deferments
 −50   requests for the release of relatives drafted into the army who were deaf and dumb

−400   petitions denouncing the actions of administrative and military officials

−50   requests for the relief of laborers laid off for their participation in strikes against management

−610   miscellaneous requests for government assistance

These letters were forwarded to appropriate GVN ministries for action and the Speaker noted that of the total only 104 had been decided upon by the executive. See *Vietnam Cong-Hoa Ha-Nghi-Vien* [Republic of Vietnam Lower House], *Mot Nam Hoat Dong [One Year's Activity]* (Saigon, 1968), pp. 7-8.

12. When one of these province chiefs learned that I was visiting his province and doing a study of Lower House deputy activities he made it a point to lecture me about the nature of government in Vietnam, the problems he faced, and the action he was taking to alleviate them. I was later told that six months earlier the province chief would have had no interest in such a discussion or in the problems of the province and its population.

13. The independent observers referred to above refer to two bodies of provincial opinion: the leaders of local opinion, i.e., the organizational and religious leaders of the local community and the American advisory community within the province. Americans were consulted on the basis of the personal friendships that had developed between the deputy and the adviser and were viewed by the deputy as helpful in determining the province chief's orientation toward them and toward cooperation on the problems with which they were likely to deal. The deputy also believed that if the Americans were committed to the development of working relations then they would be able to influence the province chief to develop a similar orientation.

14. Several weeks later the heads of the families whose homes had been destroyed came to the deputy with requests for more building materials than they had received. The deputy investigated the situation and, discovering that adequate materials had been issued, reasoned that the villagers were seeking more to sell them on the black market. The deputy confronted the family heads with this opinion, and they admitted that he was right. Admonished by the deputy, the villagers rescinded their request for additional supplies. The deputy also pointed out to the people that, if everyone acted as they had, there would not be enough supplies for all who needed them and their greed would harm others whose plight was similar.

Chapter 9. Constituency Service and the
Creation of National Interests

1. See the comprehensive discussion of political institutions and public interests in Samuel P. Huntington, *Political Order in Changing Societies* (New Haven, Conn., Yale University Press, 1968), pp. 24-32.

2. See for example, Donald Lancaster, *The Emancipation of French Indochina* (London, Oxford University Press), p. 68; and Richard Betts, *The Politics of Police in Vietnam: Organization and Power in Counter-Revolution*, unpub. Senior Honors Thesis in Government, Harvard University, 1969, pp. 15-29, 30-48, 49ff.

3. The clearest description in English of Viet Cong organization to date can be found in Douglas Pike, *Viet Cong* (Cambridge, Mass., MIT Press, 1966).

4. Frances Fitzgerald, "Vietnam: The Future," *New York Review of Books*, 14 (26 Mar. 1970), 8. In addition to this particular article the few details about the program which are publicly known can be found in James P. Sterba, "The Controversial Operation Phoenix: How It Roots out Viet Cong Suspects," *New York Times* (18 Feb. 1970), p. 2; and Tom Buckley, "Phoenix: To Get Their Man Dead or Alive," *ibid.* (22 Feb. 1970), p. E3.

5. As reported by Assistant Minister of the Interior (2nd Huong cabinet), Vo huu Thu, in a speech before the Lower House on 20 June 1969 and recorded in the House Minutes of that session.

6. Fitzgerald, "Vietnam," pp. 9-10.

7. Pham Tam, "Imprisonment and Torture in South Vietnam," *Congressional Record*, (US) 115 (9 July 1969), E5763. (Emphasis in original.)

8. Deputy Do trong Nguyen, "Some Thoughts About the Guarantee of Human Rights in Vietnam," *Ha Nghi Vien*, 6 (15 Mar. 1969), 4.

9. Cap Tien, "Nhon Quyen" (Human Rights), *Cap Tien*, I (Dec. 1969), 3.

10. I am indebted to Lee Hargrave, Professor of Law at Louisiana State University and director of its legal advisory project in Vietnam for his assistance in the analysis to follow and for providing much valuable information on the Vietnamese legal system. This section is not designed to serve as a comprehensive discussion of Vietnamese law or legal history. The basic materials on the system itself can be found in a volume entitled *The Legal System of the Republic of Vietnam* (Saigon, 1967), which is an unofficial translation of the original work prepared by the Ministry of Justice in May 1967. The English edition of the volume was prepared by the Legal Administration Branch of the Public Administration Division, USAID, Saigon. In addition, two articles appear in English which discuss the Vietnamese legal system, and the reader is referred to them: see George F. Westerman and James L. McHugh, "Reaching for the Rule of Law in South Vietnam," *American Bar Association Journal*, 53 (Feb. 1967), 159-164; and Frank O'Neil, "The Vietnamese Legal System," *Public Administration Bulletin Vietnam*, No. 51 (Nov. 1969), pp. 82-90.

11. Westerman and McHugh, "Reaching for the Rule of Law," p. 160.

12. Ministry of Justice, *Legal System*, pp. 7-8.

13. *Ibid.*, pp. 24-25.

14. *Ibid.*, pp. 47-79.

15. Shortly after Diem came to power he established a system of

military tribunals with broad jurisdictional power over both military personnel who violated the code of military justice as well as over civilians "caught in the act" of jeopardizing national security. Subsequent interpretations of the legal concept of "Flagrante Delicto" have broadened it to include almost all civil and criminal offenses that come before the military courts. The Director of Military Justice, for example, observed that within the present legal system in Vietnam the broadness in competence of the military courts is an established principle: "Based on the Article 11 of Decree Law #11/62 dated 21 May 1962, the Military Field Courts have jurisdiction over flagrante delicto cases. But according to the will (i.e., interpretation) Jurists give to this decree law, the flagrante delicto distinction is not made for 'violations of the national security.' Therefore, (such) offenses are under the trial (authority) of the Military Field Courts, whether (they) are flagrante delicto or not." (Col. Nguyen van Duc, "The Concept of Flagrante Delicto and the Separation of Jurisdiction between the Military Courts," *Memorandum from the Director of Military Justice*, 23 July 1968.)

Similarly, each subsequent amendment to the law establishing military courts has not only broadened its jurisdictional competence but also streamlined its procedures in order to preclude effective defense for those tried before it. As the Minister of Justice observed at the beginning of 1969 in a televised interview: "The Law has projected a procedure for the summary trial in these (military) courts for some special crimes injurious to the national interest such as: violation of national security, speculation (with currency), bribery, etc. The right to a proper defense was not adequately provided for." (Statement of Minister of Justice Le van Thu, 3 February 1969). While the Minister went on to note that some steps had been taken to "enlarge the right of defense," experienced observers would agree that, by the end of 1969, the significance of those steps had been minimal.

16. Ministry of Justice, *Legal System,* p. 65.

17. Ly qui Chung, "The Government's Side—The Church's Side," *Tieng Noi Dan Toc* [The Voice of the People], (12 Oct. 1969).

18. See speech of Deputy Nguyen truong Nho, Lower House Debates, Minutes, Session 4 (14 Nov. 1967), p. 58.

19. Subsequently, the committee chairman became one of the House's most outspoken critics of the executive. When asked whether his concluding remarks were sincere or whether they were made tongue-in-cheek, the deputy responded that they represented the hope of all members of the committee for harmonious relations as well as being a suggestion to the executive that effective working relations could be maintained even on potentially divisive and controversial issues provided both parties sought such a relationship. The fate of the remaining twelve students, however, was not subsequently known, and the committee's work in having the five released was not publicized within the Saigon student community. Committee members themselves were also not sure if all the students had been

released. The expectation that working relations could be established with the executive was reinforced by the method by which the House sought to resolve the particular issue of the drafted students. The use of House delegations rather than the floor itself to handle differences between the two branches was an established practice of the Constituent Assembly, and, in the waning days of that body's tenure, participants in those delegations had noted an increasing desire for cordiality on the part of Premier Ky for better relations between the two bodies.

20. Speech of Deputy Le quan Hien, Lower House Minutes, Session 45 (16 Feb. 1968), p. 902.

21. This legislation was still in committee at the end of 1969, and it was acknowledged that it would take a long time to secure passage since the due process legislation was linked to the pending revision of Vietnam's Napoleonic codes. Deputies, moreover, had at least considered their case made as far as the injustices of the Phoenix program were concerned and felt that they could do little more without working to create a civilian legal framework to replace the military court system. While this would go on at the level of committee work, deputies had begun to bring forward legislation, revise local government procedures, and change thereby some of the elements which contributed to the corruption of the Phoenix program in particular and governmental unresponsiveness in general.

Chapter 10. The Bases of Political Community in South Vietnam

1. Epilogues for studies of recent South Vietnamese political developments are probably the most appropriate but least feasible form of conclusion the pace of change there would warrant. The temptation in the present case is very great to cover the events and developments associated with the 1970-71 elections, but such an enterprise will not be attempted here. First, the analytical detail that the period from 1967-1969 has received in this study could not be reproduced—short of intensive field work and political interviewing. Second, important studies of the present period are underway. Sponsored by the Asia Society, they include the original research of Victoria Schuck at Mount Holyoke College on the development and growth of the 1967 Constitution, the study of defeated candidates in the 1967 Lower House election by Jerry Silverman at McMaster University in Canada, and John Donnell's study of political party links to both the government and the peasant at Temple University. Third, I have provided an event-oriented, analytical updating of developments after 1969 in my contributions to *Asian Survey* "South Vietnam and the Politics of Self Support" (Jan. 1971), and "South Vietnam and the New Security" (Feb. 1972); a somewhat shorter analysis of the 1971 Presidential election alone can be found in my "What Went Wrong in Saigon?" *Freedom at Issue* (Jan.-Feb. 1972). These articles place the

developments described in this study in the context of the changing nature of the war.

Fundamentally, however, too little change has occurred in Vietnamese politics to warrant revision of the analysis presented here. And I have deliberately chosen not to change *Politics in War* from a book about a segment of political life in Vietnam into a general political history. The field of Vietnamese studies has been flooded by too many general studies, in my view, making it difficult for analysts to have enough detail on any one period, institution, or event to develop more profound, and less issue-oriented interpretations of Vietnamese politics. Taken together with Scigliano's and Donnell's early work on the Diem era National Assembly, and with Donnell's forthcoming *Vietnam: The Politics of Manipulation*, I intend *Politics in War* to contribute to an analytical base that has remained underdeveloped far too long and at terrible cost.

2. This appears to be the case in both well-developed and weak political and party systems. See Jack L. Walker, "A Critique of the Elitist Theory of Democracy," *American Political Science Review*, 60 (June 1966), p. 290 *et passim*; and Herbert Agar *The Price of Union* (Boston, Houghton Mifflin, 1950), *passim*.

3. Pham Thai, "Political Security," *Cap Tien* (19 Jan. 1970).

4. Congressman Ho ngoc Nhuan, "Is the Incumbent Regime Made for the People or Vice Versa?", *Tin Sang* (8 Oct. 1969).

5. "To Indulge in Politics," *Chinh Luan* (20 Jan. 1970).

6. A description of these factions can be found in my "South Vietnam: Neither War nor Peace," *Asian Survey* 10 (Feb. 1970), 107–132.

7. For an account of the development of constituency service designed for similar purposes, see Leonard D. White, *The Federalists: A Study in Administrative History* (New York, Macmillan Co., 1948), pp. 267–290, 348–358. See also White's subsequent works, *The Jeffersonians* (New York, Macmillan, 1951), *The Jacksonians* (New York, Macmillan, 1954), and *The Republican Era* (New York, Macmillan, 1958), *passim*, for an account of how constituency service was related to the development of political parties. A discussion of current practices can be found in Walter Gellhorn's *When Americans Complain* (Cambridge, Mass., Harvard University Press, 1966), pp. 57–130.

8. See Russell Betts, *Viet Cong Village Control: Some Observations on the Origins and Dynamics of Modern Revolutionary War* (Cambridge, Mass., Center for International Studies, Massachusetts Institute of Technology, Aug. 1969), *passim*.

9. Sir Robert Thompson, quoted in "A Fiercer Tom Cat," *Newsweek* (6 June 1966), p. 36.

10. See Max Weber, "Politics as a Vocation," in *From Max Weber: Essays in Sociology*, tr. H.H. Gerth and C. Wright Mills (New York, Oxford University Press, 1958), pp. 100–101.

11. See Huntington, *Political Order in Changing Societies* (New Haven, Conn., Yale University Press, 1968), pp. 397–461, esp. 416–417.

12. Huntington, *Political Order*, p. 9.

13. For a sampling of works in progress, see Allan Kornberg and Lloyd Musolf, eds., *Legislatures in Developmental Perspective* (Durham, N.C., Duke University Press, 1970); and R.G. Boynton and Chong Lim Kim, *Legislative Systems in Developing Countries* (forthcoming).

Index